THE
SUCCESS
EQUATION

THE

SUCCESS

EQUATION

UNTANGLING SKILL AND LUCK IN BUSINESS, SPORTS, AND INVESTING

MICHAEL J. MAUBOUSSIN

Harvard Business Review Press

Boston, Massachusetts

Library of Congress Cataloging-in-Publication Data

Mauboussin, Michael J., 1964-
The success equation : untangling skill and luck in business, sports, and investing / Michael J. Mauboussin.
    p. cm.
  Includes bibliographical references.
  ISBN 978-1-4221-8423-3 (alk. paper)
  1. Success. 2. Success in business. 3. Ability. 4. Fortune. 5. Decision making. I. Title.
  BF637.S8M34125 2012
  650.1—dc23

                        2012018975

The paper used in this publication meets the requirements of the American National Standard for Permanence of Paper for Publications and Documents in Libraries and Archives Z39.48-1992.

To Michelle

Skill that I asked her to wed

Luck that it was yes she said

CONTENTS

ACKNOWLEDGMENTS

I am very grateful to have had the opportunity to learn from so many thoughtful and generous people. Writing a book is a long journey that is sometimes very difficult. I am blessed by a wonderful network of friends and associates who helped me along the way.

My colleagues at Legg Mason Capital Management have not wavered in their support. Whereas I had to do some convincing to pursue my prior book, I was strongly encouraged to pursue *The Success Equation*. Particular thanks go to Jennifer Murphy, Bill Miller, and Sam Peters. LMCM's deep commitment to ongoing learning makes it a special place to be.

A number of people graciously shared their time and knowledge with me. They pointed me to useful stories, explained points, and straightened my course when I veered off it. These include Sam Arbesman, Brian Burke, Aaron Clauset, Jerker Denrell, Paul DePodesta, Doug Erwin, John Galvin, Daniel Kahneman, Michael Raynor, Matt Salganik, David Shaywitz, Tom Tango, Phil Tetlock, Duncan Watts, David Weinberger, and Richard Zeckhauser. Tom and Duncan read specific chapters and provided valuable feedback.

Scott E. Page has been a tremendous inspiration and source of encouragement from the beginning of this project. In particular, Scott put together a terrific conference at his home institution, the University of Michigan, in February 2011, dedicated to this theme. Scott is an amazing source of ideas and a great and generous friend.

It's time-consuming to read the draft of a manuscript and to provide feedback to the author. I was blessed to have a great collection of folks help me out. These include Phil Birnbaum, Michelle Mauboussin, Bill Miller, Michael Persky, Sam Peters, Al Rappaport,

Chris Wood, and an anonymous reviewer. I was particularly pleased to have Phil Birnbaum, one of my heroes in the sabermetrics community, take the time to share his thoughts and criticism.

Andrew Mauboussin, my oldest son, made a very meaningful contribution to the book. He did research on a number of topics and generated all of the simulations—work that is beyond my technical ability. He also read each of the chapters and chipped in with helpful comments. I was proud to cite the research he did with Sam Arbesman. I appreciate your contribution, Andrew.

I benefited immensely from working with Laurence Gonzales, who edited the book. Laurence is a very talented writer—*Deep Survival* is perhaps his best-known work—who improved the clarity and quality of the text throughout. It's valuable that he doesn't come from the same professional world as I do, because it allows him to be critical with fresh eyes. He's also an editor who is old school, which I love about him. No nouns as adjectives in this text. He's a terrific source of ideas and has taught me a great deal about writing. Thank you, Laurence.

It's hard for me to say enough about Dan Callahan, my colleague at Legg Mason Capital Management. Dan does it all: quality research, vivid exhibits, and great editing of early drafts. And, as a former pro baseball player, he had particular interest in, and insight into, the sports material. On top of it all, he did all this while satisfying his other analytical responsibilities within the firm. Dan has also developed a bit of side expertise: using creative approaches to generating book titles. For this book, we employed a site developed by Matt Salganik called www.allourideas.org—check it out, it's cool. Dan not only coordinated the project, he contributed the winning title, *The Success Equation*, which beat out scores of competitors. Thanks, Dan.

I loved working with Tim Sullivan, my editor at Harvard Business Review Press. Tim supported the idea for the book from the beginning and showed great aplomb in guiding the whole process. His ideas are sprinkled throughout the book and his edits left the proper material on the cutting room floor. I also received great assistance from others on the team at HBRP, including Erin Brown, Kevin Evers, Stephani Finks, and Jen Waring. Monica Jainschigg's sharp-eyed edits also tightened and improved the manuscript.

My wife, Michelle, provides steadfast love, counsel, and support. She encourages me to pursue my intellectual and athletic passions, which keep me going mentally and physically. She also offered useful comments on the initial manuscript. Michelle's mother, Andrea Maloney Schara, is integral to our family's activities, maintains a commendable desire to learn, and injects some cognitive diversity into all of our lives. Finally, I thank my children, Andrew, Alex, Madeline, Isabelle, and Patrick. I'm confident that with hard work and grit, each will successfully solve the success equation in his or her own way.

THE
SUCCE$$
EQUATION

SORTING THE SOURCES OF SUCCESS

MY CAREER WAS LAUNCHED by a trash can.

Like many seniors in college, I wasn't sure what I wanted to do for a living, but I knew that I needed a job. Drexel Burnham Lambert, an investment bank that was hot at the time, came on campus to recruit students for a new training program. My interview went well enough that I was called to the firm's headquarters in New York City. I put on my best suit and tie, polished my shoes, and headed to the Big Apple.

Early the next morning, we candidates gathered in a vast conference room and listened intently as the leader of the program told us what to expect for the day. "You will have full interviews with six members of our staff," she informed us, "and then each of you will have *ten minutes* with the senior executive in charge of our division." When it was clear that she had everyone's attention, she added, "If you want the job, you'll have to shine in that interview."

My half dozen interviews went as well as could be expected. When they were over, a member of the staff led me down a long corridor to an office paneled in dark wood, with deep wall-to-wall carpeting and a picture window overlooking a panorama of downtown Manhattan.

A sharp-eyed administrative assistant ushered me in, and the senior executive greeted me warmly. Then I saw it.

Peeking out from underneath a huge desk was a trash can bearing the logo of the Washington Redskins, a professional football team. As a sports fan who had just spent four years in Washington, D.C., and had attended a game or two, I complimented the executive on his taste in trash cans. He beamed, and that led to a ten-minute interview that stretched to fifteen minutes, during which I listened and nodded intently as he talked about sports, his time in Washington, and the virtues of athletics. His response to my opening was purely emotional. Our discussion was not intellectual. It was about a shared passion.

I got the job. My experience in the training program at Drexel Burnham was critical in setting the trajectory of my career. But after a few months in the program, one of the leaders couldn't resist pulling me aside. "Just to let you know," he whispered, "on balance, the six interviewers voted against hiring you." I was stunned. How could I have gotten the job? He went on: "But the head guy overrode their assessment and insisted we bring you in. I don't know what you said to him, but it sure worked." My career was launched by a trash can. That was pure luck, and I wouldn't be writing this if I hadn't benefited from it.

The Boundaries of Skill and Luck

Much of what we experience in life results from a combination of skill and luck. A basketball player's shot before the final buzzer bounces out of the basket and his team loses the national championship. A pharmaceutical company develops a drug for hypertension that ends up as a blockbuster seller for erectile dysfunction. An investor earns a windfall when he buys the stock of a company shortly before it gets acquired at a premium. Different levels of skill and of good and bad luck are the realities that shape our lives. And yet we aren't very good at distinguishing the two.

Part of the reason is that few of us are well versed in statistics. But psychology exerts the most profound influence on our failure to identify what is due to skill and what is just luck. The mechanisms that our minds use to make sense of the world are not well suited to accounting for the relative roles that skill and luck play in the events we see taking shape around us. Let me start with some examples that are clearly controlled by either luck or skill.

The drawing for Powerball, a multistate lottery, went off uneventfully on the evening of Wednesday, March 30, 2005. The first five balls came through the clear tubes: 28, 39, 22, 32, 33. The final ball, which came from a separate machine, clicked into place: 42. The whole process took less than a minute.

Sue Dooley, the staff member who was overseeing the drawing that night, rolled the machines back into the vault and drove from the television studio to the Powerball headquarters five miles away. Based on the statistics, she expected that perhaps one ticket would take home that day's jackpot of $84 million and that three or four people would have picked five of the six numbers correctly, winning second place.

She turned on her computer and waited for the states to report their results. The trickle of winners she had expected was actually a torrent. In total, there were 110 second-place winners. The statisticians employed by Powerball had warned that six or seven times the predicted figure was well within the realm of chance, but an outcome nearly thirty times the expectation appeared statistically impossible. Another oddity was that nearly all of the winning tickets had the same sixth number, 40. Truth be told, the officials at Powerball would have preferred it if the winners had picked all six numbers correctly, because the jackpot is split evenly among them. No matter how many people win, it costs Powerball the same amount. But each winner of the second prize receives a set amount, which meant that in this case, Powerball had to pay out $19 million more than it had anticipated.

Dooley called her boss and together they puzzled over possible explanations, including numbers shown on television, pattern plays, lottery columns, and even fraud. None of them checked out. The next morning, they got their first inkling of what had happened. When a staff member at a prize office in Tennessee asked a winner where he had gotten his numbers, he answered, "From a fortune cookie." Later a winner in Idaho said the same thing, and shortly thereafter winners in Minnesota and Wisconsin echoed the reply. Jennifer 8. Lee, a reporter from the *New York Times*, jumped on the story and traced the fortune cookies with the winning numbers back to the factory of Wonton Food in Long Island City, New York. Derrick Wong, a vice president at the company, explained that they had put numbers in a bowl and randomly picked out six of them. Since generating the number sequences takes time, the company printed the same numbers on different fortunes so as to save labor on the 4 million cookies the factory produced each day.[1] Each of those very lucky winners took home between $100,000 and $500,000, according to how much they had bet.

Marion Tinsley won a lot, too, but it wasn't because he was lucky. Tinsley was known as the greatest player of checkers (also known as draughts) in the world. In 1948 he was crowned as the United States champion; shortly before his death in 1994, he tied Don Lafferty and a computer program named *Chinook* for first place. In the intervening forty-five years, Tinsley lost only seven individual games for a near-perfect record. In two of those games he was defeated by *Chinook*. Despite the fact that he didn't play for long periods of time (he was a professor of mathematics at Florida State and Florida A&M Universities), he reigned as world champion in three separate decades.[2]

Tinsley's success resulted from years of deliberate practice. In his youth, Tinsley spent eight hours a day, five days a week, studying checkers, and he continued to study the game, though less intensely, throughout his life. He cultivated a prodigious memory that allowed him to recall the flow of games he had played decades earlier. Tinsley was fiercely competitive and claimed that he could beat all comers, man or machine, as long as his health didn't fail him.[3]

The Sources of Success

Both those who won the Powerball lottery and Marion Tinsley enjoyed great success. But it's easy to see that the causes of the two types of success differed markedly. The lottery outcome that day was a matter of pure good luck for the 110 winners and pure bad luck for Powerball. But Tinsley's success was almost entirely the result of skill. With all the luck in the world, you would have almost no chance of winning if Tinsley were across the table from you. For practical purposes, we can regard Tinsley's success as all skill. Unfortunately, most things in life and business are not that clear. Most of the successes and failures we see are a combination of skill and luck that can prove maddeningly difficult to tease apart.

The purpose of this book is to show you how you can understand the relative contributions of skill and luck and how to use that understanding in interpreting past results as well as making better decisions in the future. Ultimately, untangling skill and luck helps with the challenging task of prediction, and better predictions lead to greater success.

Skill, Luck, and Prediction

Shortly after winning the Nobel Prize in Economics in 2002, Daniel Kahneman, a retired professor of psychology at Princeton, was asked which of his 130-plus academic papers was his all-time favorite.[4] He chose "On the Psychology of Prediction," a paper he cowrote with the late Amos Tversky that was published in *Psychological Review* in 1973. The paper argues that intuitive judgments are often unreliable because people base predictions on how well an event seems to fit a story. They fail to consider either how reliable the story is or what happened before in similar situations. More formally, Kahneman and Tversky argue that three types of information are relevant to statistical prediction. The first is prior information, or the base rate.

For example, if 85 percent of the taxicabs in a city are green, then 85 percent is the base rate. Absent any other information, you can assume that whenever you see a taxicab there's an 85 percent chance that it will be green. The second type of information is the specific evidence about an individual case. The third type of information is the expected accuracy of the prediction, or how precise you expect it to be given the information you have.[5]

I had a conversation with a doctor that illustrates these three types of information. He mentioned that he had a treatment for improving a specific ailment that succeeded about 50 percent of the time (the base rate). But he added that he could induce almost any patient to undergo the treatment if he simply told them, "The last patient who was treated this way is doing great!" (specific evidence about an individual case). For the patients who were evaluating the treatment, the story of success swamped the statistics.

The key to statistical prediction is to figure out how much weight you should assign to the base rate and specific case. If the expected accuracy of the prediction is low, you should place most of the weight on the base rate. If the expected accuracy is high, you can rely more on the specific case. In this example, the doctor gave the patient no reason to believe that the procedure had better than a 50/50 chance of working for him. So the patient should place almost no weight on the specific evidence that it worked for one patient, and should rely instead on the base rate in making his decision.

Here's how the weighting of the base rate and the specific case relate to skill and luck. When skill plays the prime role in determining what happens, you can rely on specific evidence. If you're playing checkers against Marion Tinsley, you can easily predict the winner on the basis of your knowledge of Tinsley's deadly skill. In activities where luck is more important, the base rate should guide your prediction. If you see someone win a million dollars, that doesn't change the odds of winning the lottery. Just because someone wins at roulette, it doesn't help you to guess where the ball will end up on the next spin.

Unfortunately, we don't usually think this way. When we make predictions, we often fail to recognize the existence of luck, and as a consequence we dwell too much on the specific evidence, especially recent evidence. This also makes it tougher to judge performance. Once something has happened, our natural inclination is to come up with a cause to explain the effect. The problem is that we commonly twist, distort, or ignore the role that luck plays in our successes and failures. Thinking explicitly about how luck influences our lives can help offset that cognitive bias.

Quantifying Luck's Role in the Success Equation

The starting place for this book is to go beyond grasping the general idea that luck is important. Then we can begin to figure out the extent to which luck contributes to our achievements, successes, and failures. The ultimate goal is to determine how to deal with luck in making decisions.

This book has three parts:

- Chapters 1 through 3 set up the foundation. I start with some working definitions of skill and luck, examining the types of interactions where luck is relevant and noting where our methods to sort skill and luck may not work. I then turn to why we have such a difficult time comprehending the influence that luck exerts. The basic challenge is that we love stories and have a yearning to understand the relationship between cause and effect. As a result, statistical reasoning is hard, and we start to view the past as something that was inevitable. The section finishes by looking at the continuum from all-luck to all-skill. I examine a basic model to help guide intuition. These ideas include the paradox of skill and what determines the *rate* of reversion to the mean.

- Chapters 4 through 7 develop the analytical tools necessary to understand luck and skill. I open with methods for placing activities on the luck-skill continuum. Where an activity falls on that continuum provides a great deal of insight into how to deal with it. I then look at how skill changes over time. Simply put, skill tends to follow an arc: it improves for some time, peaks, and then glides lower. Next, I turn attention to the distributions—or the range of values—of luck. In activities where the results are independent of one another, simple models effectively explain what we see. But when a past result affects a future result, predicting winners becomes very difficult. The most skillful don't always win. I close this part by showing the difference between a useless statistic and a useful one. Useful statistics are persistent (the past correlates highly with the present) and predictive (doing well or poorly correlates strongly with the desired goal). As we will see, many statistics fail this basic test.

• Chapters 8 through 11 offer concrete suggestions about how to take the findings from the first two parts of this book and put them to work. I begin by outlining ways to improve skill. Where little luck is involved, deliberate practice is essential to developing skill. Where luck is rampant, we must think of skill in terms of a process, because the results don't provide clear feedback. Checklists can also be of great value because they improve execution and can guide behavior under stressful circumstances. I then look at how to cope with luck. When you are the favorite, for example, you want to simplify the game so that you can overwhelm your opponent. If you are the underdog, you want to inject luck by making the game more complex. Because luck is in part what remains unexplained, controlled tests allow for a more accurate reading on causality. If you want to know if an advertisement worked, for example, you need to consider the purchasing behavior of those who saw the ad versus those who didn't. This part also includes an in-depth discussion of reversion to the mean, an idea that most people believe they understand, even though their behavior shows that they don't. The book finishes with ten concrete tips on how to overcome the psychological, analytical, and procedural barriers in untangling skill and luck.

This analysis of skill and luck will focus on business, sports, and investing because these are the areas I know best. Naturally, these realms are quite different. Sports are the easiest activities to analyze because the rules are relatively stable over time and there is lots of data. Other social processes, including business, have fewer rules and boundaries than sports and therefore tend to be more complex. Still, many of the same analytical methods are valid.[6] Markets in general are the most difficult to analyze because prices are established through the interaction of a large number of individuals. Here again, the nature of the problem may be somewhat different from sports, but many of the tools for sorting out the relative influence of skill and luck still apply.

Part of the fun and challenge of analyzing skill and luck is that it's a multidisciplinary endeavor. Statisticians, philosophers, psychologists, sociologists, corporate strategists, professors of finance, economists, and sabermetricians (those who apply statistical methods to the study of sports) all have something to contribute to the discussion.[7] Unfortunately, the people within these disciplines don't always reach outside their fields. You will see ideas from each of these disciplines, and I'm hopeful that bringing them together will lead to a sounder and more balanced approach to analyzing decisions and interpreting the results.

Untangling skill and luck is an inherently tricky exercise, and there are plenty of limitations, including the quality of the data, the sizes of samples, and the fluidity of the activities under study. The argument here is not that you can precisely measure the contributions of skill and luck to any success or failure. But if you take concrete steps toward attempting to measure those relative contributions, you will make better decisions than people who think improperly about those issues or who don't think about them at all. That will give you an enormous advantage over them. Some statisticians, especially in the world of sports, come across as know-it-alls who are out of touch with the human side of things. This characterization is unfair. Statisticians who are serious about their craft are acutely aware of the limitations of analysis. Knowing what you can know and knowing what you can't know are both essential ingredients of deciding well. Not everything that matters can be measured, and not everything that can be measured matters.

While there are wide swaths of human activity where the ideas in this book are hard to apply, the ideas have concrete application in some important areas and should serve as a template for thinking about decisions beyond the scope of this book. Luck may explain that you met your future wife after your buddy lured you out on a Thursday night, but this book will have little to directly say about that or other issues of love, health, and happiness. We need to define the activity we're talking about and what measures we need to use to evaluate that activity effectively.

In his book *The Theory of Gambling and Statistical Logic*, Richard Epstein, a game theorist trained in physics, notes that there is no way to assure that you'll succeed if you participate in an activity that combines skill and luck. But he does say, "It is gratifying to rationalize that we would rather lose intelligently than win ignorantly."[8] Luck may or may not smile on us, but if we stick to a good process for making decisions, then we can learn to accept the outcomes of our decisions with equanimity.

CHAPTER 1

SKILL, LUCK, AND THREE EASY LESSONS

L ET ME START with a story that is likely to be familiar to you.

One of the greatest computer programmers of all time grew up near Seattle, Washington. He saw an upstart company, Intel, making computers on a chip and was among the first people to see the potential of these so-called microcomputers. He dedicated himself to writing software for the new device and, by one account, "He wrote the software that set off the personal computer revolution."[1]

In the mid 1970s, he founded a company to sell software for microcomputers. In the early history of the company, "the atmosphere was zany," and "people came to work barefoot, in shorts," and "anyone in a suit was a visitor."[2] But the company was soon highly profitable, and by 1981 its operating system had a dominant share of the market for personal computers that used Intel microprocessors.

For all of its early triumphs, the company's watershed moment came when IBM visited in the summer of 1980 to discuss an operating system for its new PC. After some negotiation, the two companies struck a deal. In August 1981, retailers offered the company's software alongside the brand new IBM PC, and the company's fate was sealed. The rest is history, as they say.

In case this story's not familiar, here's the ending. This pioneer of computer technology entered a biker bar in Monterey, California, on July 8, 1994, wearing motorcycle leathers and Harley-Davidson patches. What happened next is unclear, but he suffered a traumatic blow to the head from either a fight or a fall. He left under his own power but died three days later from the injury, complicated by his chronic alcoholism. He was fifty-two years old. He is buried in Seattle and has an etching of a floppy disk on his tombstone. His name is Gary Kildall.[3]

You'd be excused for thinking that the first part of the story is about Bill Gates, the multibillionaire founder of Microsoft. And it is certainly tantalizing to ask whether Gary Kildall could have been Bill Gates, who at one point was the world's richest man. But the fact is that Bill Gates made astute decisions that positioned Microsoft to prevail over Kildall's company, Digital Research, at crucial moments in the development of the PC industry.

When IBM executives first approached Microsoft about supplying an operating system for the company's new PC, Gates actually referred them to Digital Research. There are conflicting accounts of what happened at the meeting, but it's fairly clear that Kildall didn't see the significance of the IBM deal in the way that Gates did.

IBM struck a deal with Gates for a lookalike of Kildall's product, CP/M-86, that Gates had acquired. Once it was tweaked for the IBM PC, Microsoft renamed it PC-DOS and shipped it. After some wrangling by Kildall, IBM did agree to ship CP/M-86 as an alternative operating system. IBM also set the prices for the products. No operating system was included with the IBM PC, and everyone who bought a PC had to purchase an operating system. PC-DOS cost $40. CP/M-86 cost $240. Guess which won.

But IBM wasn't the direct source of Microsoft's fortune. Gates did cut a deal with IBM. But he also kept the right to license PC-DOS to other companies. When the market for IBM PC clones took off, Microsoft rocketed away from the competition and ultimately enjoyed a huge competitive advantage.

When asked how much of his success he would attribute to luck, Gates allowed that it played "an immense role." In particular, Microsoft was launched at an ideal time: "Our timing in setting up the first software company aimed at personal computers was essential to our success," he noted. "The timing wasn't entirely luck, but without great luck it wouldn't have happened."[4]

Defining Skill and Luck

The first step in untangling skill and luck is to define the terms. This is not a simple task and can quickly devolve into heated philosophical debates.[5] We can avoid those, since pragmatic definitions are all that we need to think clearly about the past, present, and future results of our actions and to improve the way we make the decisions that lead to those actions.

But first things first. Before we can speak of skill and luck, we have to settle on the specific activity we're talking about. We can analyze what athletes, executives, or investors do. We just have to be clear on what elements of performance we are considering. Next, we want to agree on the measures of performance. For athletes, it is winning games. For executives, it is developing strategies that create value. The benefit of measurement is that it allows us to assign specific values to skill and luck.

Now we can turn to definitions.

Luck

Let's start with luck.

We can probably do a bit better than the average dictionary that defines *luck* as "events or circumstances that work for or against an individual."[6] This is a good starting point, but we can be a little more specific. Luck is a chance occurrence that affects a person or a group (e.g., a sports team or a company). Luck can be good or bad.

Furthermore, if it is reasonable to assume that another outcome was possible, then a certain amount of luck is involved. In this sense, luck is out of one's control and unpredictable.[7]

For example, suppose that a teacher asks her students to learn one hundred facts. One student—call him Charlie—memorizes eighty of those facts, figuring that he'll always score 80 and earn a grade of B. Charlie likes this course, but his life doesn't depend on it, as long as he doesn't get a C. In this school, if you get a C, you fail the class. So a B is good enough for Charlie. Think of his strategy as employing true skill, because luck plays no role in how Charlie will perform on the test. He either knows the answer or he doesn't. And he can predict the consequences of his efforts.

However, instead of asking the class for all hundred facts, the devious teacher writes her test by randomly selecting twenty pieces of information out of the one hundred. Charlie's entire score is now dependent on which of those twenty facts match the ones he memorized. If you look at his predicament statistically, he has about a two-thirds chance of scoring somewhere between 75 and 85 percent. A grade of 85 would be okay, a high B. But a grade of 75 would not. Making matters worse, he has about a 30 percent chance of scoring either 90 or higher or 70 or lower. Suddenly, his perfect knowledge of those eighty facts can't shield him from luck.

His performance on the test is beginning to seem like a crap shoot. He'd be fine with scoring 90, of course, but he'll be doomed if he scores 70 or lower. In theory, Charlie could score zero if the teacher, just by chance, chose only the twenty facts that he failed to memorize. He could also score 100 if she chose none of those twenty. But the probabilities of those two extremes are vanishingly small. So Charlie's skill can easily be measured as 80 percent of perfect under one set of conditions. But under a second set of conditions, his score can vary wildly. Moreover, under the second set of conditions, measuring his skill in any meaningful way based solely on his score is much more difficult.

The second set of conditions introduces the element of luck into the process. And it satisfies the definition as I've stated it so far.

- The grade affects the student.

- It is either good or bad (he scores either above or below 80).

- It is reasonable to assume that another result was possible if only the teacher had selected different questions.

Standardized tests scores, including the SAT Reasoning Test used for admission to college in the United States, reflect the influence of luck in the same way. That's why the admissions officers who assess those tests recognize that the scores are an imprecise measure of true skill.[8] Introducing a little bit of luck into a system can make the level of genuine skill very difficult to measure.

In this case, we assumed that Charlie's skill was fixed and not subject to variation. In fact, his declarative memory was very accurate. He knew eighty facts. If he was asked for them, he could regurgitate them reliably. We introduced the element of luck by varying the number of questions the teacher chose.

Skill was fairly well fixed in Charlie's example, but luck can also arise through the normal variation in other kinds of skill. Consider a basketball player who makes 70 percent of her free-throw shots over a long season. You wouldn't expect that player to make seven out of every ten shots she takes. Rather, some nights she might make 90 percent of her free throws and other nights only 50 percent. Even if she trains constantly at improving her free throws, she'll experience the variation that arises from the workings of the neuromuscular system, which relies on a completely different system of memory from the one that allows us to recall facts. An athlete can reduce that variation in performance through practice, but removing it altogether is virtually impossible.[9]

Randomness and luck are related, but there is a useful distinction between the two. You can think of randomness as operating at the level of a system and luck operating at the level of the individual. Say you ask a hundred people to call five consecutive tosses of a fair coin. The order of how heads and tails fall will be random, and we can estimate that a handful of people will call all five tosses correctly. But if you are one among the hundred and happen to get them all right, you are lucky.

My definition suggests that it is useful to develop an attitude of equanimity toward luck. The consequences of our efforts, both good and bad, reflect an element within our control—skill—and an element outside of our control—luck. In this sense, luck is a residual: it's what is left over after you've subtracted skill from an outcome. Realizing good or bad luck says nothing about you as a person. If you've benefited from good luck, be happy about it and prepare for the day when your luck runs out. And don't feel affronted when you suffer from bad luck. Provided that you have approached the activity in the correct fashion, you want to shrug off the poor results and go about your business in the same fashion in the future.

Most people have a general sense that luck evens out over time. That may be true in the grand scheme of things. But the observation doesn't hold for any individual, and the timing of luck can have a large cumulative effect. One well-documented example is the timing of graduation from college. Students who graduate at times of relative prosperity have an easier time getting jobs and enjoy higher pay than students who graduate during a recession or depression. Lisa Kahn, an economist at the Yale School of Management, studied this effect. For white male students at the time of graduation, the unemployment rate can be used to predict a loss of earnings. For each percentage point of unemployment, the graduate will earn 6 to 7 percent less. Fifteen years later, he'll still be below par.[10] The difference in what people earn is strongly influenced by whether or not the economy is weak or strong when they graduate from college. In other words, it's a matter of luck.

Making Your Own Luck

Since luck is intimately intertwined in all of our lives, it comes as no surprise that there are plenty of aphorisms that address luck:

- "You make your own luck."

- "Luck is what happens when preparation meets opportunity."

- "I'm a great believer in luck, and I find the harder I work, the more I have of it."[11]

Preparation and hard work are essential elements of skill. They often lead to good outcomes. But the aphorisms don't really address what's happening. If you prepare and work hard, you are successful not because your luck improves. Luck doesn't change at all. Only your skill improves. And you can work hard and prepare and build the best American diner on Route 66 just when the interstate highway bypasses your town and puts you out of a job.

There's another popular argument that says you can't get lucky unless you get in luck's way. For example, you can't win the lottery unless you play. On one level, of course, this is true. But it glosses over two important points. Luck can be good or bad. While winning the lottery does seem like good luck, it's hard to say that losing the lottery is bad luck. Losing the lottery is expected. Lotteries are designed to take in more money than they dole out, so they are a loser's game in the aggregate. The main issue is that putting yourself in a position to enjoy good luck also puts you in a position to lose.

The other point is that the very effort that leads to luck is a skill. Say that you need to complete ten interviews with prospective employers to receive one job offer. Individuals who seek only five interviews may not get an offer, but those who go through all ten interviews will have an offer in hand by the end of the process. Getting an offer isn't luck, it's a matter of effort. Patience, persistence, and resilience are all elements of skill.

The best-known advocate for the idea that you can create your own luck is Richard Wiseman, a professor at the University of Hertfordshire who holds Britain's Chair in the Public Understanding of Psychology. Wiseman's investigations are offbeat and fun. For example, he conducted a "scientific search" for the world's funniest joke. (The winner: Two hunters are out in the woods when one of them collapses. He doesn't seem to be breathing and his eyes are glazed. The other guy whips out his phone and calls the emergency services. He gasps, "My friend is dead! What can I do?" The operator says, "Calm down. I can help. First, let's make sure he's dead." There is a silence, then a shot is heard. Back on the phone, the guy says, "OK, now what?") He also argues that he has found "a scientifically proven way to understand, control, and increase your luck."[12]

Wiseman collected a sample of hundreds of individuals and had them rate themselves on their beliefs about luck. He then sought to explain "the different ways in which lucky and unlucky people thought and behaved" and identified the "four principles of luck." The principles include maximizing your chance opportunities, listening to your lucky hunches, expecting good fortune, and turning bad luck into good. Wiseman's research is unfailingly lively and provocative and he comes across as an energetic and intellectually curious man. Unfortunately, good science this is not.

In one experiment, Wiseman asked people playing the U.K. National Lottery to submit a form that included information on how many tickets they intended to buy and whether they considered themselves lucky. Of the seven hundred–plus respondents, 34 percent considered themselves lucky, 26 percent unlucky, and 40 percent were neutral. Thirty-six of the respondents (about 5 percent) won money that night, split evenly between the lucky and unlucky people. Individuals lost £2.50 on average, just as you would expect according to the number of tickets purchased. Wiseman points out that this experiment shows that lucky people aren't psychic (just in case you thought they were); he also rules out any relationship between intelligence and luck.[13] Suffice it to say that there is no way to improve your luck, because anything you do to improve a result can reasonably be considered skill.

Skill

Now let's turn to skill. The dictionary defines *skill* as the "ability to use one's knowledge effectively and readily in execution or performance."[14] It's hard to discuss skill in a particular activity without recognizing the role of luck. Some activities allow little luck, such as running races and playing the violin or chess. In these cases, you acquire skill through deliberate practice of physical or cognitive tasks. Other activities incorporate a large dose of luck. Examples include poker and investing. In these cases, skill is best defined as a process of making decisions. So here's the distinction between activities in which luck plays a small role and activities in which luck plays a large role: when luck has little influence, a good process will always have a good outcome. When a measure of luck is involved, a good process will have a good outcome but only *over time*. When skill exerts the greater influence, cause and effect are intimately connected. When luck exerts the greater influence, cause and effect are only loosely linked in the short run.

There's a quick and easy way to test whether an activity involves skill: ask whether you can lose on purpose. In games of skill, it's clear that you can lose intentionally, but when playing roulette or the lottery you can't lose on purpose. Advocates for the legalization of online poker in the United States articulated this neat test. The law considers poker as gambling, a game of luck, and ignores the role of skill. But while luck certainly does influence who wins at poker, there should be no doubt that it is also a game of skill.[15]

Most people attain an acceptable level of skill in day-to-day activities after about fifty hours of training and practice. Examples include driving a car, learning to type, or playing a sport with basic proficiency. The process of acquiring a skill follows three stages:[16]

- In the *cognitive stage*, you try to understand the activity and you make a lot of errors. You might imagine a golfer learning to hold the club, thinking about how to position her body for a swing, and swinging poorly at first. The cognitive stage is generally the shortest.

- Next comes the *associative stage*. In this stage, your performance improves noticeably and you make fewer errors that are more easily corrected. A golfer would make regular contact with the ball but might not have full command of the direction it goes or the distance it travels.

- Finally, there is the *autonomous stage*, where the skill becomes habitual and fluid. Now the golfer can adjust her swing to accommodate the wind or the downward slope and break of a putt.

As your learning passes through these phases, there is a change in the neural pathways that the brain employs. If you become skilled in a physical or cognitive task, your body knows what to do better than your mind, and thinking too much about what you're doing can actually lead to degradation in performance. In these activities, intuition is powerful and valuable.[17]

Most of us hit a plateau in our skills and are perfectly content to stay there. Once at that plateau, additional experience does not lead to improved results (as my play in a recreational hockey league attests). What distinguishes elite performers, or experts, from the rest of us is that they advance beyond their natural plateaus through *deliberate practice*. Unlike routine and playful performance, deliberate practice pushes people to attempt what is beyond the limits of their performance. It involves hours of concentrated and dedicated repetition. Deliberate practice also requires timely and accurate feedback, usually from a coach or teacher, in order to detect and correct errors. Deliberate practice is laborious, time-consuming, and not much fun, which is why so few people become true experts or true champions.[18]

In activities where luck plays a larger role, skill boils down to a process of making decisions. Unlike a piano virtuoso, who will per-form at a high level every night, an investor or a businessperson who makes a good decision may suffer unwelcome consequences in the short term because of bad luck. Skill shines through only if there are a sufficient number of decisions to weed out bad luck.

Jeffrey Ma was one of the leaders of a notorious team of black-jack players from the Massachusetts Institute of Technology. To make money, the team counted cards. Their system had two crucial components. First, team members fanned out and counted cards at a number of different tables in order to determine which tables were attractive. In this initial phase, the players stuck to small stakes. They were playing solely to determine if the cards that remained in the shoe had a relatively large number of high cards. The more high cards, the greater the chance that the player will win a hand. When a player found an attractive table, a teammate would join him and place large bets in order to win as much money as possible. As described in Ben Mezrich's best-selling book, *Bringing Down the House*, the team could express the attractiveness of the table and how large the bets should be with mathematical precision.[19]

Ma and his team were acutely aware of the influence that luck could have and therefore stayed focused on their decision-making process. Indeed, Ma recounts an instance when he lost $100,000 in just two rounds over the course of ten minutes, even though he played his cards just right: "The quality of the decision can be evaluated by the logic and information I used in arriving at my decision. Over time, if one makes good, quality decisions, one will generally receive better outcomes, but it takes a large sample set to prove this."[20] In other words, he has to place a lot of bets in order to win, because this game involves a lot of skill but it also involves a lot of luck.

Developing skill is hard work whether or not luck is involved. But the feedback is very different, depending on the degree to which luck plays a role. With most physical tasks, there is a high correla-tion between skill and results. If you work diligently at increasing your speed at typing, the number of words you can type each minute will increase and the number of errors you make will decline. With tasks that depend on luck, making proper decisions using good skill can produce poor results over the short term. To use Ma's example, whether his team won or lost was not a reliable form of feedback in assessing skill unless and until they played enough games. The lack of quality feedback wreaks psychological havoc, too, creating false doubt in skillful people who are making good decisions and creating false confidence in those who are doing well simply because they're experiencing a streak of good luck.

In considering skill, it is also important to distinguish between *experience* and *expertise*. There is an unspoken assumption that someone doing something for a long time is an expert. In activities that depend largely on skill, though, expertise comes only through deliberate practice, and very few individuals are willing to commit the time and effort to go beyond a plateau of performance that's good enough. The fact is, most of us generally don't need performance that's better than good enough. An experienced auto mechanic, plumber, or architect, for instance, is often all you need. On the other hand, deliberate practice is essential to reach the pinnacle as a musician or an athlete.

The confusion between experience and expertise is particularly acute in fields that are complex and where luck plays a big role. One of the signatures of expertise is an ability to make accurate predictions: an expert's model effectively ties cause to effect. By this measure, experts who deal with complex systems fare poorly.

Philip Tetlock, a professor of psychology at the University of Pennsylvania, has done detailed research on experts in political and economic fields and found that their predictions were not much better than algorithms that crudely extrapolated past events.[21] The record of people forecasting the behavior of a complex system, whether it's prices in the stock market, changes in population, or the evolution of a technology, is amazingly bad. Impressive titles and years of experience don't help, because the association between cause and effect is too murky. The conditions are changing constantly, and what happened before may not provide insight into what will happen next.

Professor Gregory Northcraft, a psychologist at the University of Illinois, sums it up: "There are a lot of areas where people who have experience think they're experts, but the difference is that experts have predictive models, and people who have experience have models that aren't necessarily predictive."[22] Distinguishing between experience and expertise is critical because we all want to understand the future and are inclined to turn to seasoned professionals with good credentials to tell us what is going to happen. The value of their predictions depends largely on the mix between skill and luck in whatever activity they're discussing.

The Luck-Skill Continuum and Three Lessons

To visualize the mix of skill and luck we can draw a continuum. On the far right are activities that rely purely on skill and are not influenced by luck. Physical activities such as running or swimming races would be on this side, as would cognitive activities such as chess or checkers. On the far left are activities that depend on luck and involve no skill. These include the game of roulette or the lottery. Most of the interesting stuff in life happens between these extremes. To provide a sense of where some popular activities belong on this continuum, I have ranked professional sports leagues on the average results of their last five seasons (see figure 1-1).[23]

FIGURE 1-1

Sports on the luck-skill continuum (one season based on an average of the last five seasons)

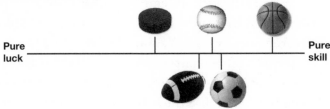

Pure luck — Pure skill

Source: Analysis by author.

Where an activity lies on the continuum has important implications for making decisions. So our initial goal is to place activities properly on the continuum between skill and luck. Naturally, there are variables that make this an elusive task. For example, the skills of athletes shift as they age, and most companies lose their competitive advantages as new technologies emerge. But having some sense of where an activity falls on the continuum is of great value. Here are some ways that untangling skill and luck can be very useful in guiding our thinking and in evaluating events.

Take Sample Size into Account

To assess past events properly, consider the relationship between where the activity is on the luck-skill continuum and the size of the sample you are measuring. One common mistake is to read more into an outcome than is justified. Howard Wainer, a distinguished research scientist for the National Board of Medical Examiners and an adjunct professor of statistics at the University of Pennsylvania, makes this point by identifying what he calls, "the most dangerous equation." Derived by Abraham de Moivre, a renowned French mathematician, the equation states that the variation of the mean (average) is inversely proportional to the size of the sample. This says that small samples display much larger variation (measured by standard deviation) than large samples in activities that involve a large dose of luck.[24] You can visualize the mean and standard deviation with the bell curve, the shape that traces the distribution. The largest number of observations is close to the top of the bell, near the mean, or average. From the top of the bell, the curve slopes down the sides symmetrically with an equal number of observations on each side. Standard deviation is a measure of how far the sides of the bell curve are from the average. A skinny bell curve has a small standard deviation, and a fat bell curve has a large standard deviation.

A small number of results tell you very little about what's going on when luck dominates, because the bell curve will look fatter for the small sample than it will for the overall population. Wainer deems this the most dangerous equation because ignorance of its lessons has misled people in a wide range of fields for a long time and has had serious consequences.

Wainer offers an example to illustrate the point: the rate at which people contract cancer of the kidney in the United States. He provides a map showing that the counties in the United States with the lowest rates tend to be rural, small, and in the Midwest, South, and West. He then shows a map of the counties with the *highest* rates. They tend to be rural, small, and in the Midwest, South, and West. This is simply de Moivre's equation at work: if you're closer to the luck side of the luck-skill continuum, small sample sizes will exhibit large variations and will lead to unreliable conclusions. Wainer then shows the rate at which people contract cancer of the kidney as a function of the population of any given county, and it is visually clear that small counties have the highest and lowest rates of incidence of cancer while large counties have rates that are closely clustered. A small population equals a small sample and therefore a wide variation.[25]

Failing to understand de Moivre's equation has led to some significant blunders in making policy. One example is the effort to improve the education of children. Seeking reform, policy makers proceeded in a seemingly sensible way by asking what kinds of schools had children who scored well on tests. The next step was to restructure other schools to look like the ones producing the outstanding students. As you would guess by now, small schools are substantially overrepresented among the schools that scored the highest. This led to a movement toward reducing the size of schools. In fact, the private and public sectors spent billions of dollars to implement a policy aimed at reducing the size of schools.

A closer look at the data shows that small schools were not only overrepresented among the schools that scored the highest, they were also overrepresented among the schools that scored the lowest. Further, Wainer offers evidence that, toward the end of their secondary education, students at larger schools actually score better on average than those at small schools, because larger schools have the resources to offer a richer curriculum, with teachers who can specialize in a subject.[26]

Here's the main point: if you have an activity where the results are nearly all skill, you don't need a large sample to draw reasonable conclusions. A world-class sprinter will beat an amateur every time, and it doesn't take a long time to figure that out. But as you move left on the continuum between skill and luck, you need an ever-larger sample to understand the contributions of skill (the causal factors) and luck.[27] In a game of poker, a lucky amateur may beat a pro in a few hands but the pro's edge would become clear as they played more hands. If finding skill is like finding gold, the skill side of the continuum is like walking into Fort Knox: the gold is right there for you to see. The luck side of the continuum is similar to the tedious work of panning for gold in the American River in California; you have to do a lot of sifting if you want to find the nuggets of gold.

Most business executives try to improve the performance of their companies. One way to do that is to observe successful companies and do what they do. So it comes as no surprise that there are a large number of books based on studies of success. Each work has a similar formula: find companies that have been successful, identify what they did to achieve that success, and share those attributes with other companies seeking similar success. The approach is intuitively appealing, which explains why the authors of these studies have sold millions of books.

Unfortunately, this approach comes with an inherent problem. Some of the companies were lucky, which means that there are no reliable lessons to learn from their successes. Michael Raynor and Mumtaz Ahmed at Deloitte Consulting teamed up with Andrew Henderson at the University of Texas to sort out how skill and luck contribute to the way that companies perform. First, the researchers studied over twenty thousand companies from 1965–2005 to understand the patterns of performance, including what you would expect to see as the result of luck. They concluded that there were more companies that sustained superior performance than luck alone could explain.

Next, they examined the 288 companies that were featured in thirteen popular books on high performance and tested them to see how many were truly great. Of the companies they were able to categorize, they found that fewer than 25 percent could confidently be called superior performers. Raynor, Ahmed, and Henderson write, "Our results show that it is easy to be fooled by randomness, and we suspect that a number of the firms that are identified as sustained superior performers based on 5-year or 10-year windows may be random walkers rather than the possessors of exceptional resources."[28]

The authors of those how-to studies found success and interpreted it to create lessons that they could peddle to a credulous audience. Yet only a small percentage of the companies they identified were truly excellent. Most were simply the beneficiaries of luck. At the end of the day, the advice for management is based on little more than patterns stitched together out of chance occurrences. You have to untangle skill and luck to know what lessons you can take from history. Where skill is the dominant force, history is a useful teacher. For example, by well-established methods, you can train yourself to play music, speak a language, or compete in athletic games such as tennis and golf. Where luck is the dominant force, however, history is a poor teacher.

At the heart of making this distinction lies the issue of feedback. On the skill side of the continuum, feedback is clear and accurate, because there is a close relationship between cause and effect. Feedback on the luck side is often misleading because cause and effect are poorly correlated in the short run. Good decisions can lead to failure, and bad decisions can lead to success. Further, many of the activities that involve lots of luck have changing characteristics. The stock market is a great example. What worked in the past may not work in the future.

An understanding of where an activity is on the luck-skill continuum also allows you to estimate the likely rate of reversion to the mean. Any activity that combines skill and luck will eventually revert to the mean. This means that you should expect a result that is above or below average to be followed by one that is closer to the average. Recall Charlie, the student who knew eighty out of one hundred facts but was tested on only twenty of them. If he scored a 90 on the first test because the teacher happened to select mostly questions he could answer, you would expect the score on the second test to be closer to 80, as his good luck would be unlikely to last.[29]

The important point is that the expected rate of reversion to the mean is a function of the relative contributions of skill and luck to a particular event. If what happens is mostly the result of skill, then reversion toward the mean is scant and slow. If you're a highly skilled NBA player making free-throw shots, your shooting percentage will stand well above the average most of the time. Sometimes your performance will move back toward the average, but not by very much. If the outcome is mostly due to luck, reversion to the mean will be pronounced and quick. If you're playing roulette and win five times, you're better off leaving the table, because you can be sure you're going lose as the number of plays increases. These concepts are important and are often overlooked in business, sports, and investing, not to mention in the casino.

Take another example from sports. Tennis is largely a game of skill. Top professional men players hit in excess of six hundred shots during a best-of-five set match, providing plenty of opportunity for skill to shine through (large sample). As a consequence, the ranking of the best tennis players tends to persist from year to year. For instance, Roger Federer, one of the greatest players of all time, spent a total of 288 weeks—longer than five years—in the number-one spot. A look at the four top-rated players at the end of 2010 reveals that they were the same as at the end of 2009, with the only difference being that the top two players swapped spots. The same four players appeared in 2011. Reversion to the mean is muted because skill exerts the most powerful influence over who wins.

Baseball is another story. Even though its professional players are extremely skillful, baseball is a sport that involves a lot of luck. A pitcher can throw well but fail to get supporting runs from his teammates and thereby lose a game. A batter can put a ball into play and a slight difference in trajectory will determine whether it's a hit or an out. Over a long, 162-game season, the best teams in baseball rarely win more than 60 percent of their games, as reversion to the mean powerfully drives the outcomes back toward the average. In sharp contrast to tennis, baseball has a lot of randomness. Only the New York Yankees were one of the top four teams in 2009, 2010, and 2011 (based on wins), and they made it by a slim margin in 2010. Because there are nine defensive players on the field at any given time, and each player's performance fluctuates, one player's skill can easily be canceled out by another's mistake, driving the whole system back toward the average. So no matter how skillful the individual players, a system like this tends to look and behave much more like a game of chance than tennis does.

Naturally, for any particular individual or organization skill will change over time. The performance of a great athlete fades with age and a company's competitive advantage eventually gets whittled away. But from period to period, a sense of the ratio of skill to luck is of great value in anticipating the rate of reversion to the mean.

Interactions Vary, but the Lessons Remain

Some of the interactions featured in this book are focused on the individual, including cognitive tasks (music), physical tasks (gymnastics), or tasks in which an individual interacts with a system (the lottery). These activities tend to have a high degree of independence, which means that whatever happens next is not influenced by what happened in the past. In those cases, the skill of the players tends to dictate the results.

Still other activities have one person or entity competing against a few others. A company launching a new product amid a handful of rivals is one example. So is a team competing in a league, or even the performance of a player on a team. In these instances, what happened in the past does influence the future, a process known as *path dependence*.

Finally, there are cases in which one person competes with a crowd. Examples include betting on sports and investing, where an individual pits his or her skill against the collective skill of the crowd. History shows us that crowds can be wise or whimsical.

So far, I have depicted events as if they follow distributions that are known. For example, de Moivre's equation applies to events that follow a normal, or bell-shaped, distribution but doesn't apply in cases where some events are extreme outliers. The real world is messy, and there are myriad distributions that depart from the simple bell curve, as we will see. But if we approach these activities properly, the effort of untangling skill and luck will yield insights into how to assess past events and anticipate the future.

Limits of the Methods

Nassim Taleb offers a useful way to figure out where statistical tools are likely to work and where they fail. He introduces a 2×2 matrix, where the rows distinguish between activities that can have extreme variation and those that have a narrower range of possibilities.[30] The narrow distributions are the ones that de Moivre's equation handles superbly. The distribution of stature is a classic example, as the ratio between the tallest and shortest human on record is only 5:1. But extreme variation is a lot more difficult to deal with. For example, the distribution of wealth has extreme outcomes. The net worth of Bill Gates, in excess of $50 billion, is more than 500,000 times more than the median net worth of all Americans.

The columns of the matrix are the payoffs, and distinguish between the simple and the complex. Binary payoffs are simple: the team wins or loses; the coin comes up heads or tails. Again, modeling these payoffs mathematically is relatively straightforward. Complex payoffs would include the casualties from a war. You may be able to predict a war, but there's no reliable way to measure its effect. Figure 1-2 summarizes the matrix.

FIGURE 1-2

Taleb's four quadrants

	Simple payoffs	Complex payoffs
Narrow outcomes	I Extremely safe	II (Sort of) safe
Extreme outcomes	III Safe	IV Black swan domain

Source: Nassim Nicholas Taleb, *The Black Swan: The Impact of the Highly Improbable* (New York: Random House, 2010), 365.

Statistical methods tend to work well in quadrants one through three, and most of what we will be dealing with falls into one of those quadrants. Dealing with quadrant four is far more difficult, and there is a natural and frequently disastrous tendency to apply naively the methods of the first three quadrants to the last. While most of our discussion will dwell on areas where statistics can be helpful, we will also discuss ways to cope with activities in the fourth quadrant.

CHAPTER 2

WHY WE'RE SO BAD AT DISTINGUISHING SKILL FROM LUCK

AS PART OF A LECTURE that he delivers to the general public, Simon Singh, a British author who writes about science and math, plays a short snippet from Led Zeppelin's famous rock song, "Stairway to Heaven." Most of the people in the audience are familiar with the tune, and some know the lyrics well enough to sing along.

He then plays the same song backward. As you would expect, it sounds like gibberish. He follows by earnestly asking how many heard the following lyrics in the backward version:

It's my sweet Satan. The one
whose little path would make me
sad whose power is Satan.
Oh, he'll give you, give you 666.
There was a little toolshed where
he made us suffer, sad Satan.

The words are a little odd, but the satanic theme is clear. Even so, no one in the audience had heard those words the first time through. But then Singh replays the backward clip, and this time he displays the pseudo lyrics on a screen and highlights them so that everyone can follow along. And sure enough, the audience unmistakably hears the words, where before they had heard nothing. The first time through, the backward version was an incoherent mess. But once Singh told the audience what might be there, the previously unintelligible gibberish was transformed into clear speech.[1]

Singh's demonstration provides an important clue to why we have a hard time understanding the roles of skill and luck. Our minds have an amazing ability to create a narrative that explains the world around us, an ability that works particularly well when we already know the answer. There are a couple of essential ingredients in this ability: our love of stories and our need to connect cause and effect. The blend of those two ingredients leads us to believe that the past was inevitable and to underestimate what else might have happened.

Stories, Causality, and the Post Hoc Fallacy

John Lewis Gaddis, a professor of history at Yale, creates a vivid image of how we represent time. He suggests that the future is a zone where skill and luck coexist independently. Almost everyone recognizes that many more things could happen than will happen. A wide range of events might occur, but won't. These possibilities come down a funnel to the present, which fuses skill and luck to create whatever happens. The conversion of a range of alternatives into a single event is the process that makes history.[2]

For example, you undoubtedly trust your skill at driving well enough to get to the grocery store and back without dying. But when you pull out onto the road, you're facing a wide range of possible histories for this journey. In one of them, the engine falls off of the Boeing 767 going overhead and lands on your car and kills you. In another, you turn in front of a motorcyclist you happen not to see, and you kill him. In yet another, a tractor trailer loses its brakes and plows into you from behind, putting you in the hospital for a month. In fact, in this instance, you drive to the store, buy your groceries, and go home. The history of this event was that you didn't die. Was it your skill as a driver that saved your life? Or was it luck?

If we look into the past, skill and luck appear to be inextricably fixed, even though the history that we lived through was but one of many possible histories that could have occurred. While we are capable of contemplating a future pulsating with possibility, we quickly forget that our experience was one of many that could have been. As a consequence, often we draw lessons from the past that are wrong. For example, you could conclude that you're such a skill-ful driver that you really stand no chance of being in an accident. That's a very dangerous conclusion.

Humans love stories.[3] They are one of the most powerful and emotive ways that we communicate with one another. Our parents told us stories, and we tell them to our children. People tell stories to teach lessons or to codify the past. The oral tradition of storytelling goes back thousands of years and predates writing. All stories have common elements. There is a beginning, some inciting episode that launches a sequence of events. The storyteller explains why events unfolded as they did, though he may be inventing those causes. As the story proceeds, the action rises. Complications occur. Interesting stories have an element of suspense and surprise. We get invested in a story when there is something at stake, when the tension mounts, and when events occur that upset our expectations. And stories have a climax and a resolution: the protagonist wins or loses, and then the tension is released as things settle down once more.

The need to connect cause and effect is deeply ingrained in the human mind.[4] When we see an effect, we naturally seek the cause. Michael Gazzaniga, a professor of psychology at the University of California, Santa Barbara, has worked with patients who have undergone surgery to sever the corpus callosum, the bundle of nerves that connects the right and left hemispheres of the brain. This sur-gery is a treatment for severe epilepsy. Gazzaniga and his colleagues were able to learn just how each hemisphere functions because in these patients the two halves of the brain cannot communicate with each other and so must function in isolation.

One of their main conclusions was that the left hemisphere "includes a special region that interprets the inputs we receive every moment and weaves them into stories to form an ongoing narrative of our self-image and our beliefs."[5] Gazzaniga calls this region the *interpreter*. One of the left hemisphere's main jobs is to make sense of the world by finding a cause for every effect, even if the cause is nonsensical.

In one experiment, Gazzaniga showed a split-brain patient two cards with images on them. The patient's left eye (controlled by the right hemisphere) saw a snowy scene. The patient's right eye (controlled by the left hemisphere) saw a chicken's foot. When asked to pick a card that related to what he saw, the patient picked a shovel with his left hand (right hemisphere) and a chicken with his right hand (left hemisphere). In other words, each hemisphere independently came up with an appropriate response. For example, the right hemisphere correctly chose something related to what it had seen: a snow shovel for the snow. However, in most people, the right hemisphere has no ability to express language. And all the left hemisphere knew about was a chicken's foot and the image of a shovel that it inexplicably chose. How could he resolve the conflict? Make up a story. When the researchers asked the patient why he picked what he did, the interpreter in the left brain kicked into gear: "Oh, that's simple. The chicken claw goes with the chicken, and you need a shovel to clean out the chicken shed." Rather than saying, "I don't know," the left hemisphere made up a response based on what it knew.[6]

Steven Pinker, a psychologist at Harvard, calls this part of the left hemisphere the *baloney-generator*. He wrote, "The spooky part is that we have no reason to believe that the baloney-generator in the patient's left hemisphere is behaving any different from *ours* as *we* make sense of the inclinations emanating from the rest of *our* brains. The conscious mind—the self or soul—is a spin doctor, not the commander in chief."[7] Gazzaniga's patient simply reveals what's going on in all of our heads.

To explain the past, we also naturally apply the essential elements of stories: a beginning, an end, and a cause.[8] As events in our world unfold, we don't—really, can't—know what's happening. But once we know the ending, we stand ready to create a narrative to explain how and why events unfolded as they did.[9] For our purpose, the two critical elements required for analyzing the past are that we already know the ending and that we want to understand the cause of what happened. Those two elements are what get us into trouble. Most of us will readily believe that this happens to others. But we are much more reluctant to admit that we can fall prey to the same bias.

We often assume that if event A preceded event B, then A caused B. Even Nassim Taleb, who has done a great deal to raise the awareness of the role of randomness and luck in our daily lives, points the finger at himself in this regard. He tells this story: Every day, he used to take a cab to the corner of Park Avenue and 53rd Street in New York City and take the 53rd Street entrance to go to work. One day, the driver let him out closer to the 52nd Street entrance and threw Taleb off his routine. But that day, he had great success at his job trading derivatives. So the next day, he had the cab driver drop him off on the corner of Park and 52nd Street so that he could extend his financial success. He also wore the same tie he had worn the day before. He obviously knew intellectually that where he got out of the cab and which tie he wore had nothing to do with trading derivatives, but he let his superstition get the best of him. He admitted that, deep down, he believed that where he entered the building and what tie he wore were causing him to succeed. "On the one hand, I talked like someone with strong scientific standards," he continued. "On the other, I had closet superstitions just like one of these blue-collar pit traders."[10] Taleb entered the building from 52nd Street and then made money; therefore entering the building from 52nd Street caused him to make money. That faulty association is known as the *post hoc fallacy*. The name comes from the Latin, *post hoc ergo propter hoc*, "after this, therefore because of this." A lot of the science done in the last two hundred years has been aimed at doing away with that mistaken way of thinking.

Knowing the end of the story also leads to another tendency, one that Baruch Fischhoff, a professor of psychology at Carnegie Mellon

University, calls *creeping determinism*. This is the propensity of individuals to "perceive reported outcomes as having been relatively inevitable."[11] Even if a fog of uncertainty surrounded an event before it unfolded, once we know the answer, that fog not only melts away, but the path the world followed appears to be the only possible one.

Here is how all of this relates to skill and luck: even if we acknowledge ahead of time that an event will combine skill and luck in some measure, once we know how things turned out, we have a tendency to forget about luck. We string together the events into a satisfying narrative, including a clear sense of cause and effect, and we start to believe that what happened was preordained by the existence of our own skill. There may be an evolutionary reason for this. In prehistoric times, it was probably better for survival to take the view that we have some control over events than to attribute everything to luck and give up trying.

John Glavin is a professor of English at Georgetown University who teaches courses in writing for the stage and screen. Glavin spends a great deal of time understanding what makes for a great narrative and emphasizes that stories are vehicles for communicating how to act. We use stories, especially those about history, to learn what to do. "Narrative is deeply connected with ethics," he notes, "and narratives tell us how we should and should not behave." But when we try to learn from history, we naturally look for causes even when there may be none. Glavin adds, "For a story to work, someone has to be responsible."[12] History is a great teacher, but the lessons are often unreliable.

Undersampling and Sony's Miraculous Failure

The most common method for teaching a manager how to thrive in business is to find successful businesses, identify the common practices of those businesses, and recommend that the manager imitate them. Perhaps the best-known book about this method is Jim Collins's *Good to Great*. Collins and his team analyzed thousands of companies and isolated eleven whose performance went from good to great. They then identified the concepts that they believed had caused those companies to improve—these include leadership, people, a fact-based approach, focus, discipline, and the use of technology— and suggested that other companies adopt the same concepts to achieve the same sort of results. This formula is intuitive, includes some great narrative, and has sold millions of books for Collins.[13]

No one questions that Collins has good intentions. He really is trying to figure out how to help executives. And if causality were clear, this approach would work. The trouble is that the performance of a company always depends on *both* skill and luck, which means that a given strategy will succeed only part of the time. So attributing success to any strategy may be wrong simply because you're sampling only the winners. The more important question is: How many of the companies that tried that strategy actually succeeded?

Jerker Denrell, a professor of strategy at Oxford, calls this the *undersampling of failure*. He argues that one of the main ways that companies learn is by observing the performance and characteristics of successful organizations. The problem is that firms with poor performance are unlikely to survive, so they are inconspicuously absent from the group that any one person observes. Say two companies pursue the same strategy, and one succeeds because of luck while the other fails. Since we draw our sample from the outcome, not the strategy, we observe the successful company and assume that the strategy was good. In other words, we assume that the favorable outcome was the result of a skillful strategy and overlook the influence of luck. We connect cause and effect where there is no connection.[14] We don't observe the unsuccessful company because it no longer exists. If we had observed it, we would have seen the same strategy failing rather than succeeding and realized that copying the strategy blindly might not work.

Denrell illustrates the idea by offering a scenario in which firms that pursue risky strategies achieve either high or low performance, whereas those that choose low-risk strategies achieve average performance. A high-risk strategy might put all of a company's resources into one technology, while a low-risk strategy would spread resources across various alternatives. The best performers are those that bet on one option and happen to succeed, and the worst performers are those that make a similar bet but fail. As time passes, the successful firms thrive and the failed firms go out of business or get acquired.

Someone attempting to draw lessons from this observation would therefore see only those companies that enjoyed good performance and would infer, incorrectly, that the risky strategies led to high performance. Denrell emphasizes that he is not judging the relative merits of a high- or low-risk strategy. He's saying that you need to consider a full sample of strategies and the results of those strategies in order to learn from the experiences of other organizations. When luck plays a part in determining the consequences of your actions, you don't want to study success to learn what strategy was used but rather study strategy to see whether it consistently led to success.

In chapter 1, we met Michael Raynor, a consultant at Deloitte. Raynor defines what he calls the *strategy paradox*—situations where "the same behaviors and characteristics that maximize a firm's probability of notable success also maximize its probability of failure." To illustrate this paradox, he tells the story of Sony Betamax and MiniDiscs. At the time those products were launched, Sony was riding high on the success of its long string of winning products from the transistor radio to the Walkman and compact disc (CD) player. But when it came to Betamax and MiniDiscs, says Raynor, "the company's strategies failed not because they were bad strategies but because they were *great* strategies.[15]

The case of the MiniDisc is particularly instructive. Sony developed MiniDiscs to replace cassette tapes and compete with CDs. The disks were smaller and less prone to skip than CDs and had the added benefit of being able to record as well as play music. Announced in 1992, MiniDiscs were an ideal format to replace cassettes in the Walkman to allow that device to remain the portable music player of choice.

Sony made sure that the MiniDisc had a number of advantages that put it in a position to be a winner. For example, existing CD plants could produce MiniDiscs, allowing for a rapid reduction in the cost of each unit as sales grew. Furthermore, Sony owned CBS Records, so it could supply terrific music and make even more profit. The strategy behind the MiniDisc reflected the best use of Sony's vast resources and embodied all of the lessons that the company had learned from the successes and failures of past products.

But just as the MiniDisc player was gaining a foothold, seemingly out of nowhere, everyone had tons of cheap computer memory, access to fast broadband networks, and they could swap files of a manageable size that contained all their favorite music essentially for free. Sony had been hard at work on a problem that vanished from beneath their feet. Suddenly, no one needed cassette tapes. No one needed disks either. And no one could possibly have foreseen that seismic shift in the world in the 1990s. In fact, much of it was unimaginable. But it happened. And it killed the MiniDisc. Raynor asserts, "Not only did everything that could go wrong for Sony actually go wrong, everything that went wrong *had* to go wrong in order to sink what was in fact a brilliantly conceived and executed strategy. In my view, it is a miracle that the MiniDisc did not succeed."[16]

One of the main reasons we are poor at untangling skill and luck is that we have a natural tendency to assume that success and failure are caused by skill on the one hand and a lack of skill on the other. But in activities where luck plays a role, such thinking is deeply misguided and leads to faulty conclusions.

Most Research Is False

In 2005, Dr. John Ioannidis published a paper, titled "Why Most Published Research Findings Are False," that shook the foundation of the medical research community.[17] Ioannidis, who has a PhD in biopathology, argues that the conclusions drawn from most research suffer from the fallacies of bias, such as researchers wanting to come to certain conclusions or from doing too much testing. Using simulations, he shows that a high percentage of the claims made by researchers are simply wrong. In a companion paper, he backed up his contention by analyzing forty-nine of the most highly regarded scientific papers of the prior thirteen years, based on the number of times those papers were cited. Three-quarters of the cases where researchers claimed an effective intervention (for example, vitamin E prevents heart attacks) were tested by other scientists. His analysis showed a stark difference between randomized trials and observational studies. In a randomized trial, subjects are assigned at random to one treatment or another (or none). These studies are considered the gold standard of research, because they do an effective job of finding genuine causes rather than simple correlations. They also eliminate bias in many cases, because the people running the experiment don't know who is getting which treatment. In an observational study, subjects volunteer for one treatment or another and researchers have to take what is available. Ioannidis found that more than 80 percent of the results from observational studies were either wrong or significantly exaggerated, while about three-quarters of the conclusions drawn from randomized studies proved to be true.[18]

Ioannidis's work doesn't touch on skill as we have defined it, but it does address the essential issue of cause and effect. In matters of health, researchers want to understand what causes what. A randomized trial allows them to compare two groups of subjects who are similar but who receive different treatments to see whether the treatment makes a difference. By doing so, these trials make it less likely that the results derive from luck. But observational studies don't make the same distinction, allowing luck to creep in if the researchers are not very careful in their methods. The difference in the quality of the findings is so dramatic that Ioannidis recommends a simple approach to observational studies: ignore them.[19]

The dual problems of bias and conducting too much testing are substantial, and by no means limited to medical research.[20] Bias can arise from many factors. For example, a researcher who is funded by a drug company may have an incentive to find that the drug works and is safe. While scientists generally believe themselves to be objective, research in psychology shows that bias is most often subconscious and nearly unavoidable. So even if a scientist believes he is behaving ethically, bias can exert a strong influence.[21] Furthermore, a bit of research that grabs headlines can be very good for advancing an academic's career.

Doing too much testing can cause just as much trouble. There are standard methods to deal with testing too much, but not all scientists use them. In much of academic research, scientists lean heavily on tests of statistical significance. These tests are supposed to indicate the probability of getting a result by chance (more formally, when the null hypothesis is true). There is a standard threshold that allows a researcher to claim that a result is significant. Here's where the trouble starts: if you test enough relationships, you will eventually find a few that pass the test but that are not really related as cause and effect.[22]

One example comes from a paper published in *The Proceedings of the Royal Society B*, a peer-reviewed journal. The article suggests that women who eat breakfast cereal are more likely to give birth to boys than girls.[23] The paper naturally generated a great deal of attention, especially in the media. Stan Young, a statistician at the National Institute of Statistical Sciences, along with a pair of colleagues, reexamined the data and concluded that the finding was likely the product of chance as a result of testing too much. The basic idea is that if you examine enough relationships, some will pass the test of statistical significance by virtue of chance. In this case, there were 264 relationships (132 foods and two time periods), and the plot of expected values of statistical significance between the various relationships was completely consistent with randomness. Young and his collaborators conclude flatly that their analysis "shows that the [findings] claimed as significant by the authors are easily the result of chance."[24]

So if we don't consider a sample that is large enough, we can miss the fact that a single strategy can always give rise to unanticipated results, as we saw in the case of the Sony MiniDisc. In contrast, we can comb through lots of possible causes and pick one that really has nothing to do with the effect we observe, such as women eating cereal and having boys as opposed to girls. What's common to the two approaches is an erroneous association between the effect, which is known, and the presumed cause. In each case, researchers fail to appreciate the role of luck.

Where Is the Skill? It's Easier to Trade for Punters Than Receivers

Many organizations, including businesses and sports teams, try to improve their performance by hiring a star from another organization. They often pay a high price to do so. The premise is that the star has skill that is readily transferable to the new organization. But the people who do this type of hiring rarely consider the degree to which the star's success was the result of either good luck or the structure and support of the organization where he or she worked before. Attributing success to an individual makes for good narrative, but it fails to take into account how much of the skill is unique to the star and is therefore portable.

Boris Groysberg, a professor of organizational behavior at Harvard Business School, has studied this topic in depth. His research shows that organizations tend to overestimate the degree to which the star's skills are transferrable. His most thorough study was of analysts at Wall Street firms.[25] The primary responsibility of these analysts is to determine whether or not a given stock is attractive within the industry that they follow. (I used to be one of these analysts.) *Institutional Investor* magazine ranks the analysts annually, which provides a measure of quality.

Groysberg examined all of the moves by ranked analysts over a twenty-year period and found 366 instances of a star analyst moving to another firm. If the skill were associated solely with the analyst, you would expect the star's performance to remain stable when he or she changed jobs. That is not what the data showed. Groysberg writes,

"Star analysts who switched employers paid a high price for jumping ship relative to comparable stars who stayed put: overall, their job performance plunged sharply and continued to suffer for at least five years after moving to a new firm."[26] He considered a number of explanations for the deterioration in performance and concluded that the main factor was that they left behind a good fit between their skills and the resources of their employer.

General Electric is a well-known source of managerial talent, and its alumni are disproportionately represented among CEOs in the S&P 500. Groysberg and his colleagues tracked the performance of twenty managers from GE that other organizations hired as chairman, CEO, or CEO-designate between 1989 and 2001. They found a stark dichotomy. Ten of the hiring companies resembled GE, so the skills of the executives were neatly transferable and the companies flourished. The other ten companies were in lines of business different from GE. For example, one GE executive went to a company selling groceries, whereas his experience had been in selling appliances. Even with a GE-trained executive at the helm, those companies delivered poor returns to shareholders. Again, developing skill is a genuine achievement. And skill, once developed, has a real influence on what we can do and how successful we are. But skill is only one factor that contributes to the end result of our efforts. The organization or environment in which a CEO works also has an influence. The evidence shows that employers systematically overestimate the power of an individual's skill and underestimate the influence of the organization in which he or she operates.

Along with some fellow researchers, Groysberg showed this point neatly by analyzing the performance of players who switched teams in the National Football League. They compared wide receivers with punters in the period between 1993 and 2002. Since each team has eleven players on the field at a time, wide receivers rely heavily on the strategy of the team and on interaction with their teammates, factors that can vary widely from team to team. Punters pretty much do the same thing no matter which team they play for, and have more limited interaction with teammates. The contrast in interaction allowed the scientists to separate an individual's skill from the influence of the organization on performance. They found that star wide receivers who switched teams suffered a decline in performance for the subsequent season compared with those who stayed with the team. Their performance then improved as they adjusted to their new team. Whether a punter changed teams or stayed put had no influence on his performance. Punters are more portable than wide receivers.[27]

As with testing too much or too little, the difficulty in determining the portability of a skill lies in the relationship between cause and effect. Groysberg's work dwells on stars and finds that the organizations that support them contribute meaningfully to their success. Yet we see people consistently overestimate skill in fields as diverse as catching touchdown passes and selling motorcycles.

Stories Can Obscure Skills

We re-create events in the world by creating a narrative that is based on our own beliefs and goals. As a consequence, we often struggle to understand cause and effect, and especially the relative contributions of skill and luck in shaping the events we observe.[28] As we've seen, we may make the mistake of drawing conclusions from samples that are too small. We may fail to consider all of the causes that might lead to particular events. We might test too much—so much, in fact, that we wind up finding causes where we're simply seeing the results of chance. Or we may look at high performance and believe we are seeing a star with exceptional skill, when in reality we are seeing the combined effects of skill and the powerful influence that an organization can exert on someone. All of these mistakes are manageable, but it is critical to learn about them and to see where they apply if we are going to overcome them. The effort of untangling skill from luck, even with its practical difficulties, still yields great value when we are trying to improve the way we make decisions.

CHAPTER 3

THE LUCK-SKILL CONTINUUM

I N 2006, TRADINGMARKETS, a company that helps people trade stocks, asked ten Playboy Playmates to select five stocks each. The idea was to see if they could beat the market. The winner was Deanna Brooks, Playmate of the Month in May 1998. The stocks she picked rose 43.4 percent, trouncing the S&P 500, which gained 13.6 percent, and beating more than 90 percent of the money managers who actively try to outperform a given index. Brooks wasn't the only one who fared well. Four of the other ten Playmates had better returns than the S&P 500 while less than a third of the active money managers did.[1]

Although the exercise was presumably a lighthearted effort at attracting attention, the results raise a serious question: How can a group of amateurs do a better job of picking stocks than the majority of dedicated professionals? You would never expect amateurs to outperform professional dentists, accountants, or athletes over the course of a year. In this case, the answer lies in the fact that investing is an activity that depends to a great deal on luck, especially over a short period of time. In this chapter, I'll develop a simple model that will allow us to take a more in-depth look at the relative contributions of luck and skill. I'll also provide a framework for thinking about extreme outcomes and show how to anticipate the rate of reversion to the mean. A deeper discussion of the continuum between luck and skill can help us to avoid some of the mistakes described in chapters 1 and 2 and to make better decisions.

Sample Size, Not Time

Visualizing the continuum between luck and skill can help us to see where an activity lies between the two extremes, with pure luck on one side and pure skill on the other. In most cases, characterizing what's going on at the extremes is not too hard. As an example, you can't predict the outcome of a specific fair coin toss or payoff from a slot machine. They are entirely dependent on chance. On the other hand, the fastest swimmer will almost always win the race. The outcome is determined by skill, with luck playing only a vanishingly small role (for example, the fastest swimmer could contract food poisoning in the middle of a match and lose). But the extremes on the continuum capture only a small percentage of what really goes on in the world. Most of the action is in the middle, and having a sense of where an activity lies will provide you with an important context for making decisions.

As you move from right to left on the continuum, luck exerts a larger influence. It doesn't mean that skill doesn't exist in those activities. It does. It means that we need a large number of observations to make sure that skill can overcome the influence of luck. So Deanna Brooks would have to pick a lot more stocks and outperform the pros for a lot longer before we'd be ready to say that she is skillful at picking stocks. (The more likely outcome is that her performance would revert to the mean and look a lot more like the average of all investments.) In some endeavors, such as selling books and movies, luck plays a large role, and yet best-selling books and blockbuster movies don't revert to the mean over time. We'll return to that subject later to discuss why that happens. But for now we'll stick to areas where luck does even out the results over time.

When skill dominates, a small sample is sufficient to understand what's going on. When Roger Federer was in his prime, you could watch him play a few games of tennis and know that he was going to win against all but one or two of the top players. You didn't have to watch a thousand games. In activities that are strongly influenced by luck, a small sample is useless and even dangerous. You'll need a large sample to draw any reasonable conclusion about what's going to happen next. This link between luck and the size of the sample makes complete sense, and there is a simple model that demonstrates this important lesson. Figure 3-1 shows a matrix with the continuum on the bottom and the size of the sample on the side. In order to make a sound judgment, you must choose the size of your sample with care.

We're naturally inclined to believe that a small sample is representative of a larger sample. In other words, we expect to see what we've already seen. This fallacy can run in two directions. In one direction, we observe a small sample and believe, falsely, that we know what all of the possibilities look like. This is the classic problem of *induction*, drawing general conclusions from specific

FIGURE 3-1

Sample size and the luck-skill continuum

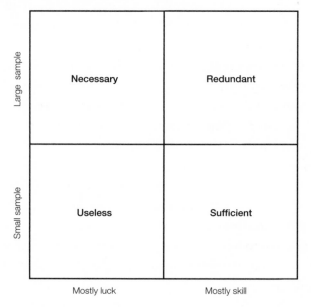

Source: Analysis by author.

observations. We saw, for instance, that small schools produced students with the highest test scores. But that didn't mean that the size of the school had any influence on those scores. In fact, small schools also had students with the lowest scores.

In many situations we have only our observations and simply don't know what's possible.[2] To put it in statistical terms, we don't know what the whole distribution looks like. The greater the influence luck has on an activity, the greater our risk of using induction to draw false conclusions. To put this another way, think of an investor who trades successfully for a hundred days using a particular strategy. He will be tempted to believe that he has a fail-safe way to make money. But when the conditions of the market change, his profits will turn to losses. A small number of observations fails to reveal all of the characteristics of the market.

We can err in the opposite direction as well, unconsciously assuming that there is some sort of cosmic justice, or a scorekeeper in the sky who will make things even out in the end. This is known as the *gambler's fallacy*. Say you're watching a coin being tossed. Heads comes up three times in a row. What do you think the next toss will show? Most people will say tails. It feels as if tails is overdue. But it's not. There is a 50-50 chance of both heads and tails on every toss, and one flip has no influence on any other. But if you toss the coin a million times, you will, in fact, see about half a million heads and half a million tails. Conversely, in the universe of the possible, you might see heads come up a hundred times in a row if you toss the coin long enough.

It turns out that many things in nature do even out, which is why we have evolved to think that all things balance out. Several days of rain are likely to be followed by fair weather. But in cases near the side of the continuum where outcomes are independent of one another, or close to being so, the gambler's fallacy is alive and well. This influence casts its net well beyond naive gamblers and ensnares trained scientists, too.[3]

When you're attempting to select the correct size of a sample to analyze, it's natural to assume that the more you allow time to pass, the larger your sample will be. But the relationship between the two is much more complicated than that. In some instances, a short amount of time is sufficient to gather a relatively large sample, while in other cases a lot of time can pass and the sample will remain small. You should consider time as independent from the size of the sample.

Evaluation of competition in sports illustrates this point. In U.S. men's college basketball, a game lasts forty minutes and each team takes possession of the ball an average of about sixty-five times during the game. Since the number of times each team possesses the ball is roughly equal, possession has little to do with who wins. The team that converts possessions into the most points will win. In contrast, a men's college lacrosse game is sixty minutes long but each team takes possession of the ball only about thirty-three times. So in basketball, each team gets the ball almost twice a minute, while in lacrosse each team gets the ball only once every couple of minutes or so. The size of the sample of possessions in basketball is almost double that of lacrosse. That means that luck plays a smaller role in basketball, and skill exerts a greater influence on who wins. Because the size of the sample in lacrosse is smaller and the number of interactions on the field so large, luck has a greater influence on the final score, even though the game is longer.[4]

The Two-Jar Model

Imagine that you have two jars filled with balls.[5] Each ball has a number on it. The numbers in one jar represent skill, while the numbers in the other represent luck. Higher numbers are better. You draw one ball from the jar that represents skill, one from the jar that represents luck, and then add them together to get a score. Figure 3-2 shows a case where the numbers for skill and luck follow a classic bell curve. But the numbers can follow all sorts of distributions. The idea is to fill each jar with numbers that capture the essence of the activity you are trying to understand.

FIGURE 3-2

A simple example of skill and luck distributions

Skill	Luck

Source: Analysis by author.

To represent an activity that's completely dependent on skill, for instance, we can fill the jar that represents luck with zeros. That way, only the numbers representing skill will count. If we want to represent an activity that is completely dependent on luck, such as roulette, we fill the other jar with zeros. Most activities are some blend of skill and luck.

Here's a simple example. Let's say that the jar representing skill has only three numbers, −3, 0, and 3, and that the jar representing luck has −4, 0, and 4. We can easily list all of the possible outcomes, from −7, which reflects poor skill and bad luck, to 7, the combination of excellent skill and good luck. (See figure 3-3.) Naturally, anything real that we model would be vastly more complex than this example, but these numbers suffice to make several crucial points.

It is possible to do poorly in an activity even with good skill if the influence of luck is sufficiently strong and the number of times

FIGURE 3-3

Simple jar model

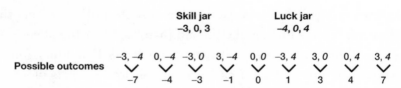

	Skill jar −3, 0, 3			Luck jar −4, 0, 4				
Possible outcomes −3, −4	0, −4	−3, 0	3, −4	0, 0	−3, 4	3, 0	0, 4	3, 4
∨	∨	∨	∨	∨	∨	∨	∨	∨
−7	−4	−3	−1	0	1	3	4	7

Source: Analysis by author.

you draw from the jars is small. For example, if your level of skill is 3 but you draw a −4 from the jar representing luck, then bad luck trumps skill and you score −1. It's also possible to have a good outcome without being skilled. Your skill at −3 is as low as it can be, but your blind luck in choosing 4 gives you an acceptable score of 1.

Of course, this effect goes away as you increase the size of the sample. Think of it this way: Say your level of skill is always 3. You draw only from the jar representing luck. In the short run, you might pull some numbers that reflect good or bad luck, and that effect may persist for some time. But over the long haul, the expected value of the numbers representing luck is zero as your draws of balls marked 0, 4, and −4 even out. Ultimately your level of skill, represented by the number 3, will come through.[6]

The Paradox of Skill—More Skill Means Luck Is More Important

This idea also serves as the basis for what I call the *paradox of skill*. As skill improves, performance becomes more consistent, and therefore luck becomes more important. Stephen Jay Gould, a renowned paleontologist at Harvard, developed this argument to explain why no baseball player in the major leagues has had a batting average of .400 or more for a full season since Ted Williams hit .406 in 1941 while playing for the Boston Red Sox.[7] Gould started by considering some common explanations. The first was that night games, distant travel, diluted talent, and better pitching had all impeded batters. While those factors may have had some influence on the results, none are sufficient to explain the failure to achieve a .400 average. Another possibility was that Williams was not only the best hitter of his era, but that he was better than any other hitter to come along since then. Gould quickly dismissed that argument by showing that in every sport where it can be measured, performance had steadily improved over time. Williams, as good as he was in his era, would certainly not stand out as much if he were to be compared with players today.

At first glance, that may seem contradictory. But the improvement in performance since 1941 may not be as apparent in baseball as it is in other sports because batting average has remained relatively stable, at around .260–.270, for decades. But the stable average masks two important developments. First, batting average reflects not individual skill but rather the interaction between pitchers and hitters. It's like an arms race. As pitchers and hitters both improve their skills on an absolute basis, their relative relationship stays static. Although both pitchers and hitters today are some of the most skillful in history, they have improved in lockstep.[8] But that lockstep was not ordained entirely by nature. The overseers of Major League Baseball have had a hand in it. In the late 1960s, for example, when it appeared that pitchers were getting too good for the batters, they changed the rules by lowering the pitcher's mound by five inches and by shrinking the strike zone, allowing the hitters to do better. Thus the rough equilibrium between pitchers and hitters reflects the natural evolution of the players as well as a certain amount of intervention from league officials.

Gould argues that there are no more .400 hitters because all professional hitters have become more skillful, and therefore the difference between the best and worst has narrowed. Training has improved greatly in the last sixty years, which has certainly had an effect on this convergence of skills. In addition, the leagues began recruiting players from around the world, greatly expanding the pool of talent. Hungry kids from the Dominican Republic (Sammy Sosa) and Mexico (Fernando Valenzuela) brought a new level of skill to the game. At the same time, luck continued to play a meaningful role in determining an individual player's batting average. Once the pitcher lets go of a ball, it is still hard to predict whether the batter, however skilled, will connect with it and what will happen if he does.

The key idea, expressed in statistical terms, is that the variance of batting averages has shrunk over time, even as the skill of the hitters has improved. Figure 3-4 shows the standard deviation and coefficient of variation for batting averages by decade since the 1870s.

FIGURE 3-4

Reduction in standard deviation in Major League Baseball batting averages

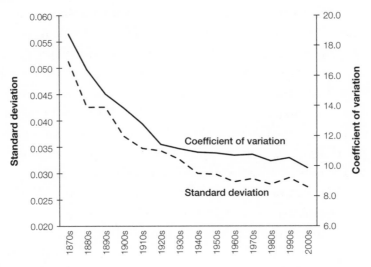

Source: Analysis by author.

Variance is simply standard deviation squared, so a reduction in standard deviation corresponds to a reduction in variance. The coefficient of variation is the standard deviation divided by the average of all the hitters, which provides an effective measure of how scattered the batting averages of the individual players are from the league average. The figure shows that batting averages have converged over the decades. While Gould focused on batting average, this phenomenon is observable in other relevant statistics as well. For example, the coefficient of variation for earned run average, a measure of how many earned runs a pitcher allows for every nine innings pitched, has also declined over the decades.[9]

This decline in variance explains why there are no more .400 hitters. Since everybody gets better, no one wins quite as dramatically. In his day, Williams was an elite hitter and the variance was large enough that he could achieve such an exalted average. Today, the variance has shrunk to the point that elite hitters have only a tiny probability of matching his average. If Williams played today and had the same level of skill that he had in 1941 relative to other players, his batting average would not come close to .400.

Hitting a baseball in the major leagues is one of the hardest tasks in all of sports. A major league pitcher throws a baseball at speeds of up to one hundred miles an hour with the added complication of sideways or downward movement as it approaches the plate. The paradox of skill says that even though baseball players are more skillful than ever, skill plays a smaller role in determining batting averages than it did in the past. That's because the difference between success and failure for the batter has come to depend on a mistake of only fractions of an inch in where he places his bat or thousandths of a second in his timing in beginning an explosive and nearly automatic swing. But because everyone is uniformly more skillful, the vagaries of luck are more important than ever.

You can readily see how the paradox of skill applies to other competitive activities. A company can improve its absolute performance, for example, but will remain at a competitive parity if its rivals do the same.[10] Or if stocks are priced efficiently in the market, luck will determine whether an investor correctly anticipates the next price move up or down. When everyone in business, sports, and investing copies the best practices of others, luck plays a greater role in how well they do.

For activities where little or no luck is involved, the paradox of skill leads to a specific and testable prediction: over time, absolute performance will steadily approach the point of physical limits, such as the speed with which one can run a mile. And as the best competitors confront those limits, the relative performance of the participants will converge. Figure 3-5 shows this idea graphically. As time goes on, the picture evolves from one that looks like the left side to one that looks more like the right side. The average of the distribution of skill creeps toward peak performance and the slope of the right tail gets steeper as the variance shrinks, implying results that are more and more alike.

We can test this prediction to see if it is true. Consider running foot races, especially the marathon, one of the oldest and most popular

FIGURE 3-5

The paradox of skill leads to clustered results

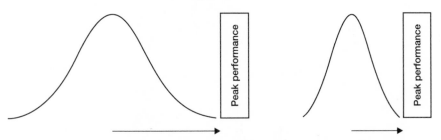

Over time, the average distance from peak performance shrinks and results cluster.

Source: Analysis by author.

sports events in history. The race covers 26 miles and 385 yards. It was introduced as an original Olympic event in 1896, roughly fifteen hundred years after—legend has it—Pheidippides ran to his home in Athens from the battlefield of Marathon, where his country-men had just defeated the Persians. When Pheidippides arrived, he proclaimed, "We have won!" He then dropped dead.

John Brenkus, host of *Sports Science* for the television network ESPN, speculates on the limits of human performance in his book *The Perfection Point*. After giving consideration to a multitude of physical factors, he concludes that the fastest time that a human can ever run a marathon is 1 hour, 57 minutes, and 58 seconds.[11] As I write this, the world record, held by Patrick Makau of Kenya, is 2 hours, 3 minutes, and 38 seconds. So Makau's record is 5 minutes and 40 seconds slower than what is theoretically possible, according to Brenkus.

Figure 3-6 shows two results from each men's Olympic mara-thon from 1932 to 2008. The first is the time of the winner. That time dropped by about twenty-five minutes during those years. This trans-lates into a pace that is almost one minute faster each mile, which (as you runners out there know) is a substantial increase, even considering that it was achieved over three-quarters of a century. The figure also shows the difference between the time of the gold

FIGURE 3-6

Men's Olympic marathon times and the paradox of skill

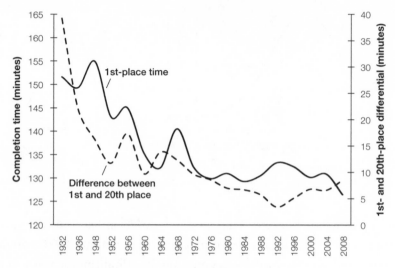

Source: www.olympicgamesmarathon.com and analysis by author.

medalist and the man who came in twentieth. As the paradox of skill predicts, that time has narrowed from close to forty minutes in 1932 to around nine minutes in 2008. So as everyone's skill has improved, the performance of the person who finished in twentieth place and the winner has converged.

The two-jar model shows that luck can overwhelm skill in the short term if the variance of the distribution of luck is larger than the variance of the distribution of skill. In other words, if everyone gets better at something, luck plays a more important role in determining who wins. Let's return to that model now.

The Ingredients of an Outlier

Note that the extreme values in the two-jar model are −7 and 7. The only way to get those values is to combine the worst skill with the worst luck or the best skill with the best luck. Since the poorest performers generally die off in a competitive environment, we'll concentrate on the best. The basic argument is easy to summarize: great success combines skill with a lot of luck. You can't get there by relying on either skill or luck alone. You need both.

This is one of the central themes in Malcolm Gladwell's book, *Outliers*. As one of his examples, Gladwell tells the story of Bill Joy, the billionaire cofounder of Sun Microsystems, who is now a partner in the venture capital firm Kleiner Perkins. Joy was always exceptionally bright. He scored a perfect 800 on the math section of the SAT and entered the University of Michigan at the age of sixteen. To his good fortune, Michigan had one of the few computers in the country that had a keyboard and screen. Everywhere else, people who wanted to use a computer had to feed punched cards into the machine to get it to do anything (or more likely, wait for a technician to do it). Joy spent an enormous amount of time learning to write programs in college, giving him an edge when he entered the PhD program for computer science at the University of California, Berkeley. By the time he had completed his studies at Berkeley, he had about ten thousand hours of practice in writing computer code.[12] But it was the combination of his skill and good luck that allowed him to start a software company and accrue his substantial net worth. He could have been just as smart and gone to a college that had no interactive computers. To succeed, Joy needed to draw winning numbers from both jars.

Gladwell argues that the lore of success too often dwells on an individual's personal qualities, focusing on how grit and talent paved the way to the top. But a closer examination always reveals the substantial role that luck played. If history is written by the winners, history is also written *about* the winners, because we like to see clear cause and effect. Luck is boring as the driving force in a story. So when talking about success, we tend to place too much emphasis on skill and not enough on luck. Luck is there, though, if you look. A full account of these stories of success shows, as Gladwell puts it, that "outliers reached their lofty status through a combination of ability, opportunity, and utter arbitrary advantage."[13] This is precisely what the two-jar model demonstrates.

Outliers show up in another way. Let's return to Stephen Jay Gould, baseball, and the 1941 season. Not only was that the year that Ted Williams hit .406, it was the year that Joe DiMaggio got a hit in fifty-six straight games. Of the two feats, DiMaggio's streak is considered the more inviolable.[14] While no player has broached a .400 batting average since Williams did, George Brett (.390 in 1980) and Rod Carew (.388 in 1977) weren't far off. The closest that anyone has approached to DiMaggio's streak was in 1978, when Pete Rose hit safely in forty-four games, only 80 percent of DiMaggio's record.

"Long streaks are, and must be, a matter of extraordinary luck imposed on great skill," wrote Gould.[15] That's exactly how you generate a long streak with the two jars. Here's a way to think about it: Say you draw once from the jar representing skill and then draw repeatedly from the other. The only way to have a sustained streak of success is to start with a high value for skill and then be lucky enough to pull high numbers from then on to represent your good luck. As Gould emphasizes, "Long hitting streaks happen to the greatest players because their general chance of getting a hit is so much higher than average."[16] For instance, the probability that a .300 hitter gets three hits in a row is 2.7 percent (= $.3^3$) while the probability that a .200 hitter gets three hits in a row is 0.8 percent (= $.2^3$). Good luck alone doesn't carry the day. While not all great hitters have streaks, all of the records for the longest streaks are held by great hitters. As a testament to this point, the players who have enjoyed streaks of hits in thirty or more consecutive games have a mean batting average of .303, well above the league's long-term average.[17]

Naturally, this principle applies well beyond baseball. In other sports, as well as the worlds of business and investing, long winning streaks always meld skill and luck. Luck does generate streaks by itself, and it's easy to confuse streaks due solely to luck with streaks that combine skill and luck. But when there are differences in the level of skill in a field, the long winning streaks go to the most skillful players.

Reversion to the Mean and the
James-Stein Estimator

Using the two jars also provides a useful way to think about reversion to the mean, the idea that an outcome that is far from the average will be followed by an outcome that is closer to the average. Consider the top four combinations (–3 skill, 4 luck; 3 skill, 0 luck; 0 skill, 4 luck; and 3 skill, 4 luck) which sum to 15. Of the total of 15, skill contributes 3 (–3, 3, 0, 3) and luck contributes 12 (4, 0, 4, 4). Now, let's say you hold on to the numbers representing skill. Your skill remains the same over the course of this exercise. Now you return the numbers representing luck to the jar and draw a new set of numbers. What would you expect the new sum to be? Since your level of skill remains unchanged at 3 and the expected value of luck is zero, the expected value of the new outcome is 3. That is the idea behind reversion to the mean.

We can do the same exercise for the bottom four outcomes (–3 skill, –4 luck; 0 skill, –4 luck; –3 skill, 0 luck; and 3 skill, –4 luck). They add up to –15, and the contribution from skill alone is –3. Here, also, with a new draw the expected value for luck is zero, so the total goes from –15 to an expected value of –3. In both cases, skill remains the same but the large contributions from either good luck or bad luck shrink toward zero.

While most people seem to understand the idea of reversion to the mean, using the jars and the continuum between luck and skill can add an important dimension to this thinking. In the two-jar exercise, you draw only once from the jar representing skill; after that, your level of skill is assumed to remain the same. This is an unrealistic assumption over a long period of time but very reasonable for the short term. You then draw from the jar representing luck, record your value, and return the number to the jar. As you draw again and again, your scores reflect stable skill and variations in luck. In this form of the exercise, your skill ultimately determines whether you wind up a winner or a loser.

The position of the activity on the continuum defines how rapidly your score goes toward an average value, that is, the *rate* of reversion to the mean. Say, for example, that an activity relies entirely on skill and involves no luck. That means the number you draw for skill will always be added to zero, which represents luck. So each score will simply be your skill. Since the value doesn't change, there is no reversion to the mean. Marion Tinsley, the greatest player of checkers, could win all day long, and luck played no part in it. He was simply better than everyone else.

Now assume that the jar representing skill is filled with zeros, and that your score is determined solely by luck; that is, the outcomes will be dictated solely by luck and the expected value of every incremental draw for skill will be the same: zero. So every subsequent outcome has an expected value that represents complete reversion to the mean. In activities that are all skill, there is no reversion to the mean. In activities that are all luck, there is complete reversion to the mean. So if you can place an activity on the luck-skill continuum, you have a sound starting point for anticipating the rate of reversion to the mean.

In real life, we don't know for sure how skill and luck contribute to the results when we make decisions. We can only observe what happens. But we can be more formal in specifying the rate of reversion to the mean by introducing the *James-Stein estimator* with a focus on what is called the *shrinking factor*.[18] This construct is easiest to understand by using a concrete example. Say you have a baseball player, Joe, who hits .350 for part of the season, when the average of all players is .265. You don't really believe that Joe will average .350 forever because even if he's an above-average hitter, he's likely been the beneficiary of good luck recently. You'd like to know what his average will look like over a longer period of time. The best way to estimate that is to reduce his average so that it is closer to .265. The James-Stein estimator includes a factor that tells you how much you need to shrink the .350 while Joe's average is high so that his number more closely resembles his true ability in the long run. Let's go straight to the equation to see how it works:

Estimated true average = Grand average +
shrinking factor (observed average − grand average)

The *estimated true average* would represent Joe's true ability.
The *grand average* is the average of all of the players (.265), and the
observed average is Joe's average during his period of success (.350).
In a classic article on this topic, two statisticians named Bradley
Efron and Carl Morris estimated the shrinking factor for batting
averages to be approximately .2. (They used data on batting averages from the 1970 season with a relatively small sample, so consider
this as illustrative and not definitive.)[19] Here is how Joe's average
looks using the James-Stein estimator:

Estimated true average = .265 + .2 (.350 − .265)

According to this calculation, Joe is most likely going to be
batting .282 for most of the season. The equation can also be used
for players who have averages below the grand average. For
example, the best estimate of true ability for a player who is hitting
only .175 for a particular stretch is .247, or .265 + .2 (.175 − .265).

For activities that are all skill, the shrinking factor is 1.0, which
means that the best estimate of the next outcome is the prior outcome. When Marion Tinsley was playing checkers, the best guess
about who would win the next game was Marion Tinsley. If you
assume that skill is stable in the short term and that luck is not a
factor, this is the exact outcome that you would expect.

For activities that are all luck, the shrinking factor is 0, which
means that the expected value of the next outcome is the mean of
the distribution of luck. In most American casinos, the mean distribution of luck in the game of roulette is 5.26 percent, the house
edge, and no amount of skill can change that. You may win a lot for
a while or lose a lot for a while, but if you play long enough, you will
lose 5.26 percent of your money. If skill and luck play an equal role,
then the shrinking factor is 0.5, halfway between the two. So we can
assign a shrinking factor to a given activity according to where that

activity lies on the continuum. The closer the activity is to all skill, the closer the factor is to 1. The larger the role that luck plays, the closer the factor is to zero. We will see a specific example of how these shrinking factors correlate with skill in chapter 10.

The James-Stein estimator can be useful in predicting the outcome of any activity that combines skill and luck. To use one example, the return on invested capital for companies reverts to the mean over time. In this case, the rate of reversion to the mean reflects a combination of a company's competitive position and its industry. Generally speaking, companies that deal in technology (and companies whose products have short life cycles) tend to revert more rapidly to the mean than established companies with stable demand for their well-known consumer products. So Seagate Technology, a maker of hard drives for computers, will experience more rapid reversion to the mean than Procter & Gamble, the maker of the best-selling detergent, Tide, because Seagate has to constantly innovate, and even its winning products have a short shelf life. Put another way, companies that deal in technology have a shrinking factor that is closer to zero.

Similarly, investing is a very competitive activity, and luck weighs heavily on the outcomes in the short term. So if you are using a money manager's past returns to anticipate her future results, a low shrinkage factor is appropriate. Past performance is no guarantee of future results because there is too much luck involved in investing.

Understanding the rate of reversion to the mean is essential for good forecasting. The continuum of luck and skill, as our experience with the two jars has shown, provides a practical way to think about that rate and ultimately to measure it.

So far, I have assumed that the jars contain numbers that follow a normal distribution, but in fact, distributions are rarely normal. Furthermore, the level of skill changes over time, whether you're talking about an athlete, a company, or an investor. But using jars to create a model is a method that can accommodate those different distributions. Chapters 5 and 6 will examine how skill changes over time and what forms luck can take.

Visualizing luck and skill as a continuum provides a simple concept that can carry a lot of intellectual freight. It allows us to understand when luck can make your level of skill irrelevant, especially in the short term, as we saw with the Playboy Playmates. It allows us to think about extreme performance, as in the cases of Bill Joy and Joe DiMaggio. And makes it possible for us to calibrate the rate of reversion to the mean, as we did with batting averages. Each of these ideas is essential to making intelligent predictions.

Chapter 4 looks at techniques for placing activities on the continuum. It's time to make the ideas from the continuum operational.

PLACING ACTIVITIES ON THE LUCK-SKILL CONTINUUM

ONE OF MY SONS, Alex, is an avid rower. It is a sport that demands a great deal of hard work and dedication, and, as with running races, skill largely determines who wins. Alex told me that one of his coaches refuses to allow parents and other well-wishers to bid the rowers "Good luck!" before a race. The coach suggests, instead, that they encourage the rowers by saying "Good effort!" As he sees it, there is no reason to wish an athlete good luck if luck doesn't make you a winner.

If you do a search on the Internet, you will find a number of sites that claim to offer a system that allows you to win playing the slot machines. As a little research (and the lavishness of casinos) reveals, slots are a game of negative expectation. For every dollar you put in, the machine returns between eighty and ninety-eight cents. After I mentioned in a talk that there is nothing you can do to increase your odds at slots, Richard Zeckhauser, a professor of political economy at Harvard and a friend, pulled me aside and told me that there *are* professional slot machine players.[1] Well, there may be. But if they exist, there are not many of them. Whether you win or lose, playing slots in the short term is a matter of luck. The skill lies with the programmers of the machines, who must strike a balance between allowing players to win enough to encourage them to play more and ensuring that the casino makes a profit over time.[2]

Rowing is at one extreme of the continuum between luck and skill, which is why wishing the competitors good luck makes little sense. Slot machines are at the other extreme, so the idea of a system based on skill that will allow a gambler to beat slots over time is far-fetched. But most activities combine luck and skill. The extent to which the two factors contribute to outcomes is the essential issue.

To address that issue, we have to be able to place activities somewhere along the continuum that will represent the true mix of luck and skill. We'll have to consider what unit of analysis to use, what size the sample should be, and how time influences the activity in question. We can analyze activities at different levels, and the levels may represent different mixes of luck and skill. For instance, the rate at which batters strike out in baseball compared with the number of turns they take at bat may fall on one spot on the continuum, while the performance of a baseball team over a season may end up on a very different spot. The rate at which batters strike out reflects a mixture of the skill of the pitcher, the skill of the batter, and an element of luck. But neither pitcher nor batter has to interact with the other players on the team. This one-on-one contest would suggest that skill has a strong influence, while luck is a minor force.

The experience of the whole baseball team over a season is much different. Not only are there many more individual skills to consider, but the final record will be influenced by injuries (bad luck), normal fluctuations in performance (good and bad luck), and the natural element of chance that enters into any skilled performance.

When an activity is mostly skill, we need not worry much about the size of the sample unless the level of skill is changing quickly. For activities with a good dose of luck, skill is very difficult to detect with small samples. As the sample increases in size, the influence of skill becomes clearer. So you can actually place the same activity at different points along the continuum based on the size of the sample alone. Larger samples do a better job of revealing the true contributions of skill and luck.

As a simple example, consider the game of blackjack played using standard strategy. Figure 4-1 provides an estimate of the percentage of times you can expect to win assuming that you bet 100, 1,000, and 10,000 times. If a large number of players each play 100 hands of blackjack, 51 percent of them will be behind and 49 percent will come out even or ahead. But as the number of hands played by each player rises to 10,000, two-thirds of them lose and only one-third make a profit. Almost no one breaks even at that point. The more you play, the more apparent the house edge becomes.

Time is just as important as the size of your sample. Most of our measurements of time are derived from how long it takes the earth to orbit the sun: one year. Sports measure time by the season, that fraction of the year when teams compete within a particular league. Businesses generally operate with quarters and years for financial reporting and three- to ten-year periods for long-term assessments of performance and compensation. Investors also use quarters

FIGURE 4-1

Probability of winning at blackjack using standard strategy for varying numbers of bets

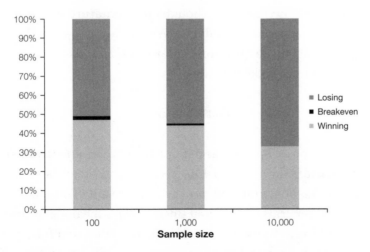

Source: David Spanier, *Easy Money: Inside the Gambler's Mind* (New York: Penguin Books, 1987), 149.

and years. Three years is the most common period of time over which to evaluate an investment manager's performance.[3]

In this chapter, we will explore three methods for placing activities on the continuum between luck and skill. We'll start by asking some basic questions about the activity. The answers should provide some solid guidance about where the activity lies on the continuum. This approach appears subjective, but provides great insight if done carefully. Next, we'll use simulation to make that placement on the continuum more precise. In this case we'll derive distributions of all skill and all luck and combine them in a proportion that matches the actual results. We'll finish by reviewing a method that is popular among sports statisticians and that closely follows the structure of the two-jar model. This approach estimates the contribution of skill by subtracting luck from the outcomes we observe. We will see, too, that we can apply these methods to the world of business and investing, even if the data are not quite as clean as they are for sports.

Placing Activities by Answering Three Questions

The first method of placing activities on the luck-skill continuum relies on simply giving some thought to the nature of the activity and the outcomes that it produces. We can learn a great deal from answering some basic questions and recognizing what the answers imply for when we make decisions.

Cause and Effect

First, ask if you can easily assign a cause to the effect you see. In some activities, the relationship of cause and effect is clear. You can repeat the behavior and get the same result. These are activities that are generally stable and linear. *Stable* means that the basic structure of the activity doesn't change over time, and *linear* means that a particular action leads to the same reaction every time. If you can easily identify the cause of a given effect, you're most likely on the skill side of the continuum. If it's hard to tell, you're on the luck side.[4]

Here's an example: As an amateur tennis player, you decide that if you simply look at the ball all the time when you're trying to return it, you'll be more successful. You keep track and find that, indeed, you're returning a lot more balls when you keep your eye on the ball. Conclusion: It's not luck. You're really improving your skill. Another example: You wear your Lucky Hat every time you go to the casino to play roulette. You win between $50 and $100 the first three times you do it. Never again will you gamble without your Lucky Hat. The trend holds for another few visits to the casino—wear the hat and win. But then one blustery Saturday, your Lucky Hat blows off your head and lands in the river, never to be seen again. That night you win $1,000 at roulette. The next weekend you're so stoked about *not* wearing your Lucky Hat that you bet heavily and lose $2,000. You get the idea. Hard to tell cause and effect here. You're way on the luck side of the continuum.

Take a more complex example. Consider two elements of a manufacturing business. The first is the actual manufacturing process. World-class manufacturers develop very clear processes that are highly repeatable and have very low error rates. There is a rich literature that applies statistical methods to manufacturing, with a goal of reducing costs.[5] One well-known case in point is the Six Sigma method, designed to reduce variation in production. A company that achieves Six Sigma ability will have fewer than 3.4 defects for every million units of goods or services. General Electric and Honeywell, among others, have saved billions of dollars by implementing the method. Manufacturing is an activity that falls near the all-skill side of the continuum. A proper process using statistical control yields a favorable outcome a very high percentage of the time.[6]

The second element of a manufacturing business is simply deciding which products to manufacture. We call this *strategy*, and even a well-conceived strategy can fail catastrophically, as we saw with the Sony MiniDisc, because success is not a linear process. It depends on a large number of factors, including competitors, technological developments, regulatory changes, general economic conditions, and the preferences of fickle customers, to name just a few. Although better strategies will lead to more successes over time, a good process provides no guarantee of a good outcome. So even within the same company, some activities will rely mostly on skill and others will depend a great deal on luck.

As a side note, as individuals advance in their careers, their duties often slide toward the luck side of the continuum. The tools that made an executive very successful as the head of manufacturing may be of little use when he is promoted to CEO, a position in which it's much more difficult to find causes for specific effects. The nature of feedback changes, too, which is also challenging. In activities strongly influenced by skill, feedback is generally clear. When luck stands between cause and effect, giving and receiving quality feedback becomes much more difficult.

The Rate of Reversion

The second question relates to a topic this book has already discussed in some detail: What is the rate of reversion to the mean? To answer this question you need some way to measure performance. You can, for example, tally up a sports team's wins and losses. You can record a company's profit or an investment manager's success at beating a benchmark such as the S&P 500. In each of these cases, you can calculate the results and get a good sense of how quickly they are moving toward the average. Slow reversion is consistent with activities dominated by skill, while rapid reversion comes from luck being the more dominant influence.

Where Prediction Is Useful

The third and final question is: Where can we predict well? In other words, where are experts useful? Answering this question requires examining and assessing the track record of expert predictions. When the predictions of experts tend to be uniform and accurate, skill is the driving factor. When experts have wide disagreement and predict poorly, lots of luck is generally involved.

Areas that have high predictability include engineering, some areas of medicine, and games such as chess and checkers. For instance, tournament chess players earn a rating based on how much they win or tie and what the opposing player's rating was at the time of the game. If you're rated two hundred points higher than your opponent, you'll be expected to win 75 percent of the time. If you win, your rating will go up a small amount. If you lose, your rating will drop by much more.[7] Therefore, your rating is a reliable predictor of how well you'll perform, even though your skill is constantly changing.

Experts are notoriously poor at predicting the outcomes of political, social, and economic systems.[8] Researchers documented that fact decades ago. But what's surprising is not their abysmal record of prediction but rather that society continues to believe them. The reason the experts are so hopelessly lost is that political, social, and economic systems are complex adaptive systems. The results you see, such as booms and busts in the stock market, emerge from the interaction of lots of individual agents. Complex adaptive systems effectively obscure cause and effect. You can't make predictions in any but the broadest and vaguest terms.[9]

Simulation: Blending Distributions
to Match the Results

In the next method for estimating the relative contributions of skill and luck, the first step is to specify what would happen if only luck were involved and then ask what would happen if what we're seeing were completely the result of skill. We can then observe the real data that has been gathered and see where it ought to fall on the continuum.

Although this approach applies elsewhere, sports again provide a convenient illustration. Let's take a look at the work of Brian Burke at Advanced NFL Stats concerning records of wins and losses in the National Football League (NFL).[10] The NFL has thirty-two teams, each of which plays sixteen games in the regular season. Let's first calculate the distribution of wins and losses if football were purely a game of luck. This assumes that the performance of each team is equivalent to drawing from a jar filled with an equal number of ones and zeros (representing luck) and a jar filled with zeros (representing skill). In other words, it's as if the flip of a coin determines the outcome of each game (see figure 4-2). The horizontal axis shows the number of wins, and the vertical axis represents frequency, or the percentage of teams in the league that are expected to win that number of games. For example, about 20 percent of the teams are expected to win half of their games for a record of 8-8, and the percentage of teams winning either all or none of their games—going either winless or undefeated—is extremely low.

The second step is to consider what the distribution of wins and losses would look like if no luck were involved. To do this, we

FIGURE 4-2

NFL record assuming pure luck

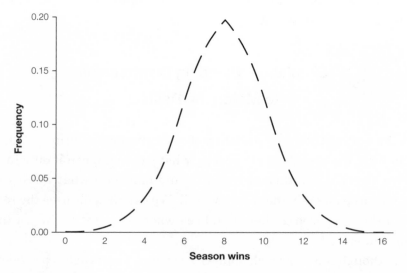

Source: Analysis by author.

randomly assign the teams a number from 1 to 32 (because there are thirty-two teams), and assume that the higher-ranked team always beats the lower-ranked team. For instance, if a team assigned a higher-skill number plays a team assigned a lower-skill number, the higher-skill team wins every time. This is equivalent to having a skill jar filled with thirty-two distinct numbers that correspond with skill and a luck jar that is filled with zeros.

We then mimic the format of the NFL schedule, mixing games within the division with games outside the division, using the league's scheduling algorithm. Next we simulate five thousand seasons and see what the distribution looks like. Figure 4-3 shows the outcome of the simulation. The distribution is relatively flat in the middle with slight dips at the ends for the very best (1 and 2) and worst (31 and 32) teams.

We then look at the actual results for all NFL teams. Figure 4-4 gathers the results for five seasons from 2007 through 2011. So now we have three distributions: one for an all-luck world, one for an all-skill world, and one that reflects the actual results.

FIGURE 4-3

NFL record assuming pure skill

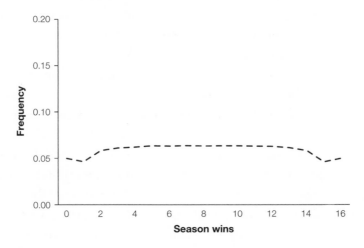

Source: Analysis by author.

FIGURE 4-4

Actual NFL record (2007–2011)

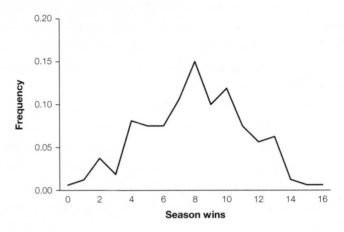

Source: Analysis by author.

We can now compare all three distributions. First, let's examine the actual results along with the luck model (figure 4-4 and
figure 4-2). We see clearly that the middle of the distribution for the
empirical results is lower than the luck model and that there are
more teams winning or losing lots of games than the luck model suggests. When we contrast the actual results with the all-skill model
(figure 4-4 and figure 4-3), we see that the middle of the empirical
results is higher than the all-skill model, but fewer teams either win
or lose all of the games they play.

So the final step is to come up with a blend of the models representing skill and luck that best fits the actual experience in the
league. Adding pure skill to the pure-luck model helps to adjust the
frequency with which any team wins or loses a large majority of its
games, while adding the pure luck to the pure-skill model raises the
middle of the distribution, making teams look more like the average.
In other words, luck pulls up the middle of the all-skill distribution
and pushes down the sides, while skill pulls down the top of all-luck
and lifts the sides. Mimicking the actual results requires combining
the two.

To blend the distribution, we need to sort out how much skill and luck contribute to the actual results. Let's assign a value to luck as a percentage of actual results. Call it p. If the result of a season rests entirely on luck, then $p = 100$ percent. If the result of a season rests entirely on skill, then $p = 0$ percent. No luck involved. If the value of luck is p and the actual results combine skill and luck, we know that the value of skill is $1 - p$. In this way, we can assume different values for p and look at the resulting distributions. We are looking for the value of p that gives us a distribution that most closely resembles the actual results. That value tells us where we are on the continuum.

In this case, the value of p that provides the best fit is 48 percent (see figure 4-5). The model that best explains the actual scores represents a bit more than half skill and a bit less than half luck. Naturally, there are many important contextual details that a model like this ignores, including home field advantage and the specifics of contests between particular teams. But the well-worn phrase "any

FIGURE 4-5

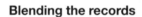

Blending the records

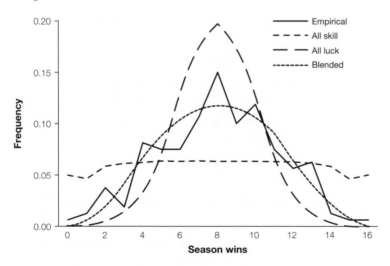

Source: Analysis by author.

given Sunday" acknowledges that upsets occur quite frequently in the NFL.

If luck contributes 48 percent to the game of football, then the models used to predict scores should be accurate about 75 percent of the time, according to Brian Burke. This is consistent with the performance of various computer models and oddsmakers.

Sports provide particularly convenient examples for this kind of analysis because the games have binary outcomes, a win or a loss. We can easily envision the distributions at the continuum's extremities. In most other contexts, such as business and investing, we don't know what the extremes look like. But this method does reinforce the essential idea that you always need to consider a null model— the simplest model that might explain the outcomes—when assessing results. In many cases, the basic question is whether luck is sufficient to explain results.

Skill = Observed Outcome – Luck

The final method for placing activities on the continuum is based on what is known as *true score theory*. That theory provides a method for measuring the relative contributions of skill and luck. It's essential to emphasize that this is a model of how the world works. We don't ever know what true skill is, and skill changes over time. For example, an athlete gains or loses skill with age. Skill also changes depending on circumstances. For example, a tennis player may be looking into the sun. That said, this approach is consistent with the two-jar model from chapter 3.[11]

The equation for true score theory is as follows:

Variance (observed) = Variance (skill) + Variance (luck)

Note that the previous approach involved specifying what the distribution of skill and luck would look like and then combining them in proportion to match the actual record of the NFL teams. Here an equation computes skill's contribution. Since we know the variance of the observed outcomes and can estimate the variance of luck, we can solve for the variance of skill:

Variance (skill) = Variance (observed) − Variance (luck)

Let's turn to a specific example. Tom Tango, a thoughtful and respected sabermetrician, describes the five steps of employing true score theory.[12] For this example, let's consider which teams in the National Basketball Association won and which ones lost. The first step is to consider a sufficiently large number of teams that have played the same number of games. We will look at the thirty teams in the NBA for the 2010–2011 season. Teams in the NBA play eighty-two games during the regular season. The second step is to examine each team's performance. For the 2010–2011 season, the Chicago Bulls had the best performance, winning more than 75 percent of their games. The Minnesota Timberwolves managed to win only 21 percent of their games, putting that team in last place. The other twenty-eight teams had winning percentages between the Timberwolves and the Bulls. The third step is to calculate the standard deviation of the winning percentages. For the 2010–2011 season, the standard deviation was 0.161. This is consistent with the average of 0.159 for the five seasons from 2006–2007 through 2010–2011. Since variance equals standard deviation squared, the variance (observed) is 0.026, or 0.161 squared.

The fourth step is to determine what the standard deviation would look like if luck were the only factor in who wins and loses these basketball games. In other words, at the beginning of the game, the referee flips a coin and whoever wins the toss wins the game. This would provide for pretty boring TV coverage, but it's going to help our calculations, because we can approximate the standard deviation of that binomial distribution with the following equation, where p is the probability of winning (0.5 in this case) and n is the number of games (eighty-two for the regular season):

$$\text{Standard deviation of luck} = \sqrt{p * \left(\frac{1-p}{n} \right)}$$

Plugging in the numbers we see that the standard deviation of luck is 0.552 and the variance of luck is 0.003, or 0.552 squared.

Now that we know two of the three variables in the equation, we can go to the final step, solving for the variance of skill:

Variance (skill) = variance (observed) − variance (luck)
Variance (skill) = 0.026 − 0.003
Variance (skill) = 0.023

This analysis allows us to look at the ratio of variance (luck) to variance (observed) in order to determine the contribution of luck. For the NBA season, the answer is about 12 percent (0.003/0.026 = 0.115). We can use this method to rank sports leagues by the relative contribution of luck in shaping the winning percentages of teams, offering a convenient way to place the leagues on the luck-skill continuum. Table 4-1 shows an estimate of the contribution of luck over one season for several sports. I derived these numbers by averaging the contributions of luck over five recent seasons. The data says that the higher the contribution of luck, the greater the equality within the league.

This method yields a modestly lower contribution for luck in professional football than the simulation did, although the results are similar. The virtue of this approach is that it is relatively simple yet

TABLE 4-1

The contribution of luck in some professional sports leagues

League	Contribution of luck	Five seasons ended
National Basketball Association	12%	2011
Premier League	31%	2011
Major League Baseball	34%	2011
National Football League	38%	2011
National Hockey League	53%	2012

Source: Analysis by author.

quite powerful. It also reinforces the point that differing amounts of luck shape the results we see in various activities. Finally, the outcomes provide us with a quick way of assessing how reliable a small sample is likely to be. Ten basketball games, for instance, reveal much more about skill than ten baseball games do.

There are some related points worth noting that this table doesn't show. The contribution of luck tends to be similar for various professional leagues within the same sport. For example, in the old American Basketball Association, which merged with the NBA in 1976, the influence of luck looked similar to that in the NBA. This is also true in hockey, football, and soccer. The contribution of luck, in other words, seems to be tied more to the activity itself than to the specific details of how a given league is organized or what rules it employs.

It is also true that the number of opportunities a team has to score will greatly determine the influence of luck on the outcome of the game. Basketball players take possession of the ball at eight or nine times the rate of football players. The more chances they have to score, the more influence skill has. Ian Stewart, a mathematician, shares a simplified model of men's tennis in his book, *Game, Set and Math*. He shows that a player with a 53 percent probability of winning each point has almost an 85 percent probability of winning the match, assuming that he has to win the best of five sets. A player who is likely to win 60 percent of his points is almost sure to win the match.[13] That's because tennis is a game in which the ball is served a large number of times. A slight advantage in skill gives you a tremendous overall advantage if you have enough chances to exercise that skill and to thereby nullify the effects of luck.

In addition, the contribution of luck has been rising steadily over time in most sports, which means that the players are all converging on an equal level of skill. This is consistent with the paradox of skill. The one exception is basketball, where it appears that equality has declined in recent decades when compared with the average before 1990. This result seems to contradict the paradox of skill. In fact, a closer examination of this trend helps explain the paradox of skill and shows why it doesn't apply to basketball.[14]

More People Help Explain the Paradox—Unless They Need to Be Really Tall

Let's do a mental exercise. We'll assume we have a league of twenty-five teams, each with twenty players, for a total of five hundred participants. Next, we will assume that we can draw from a town that has a population of one thousand athletes, who have a distribution of skill as shown in figure 4-6. The higher the number, the higher the skill.

To populate our league, we start from the right of the distribution and select the five hundred most skillful players. So we will take all 20 of the 6s, all 140 of the 5s, and all 340 of the 4s. We can then calculate that our players will have an average skill level of 4.36 with a standard deviation of 0.6. In this league, the 6s will perform head and shoulders above the rest of the players.

Now, let's say our league opens up to another town, which also has one thousand athletes distributed in the same fashion as the first town. Now we have two thousand players to pick from, and figure 4-7 shows the new distribution of talent.

FIGURE 4-6

The distribution of skill for a sample population of 1,000

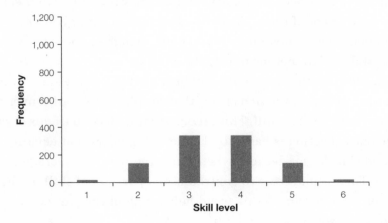

Source: Analysis by author.

FIGURE 4-7

The distribution of skill for a sample population of 2,000

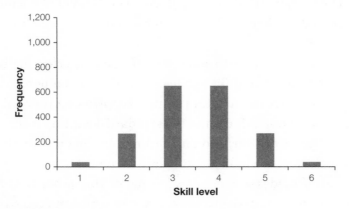

Source: Analysis by author.

To create the best league possible, we enlist all 40 of the 6s, 280 of the 5s, and 180 of the 4s. Now our average skill level is 4.72, an 8.3 percent improvement.

Finally, we add one more town with one thousand athletes and the same distribution of talent. The pool from which we can build our league is shown in figure 4-8. Our league has 60 6s, 420 5s, and

FIGURE 4-8

The distribution of skill for a sample population of 3,000

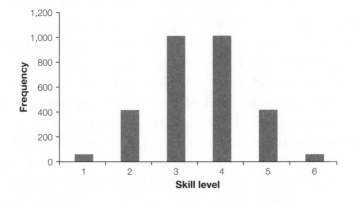

Source: Analysis by author.

only 20 4s. The league's average talent again rises, this time by 7.6 percent, to reach 5.08. The standard deviation of skill has dropped to 0.4. The 6s will still do well, but the overall level of competition has improved markedly. The 6s won't stand out so much from the other players.

If we were to continue to add towns of a similar size and distribution of talent, we would fill our league with a rising percentage of 6s until we reached the limit at twenty-five towns. At that point, the average level of talent is 6.0 and the standard deviation is zero. Luck would determine the variation in performance among our elite athletes, and the teams would all be equally strong.[15]

Baseball provides a concrete example of this process. One century ago, professional baseball players were white and came primarily from the northeastern United States. Baseball now draws players from all racial groups, and from not just the entire United States but the entire world. Just under 30 percent of players in Major League Baseball today were born outside of the United States, up from about 10 percent in the 1960s.[16] Soccer and ice hockey have experienced similar trends. In chapter 3, we observed the paradox of skill. Now we have a mechanism to help explain it: if the population of players to choose from expands and the size of the league remains constant, the average level of skill will tend to increase.

Now let's turn back to basketball, arguably the second most popular sport in the world, behind soccer. You might expect basketball to see a similar trend toward parity. When the NBA was founded in 1946, its players and coaches were all white. Today, almost 80 percent of the players are black and approximately 20 percent were born outside the United States. So, as in other major sports, basketball draws from a much larger pool of talent today than it did in years past. At first blush, the NBA certainly appears anomalous.

But there is a relatively straightforward explanation for the strong and consistent contribution of skill in the NBA: the height of the players. In most sports, the most skillful players within a wide range of heights can make it to the pros. But a relatively small percentage of men are tall enough to play in the NBA, and the average height in the league has risen over the years. Only about 2 percent of the male population is 6' 4" or taller, but more than 80 percent of NBA players meet that threshold. Average stature in the NBA is 6' 7", and 27 percent of NBA players are at least 6' 10", which is four standard deviations above normal.[17] For some context, four or more standard deviations means you'd expect about thirty-two hundred men of that height in a population of 100 million.

This mental exercise suggests that a small population of big men should lead to a wider variation of skill than a large population of smaller players. A pair of economists, David Berri and Stacey Brook, along with some colleagues, tested this prediction. They compared players who were 6' 4" or shorter with players who were 6' 10" or taller, using points scored and productivity each minute to gauge the variation. The two groups had roughly the same number of players. They found that short players had lower standard deviations in performance than the tall players did, which means that the range of scoring and productivity was smaller than it was for the big men.

The high standard deviation of the tall players appears to be an important factor in explaining why skill is the primary determinant of the results for NBA teams. Even though the NBA is more international than ever, skill levels show relatively high variance because of what Berri et al. call "the short supply of tall people."[18] Think back to our mental exercise. The NBA's need for tall players means there's a small pool of talent from which to select, so it's like drawing players from one instead of many towns. As we saw, there is a wide range of talent in one town, and the range of talent narrows as more towns are included.

The Luck-Skill Continuum in Business and Investing

I used sports to illustrate the second and third methods for placing activities on the continuum because the games are rich in data and relatively stable. The methods may not apply as neatly in business and investing, but having a sense of where an activity falls on the continuum still helps greatly in making decisions.

In a company, employees perform two broad categories of tasks, those that are repetitive and those that involve trial and error. Repetitive tasks are performed by following a recipe. Think of a worker making automobiles on an assembly line. Every time a vehicle rolls by, he attaches the same part. Employers can improve those step-by-step procedures, and following the formula will allow the employee to meet the objective. The execution of repetitive tasks is accomplished mostly through skill.

In contrast, there are no recipes for tasks that involve trial and error. Workers have to experiment to find out what works. Setting corporate strategy is an example, as is developing a new advertising campaign or managing a team of people to work on a specific project.[19] These tasks fall closer to the luck side than repetitive tasks because cause and effect are difficult to link, reversion to the mean is strong, and predicting success isn't easy.

We can also consider skill and luck on the level of the whole company. Thomas Powell, a professor of strategy at Oxford, created a useful bridge between sports and business through a novel study of parity—how the competitiveness of sports teams and companies compared to one another. Powell studied more than twenty industries in the United States and measured the degree of equality in financial performance. He then measured the level of equality of other pursuits, including many sports (baseball, tennis, hockey, basketball, cricket, golf, football, and lacrosse) as well as other competitive fields (chess, snooker, bridge). He found that those pursuits had a level of parity nearly identical to that of the companies. As he summarizes, "Performance distributions in business are statistically indistinguishable from distributions in non-business domains." Since we know that skill plays a meaningful role in sports, this research clearly suggests that skill, which often appears as competitive advantage, is also relevant in shaping business results.[20]

Researchers typically define success in business as a high and sustainable return on assets (ROA). As in other fields, success in business depends on a healthy dose of luck, so it is essential to compare results to a null model to assess the contribution of skill. The null model tells us what we should expect to see by virtue of luck alone. Research by Andy Henderson, Michael Raynor, and Mumtaz Ahmed, briefly discussed in chapter 1, does just that. They studied tens of thousands of companies over a forty-year span, amassing over 230,000 firm-years of observations of ROA. These researchers carefully structured the analysis so that it would discriminate between luck and skill in explaining how companies achieved success.

The main finding of the study is that "the results consistently indicate that there are many more sustained superior performers than we would expect through the occurrence of lucky random walks." While this is comforting because it suggests that management's actions, or skill, can lead to success, efforts are ongoing to pinpoint accurately which behaviors were the correct ones. So unlike sports, where there are some observable measures of skill (such as hitting a baseball), all we can really say today is that we cannot explain results by luck alone and that it appears that skill plays a role when companies earn a high return on their assets. The authors caution, though, that it is very easy to confuse superior performance with the results you would expect from luck.[21]

Investing is another endeavor where we could benefit from teasing apart skill and luck. We can define skill as the ability to take actions that will predictably generate a risk-adjusted return in excess of an appropriate benchmark, such as the S&P 500, over time. It is impossible for investment managers to generate returns in excess of the benchmark in the aggregate. The reason is that the market's return must simply be the sum total of the results of the managers (or close to it). Since managers charge fees for their services, the return to investors is less than that of the market.

Researchers studying the investment industry have answered each of the three questions from the first method of placing activities on the continuum between luck and skill. Prices in markets reflect the interaction of lots of investors, and we know that identifying a cause for any given effect in these kinds of systems is notoriously difficult. Booms and crashes have been consistent features of markets for centuries, and there is no simple way to anticipate the behavior of markets in the short-term.[22]

Reversion to the mean is a powerful force in investing, too. John Bogle, a luminary of the investment industry, illustrates this by ranking mutual funds in four groups based on results in the 1990s and seeing how those groups performed in the 2000s. The group that was most successful, the top fourth of the mutual funds, handily out-paced the average fund in the 1990s. But it suffered a 7.8 percent drop in relative performance since then. The bottom fourth in the 1990s showed a sharp 7.8 percent relative gain in the 2000s. This power-ful and symmetrical reversion to the mean suggests that investing involves a large dose of luck.[23]

Importantly, reversion to the mean in the investment business extends its influence well beyond the realm of mutual funds. It exerts its power over companies with small capitalization as well as large capitalization, over value and growth investing, over bonds as well as stocks; and it spans geographic boundaries. There are few corners of the investment business where reversion to the mean does not hold sway.[24]

One of the most popular topics in research on mutual funds is known as *persistence of performance*, a measure of predictability. There is some evidence of persistence in the way funds perform, but the strength of the signal is in part a function of the time period a researcher decides to measure. It's more pronounced with poor per-formers than superior performers and is weakened as academics adjust the amount earned by a mutual fund for factors that influence the price of stocks, such as the average size of the market capitaliza-tions, the valuations of the stocks, and whether the stock price has momentum.[25]

The paradox of skill is an effective way to explain why markets are so hard to beat consistently. In 1975, Charles Ellis, the founder of the consulting firm Greenwich Associates, wrote an essay called "The Loser's Game." In it, he noted: "Gifted, determined, ambitious professionals have come into investment management in such large numbers during the past 30 years that it may no longer be feasible for any of them to profit from the errors of all the others sufficiently often and by sufficient magnitude to beat the market averages."[26] Over those decades, investing went from being dominated by individuals to being dominated by institutions. As the population of skilled investors increased, the variation in skill narrowed, and luck became more important.

The more everyone's level of skill looks the same, the more you'd expect the range of excess returns for money managers to shrink. An excess return captures a fund manager's results versus a benchmark, adjusted for risk. So a money manager who earns a 10 percent return when the comparable index is up 8 percent has an excess return of 2 percentage points (assuming the risk of the manager is comparable to that of the index).

In 1998, Peter Bernstein, one of the investment industry's greatest thinkers, wrote an article inspired by Stephen Jay Gould's analysis of the dearth of .400 hitters in baseball. Bernstein surmised that as markets continued their march toward efficiency, the pattern of declining variance in excess returns should be evident for money managers. The data backed him up: the standard deviation of excess returns for mutual funds slowly and steadily declined from 1960 through 1997. In 2004, though, Bernstein reran the numbers and found that the standard deviation had exploded from roughly 10 percent in the late 1990s to almost 20 percent in 1999. That meant that there were big winners and big losers. He concluded that the .400 hitters of the investment industry were back.

But the spike in standard deviations was short-lived and attributable to strong swings in the style of investing. Specifically, large capitalization managers were narrowly focused on technology stocks in late 1999, allowing for very large gains relative to other styles of investing. And following the end of the bubble in technology stocks, small capitalization managers enjoyed relative gains that were much larger. Since Bernstein's paper was published in 2004, the standard deviations have again shrunk, consistent with his, and Gould's, original thesis.[27]

There is a big difference between saying that the short-term results of investment managers are mostly luck and saying they are *all* luck. Research shows that most active managers generate returns above their benchmark on a gross basis, but that those excess returns are offset by fees, leaving investors with net returns below those of the benchmark.[28] Considering the evidence on balance, it is reasonable to conclude that there is evidence of skill in investing. However, only a small percentage of investors possess enough skill to offset fees. As a result, investing, especially over relatively short periods of time, is more a matter of luck than of skill.

Figure 4-9 provides an estimate of where a handful of activities lie on the continuum. While we can never place an activity with pinpoint precision, the qualitative and quantitative methods in this chapter provide useful guidelines. It is essential to emphasize that it is not where activities lie per se that is important but rather what that position means for helping us to make decisions. A common mistake is to use a process for making a decision that is appropriate for activities that are nearly all skill and then apply it to an activity that is mostly luck.

FIGURE 4-9

Activities along the luck-skill continuum

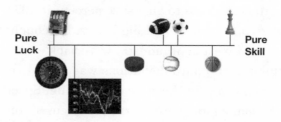

Source: Analysis by author.

CHAPTER 5

THE ARC OF SKILL

IN 2010, JAYSON WERTH had just wrapped up one of his best seasons as an outfielder for the Philadelphia Phillies, a Major League Baseball team. That December, the thirty-one-year-old player signed a seven-year deal with the Washington Nationals for $126 million, a contract that raised some eyebrows around the league. "Makes some of our contracts look good," quipped Sandy Alderson, general manager of the New York Mets, a team notorious for overpaying its players. "It's a long time and a lot of money."[1]

Scott Boras, the agent who negotiated the deal, suggested that Werth might "provide something to the franchise in addition to his performance." And Mike Rizzo, the general manager of the Nationals, sounded confident as he asserted, "We got the inside scoop on who the man is." Rizzo gushed, "Jim [Riggleman, the manager] is a great judge of character and clubhouse presence. He was very flowery in his praise of Jayson on and off the field. He feels, like I feel, Jayson's best days haven't been had yet."[2]

Rizzo's actions backed up his rhetoric. The contract calls for Werth to earn less money in the first few years of the contract and more in the last years, including the princely sum of $21 million in years five through seven. At the end of the contract, he'll be thirty-eight years old. That's a lot of money for a guy getting on in years. The question is whether Werth will deliver sufficient performance to justify his pay. As we are about to see, it's not a good bet.

So far, I have treated skill as largely static, a reasonable assumption in the short term. This chapter takes a more realistic look at how skill changes over time. Specifically, we will examine trends in performance in athletics, cognitive tasks, and business. The general pattern in all three areas is the same and is easy to summarize: old age is not your friend.

Athletic Performance: Why Werth's Worth
Is Likely to Drop

As you move through your teens and into your twenties, your athletic performance improves. If you're like most people, you'll peak in your mid- to late twenties. Then you'll go into a slow and steady decline. Various sports show different peaks in performance, reflecting the nature of each game. Sprinters, for instance, peak in their early twenties, while golfers can be highly competitive well into their thirties. But sooner or later, age takes its toll on athletes in all sports.

To get a sense of the daunting task Werth is up against every time he steps to the plate, consider the physics of baseball. Robert Adair, professor emeritus of physics at Yale University, calculates that it takes the average fastball 400 milliseconds (0.4 seconds, or less than half a second) to go from the pitcher's hand to home plate. During the first 100 to 150 milliseconds nothing visibly happens, as this is the minimum amount of time it takes for a batter to respond to a visual cue by moving a muscle. (The starting blocks of world-class sprinters have sensors, and runners who leave sooner than 100 milliseconds after the sound of the gun are disqualified for a false start.) The batter must locate the ball in space with his eye, relay that information to the brain, calculate the ball's speed and trajectory, and construct an internal representation of what the ball is doing. This process takes 75 milliseconds.

By the time the pitch has traveled almost half of the distance to the plate, the player has decided what to do: nothing, get out of the way of an errant pitch, or swing with a particular pattern of movement. This phase of his response takes 50 milliseconds. The swing itself takes about 175 milliseconds, and most players can make tiny adjustments only during the first 50 milliseconds. After that, the plane through which the bat will swing is already determined and can't be changed. If the batter's timing is off by as little as 7 milliseconds, he will hit a foul ball. Sharp eyesight and explosiveness are essential to success.[3]

Professional baseball players can see much better than the population at large. In the early 1990s, ophthalmologists tested the vision of almost four hundred players in the Los Angeles Dodgers organization. For the first round, they had equipment that measured vision only up to 20-15. People with 20-15 vision can see from a distance of 20 feet as well as an average person can see from a distance of 15 feet. A remarkable 81 percent of the players had a maximum reading on the equipment. So the researchers came back with a test that could measure vision up to 20-8, considered to be the limit of human ability. The average player had 20-13 vision, and a couple of the players had vision better than 20-9, approaching the human limit. The Major League Baseball players were also better at picking out figures from a confusing background and in judging small differences in depth.[4] Professional ballplayers rely on that extraordinary visual acuity.

There are two broad categories of muscle fibers: slow-twitch and fast-twitch. Slow-twitch fibers contract relatively slowly but are efficient at using oxygen to create energy—they don't fatigue easily. That's why they're good for endurance. They're used for activities such as running a marathon. Fast-twitch fibers transmit force with explosive speed and energy but use anaerobic metabolic systems, which means that they can't sustain the effort for long. They're the ones used for throwing a baseball or swinging a bat. As we age, the performance of both our visual systems and our fast-twitch muscle fibers declines. Because of these changes, ballplayers simply can't sustain their peak levels of power and speed as they get older.

Their performance on the field inevitably fades. Hitters may try to get more selective about the pitches they swing at in order to tip the odds back in their favor, or they may rely more on their experience to outwit the pitcher. But these mental moves only slow the slide, they don't stop it.

The age of peak performance depends on the sport. The blend of slow-twitch and fast-twitch fibers in muscles is a good way to determine the peak. With aging, the fast-twitch fibers shrink in both size and number. Slow-twitch fibers tend to maintain their size and number far longer. As a consequence, the peak of performance comes sooner for sports that require power and speed than it does for sports that rely more on endurance and coordination.

Contrast sprinters to distance runners as a case in point. Fast-twitch fiber makes up 75–80 percent of a sprinter's calf muscle, and slow-twitch fiber makes up the rest. For distance runners, the percentages are reversed: 75–80 percent of muscle is slow-twitch fiber. The ratio for the general population is about 50–50.[5] Sprinters peak around the age of twenty-three, while distance runners peak at twenty-seven. Table 5-1 shows the ages of peak performance for various sports for men and women.[6]

Within a sport, it is uncommon for an individual who is much younger, or much older, than the peak age to perform at a high level. Take tennis. Examination of the age distribution of the winners of men's Grand Slam tournaments (the Australian Open, the French Open, Wimbledon, and the U.S. Open) from 1968 through 2011 reveals that winners were twenty-four years old on average, and that twenty-four was also the most common age of a winner. Further, fewer than 5 percent of the winners in the past forty years have been older than thirty.[7]

Professional athletes get paid to perform, and it's possible to place an economic value on that performance. Indeed, the prime task of the general manager of a sports team is to field the best squad possible given his budget. So he'll search for undervalued talent and try to avoid overpaying for performance. Hiring professional

TABLE 5-1

Peak performance in various sports

	Men	Women
Swimming	20–22	23–25
Sprinting	22–24	21–23
Jumping	23–25	22–24
Medium-distance running	23–25	23–25
Basketball	24–26	
Tennis	24–26	23–25
Long-distance running	26–28	26–28
Ice hockey	26–28	
Baseball	27–29	
NFL running backs	27–29	
Soccer	27–29	
NFL receivers	29–31	
NFL quarterbacks	31–33	
Golf	30–35	

Source: Compiled by author.

baseball players is particularly tricky, because it is common for them to become free agents right around the time their performance is peaking. Age is an important consideration in any general manager's calculations.

Very few baseball players can keep up their peak performance into their late thirties. Jayson Werth and his agent appear to have convinced the Washington Nationals to parlay his terrific season at age thirty-one into a lucrative contract that would require seven more years of superior performance in order to pay off. If the work of Mother Nature and Father Time are any guide, the worth of the contract will exceed that of Werth the player.

Cognitive Performance: The Battle Between Fluid and Crystallized Intelligence

When it comes to cognitive tasks, skill is closely related to being competent at making decisions. Melissa Finucane and Christina Gullion, psychologists who have studied how people in different age groups make decisions, suggest that the keys to this competence include "understanding information, integrating information in an internally consistent manner, identifying the relevance of information in a decision process, and inhibiting impulsive responding."[8] Finucane and Gullion designed a set of tools to measure how those skills change as people age.

There are a couple of ways of conceptualizing how good someone is at making decisions. The first way suggests that competence is the result of developing expert knowledge that allows you to choose a course of action automatically. If you practice an activity long enough to internalize its salient features, you will be able to make good decisions. This type of competence is intuitive. For example, psychologists have documented how firefighters and nurses make quick, correct decisions under conditions of stress and the pressure of time.[9] Master chess players are perhaps the best-known illustration of naturalistic decision making. Expert chess players can identify the best moves rapidly and understand at a glance the relative strength of each player's position.

While aging does degrade the ability to make these types of automatic decisions, the rate of decline appears slow. Ray Fair, an economist at Yale University, studied the effect of age on the speed at which people run and swim, as well as on the quality of play in chess. His analysis showed that "the results for chess are striking in that they show much smaller rates of decline than any of the physical activities." By his estimates, a man who runs a marathon in 4 hours when he is thirty-five years old can expect to run it in 5 hours and 18 minutes when he's seventy years old, a 32 percent decline in performance. A man's chess game, in contrast, is projected to only decline by 7 percent between the ages of thirty-five and seventy.[10] The muted effect of aging on the quality of decisions in chess helps explain how Marion Tinsley was able to be the world champion in checkers for many decades. While chess and checkers are different, they share a board, have stable rules, and involve envisioning spatial relationships.

The problem with this sort of automatic decision-making apparatus is that it only works under very specific circumstances. Intuition works when the environment is stable and an individual has the opportunity to spend a great deal of time learning about it.[11] While checkers and chess provide good environments for demonstrating this sort of competence, intuition works in many occupations. For instance, physicians can rely on their intuition in many cases. Good doctors become expert at reading facial expressions and body language. But they also face situations that they haven't had the opportunity to master.

Trouble arises when individuals rely too heavily on their experience in making automatic decisions. When we age, we tend to avoid exerting too much cognitive effort and deliberating extensively over a decision that needs to be made. We gradually come to rely more on rules of thumb. This means that we make poorer choices in environments that are complex and unstable.[12] Business and investing are examples of realms where intuition often fails. Researchers who studied people making investments found that decisions about those investments grew less wise as people aged. In other words, skill declines with age. The amount of money you can make through investing follows the same arc of skill that we saw with sports (table 5-1), although at forty-two years, the peak age is quite a bit older. More pointedly, the research showed a sharp drop in performance around the age of seventy.[13]

The ability to make good decisions can also be viewed as a collection of cognitive capabilities that change with age. These abilities include fluid and crystallized intelligence, speed of process- ing, and the discipline to think twice before responding. The theory of fluid and crystallized intelligence provides a classic approach to this research.[14] *Fluid intelligence* refers to the ability to solve problems that you've never seen before. Fluid intelligence doesn't depend on something you've learned. Tests that require you to visu- alize spatial relationships, to hold facts in working memory, and to complete a series of numbers help measure fluid intelligence. For example, what is the next number in the series: 1, 5, 6, 10, 11, 15, __?*

Crystallized intelligence is the ability to use the knowledge accumulated through learning. Tests for vocabulary, geography, and history measure crystallized intelligence. Performance on general intelligence tests is a blend of intelligence as process and intelligence as knowledge.

The research on fluid and crystallized intelligence offers bad and good news (see figure 5-1). The bad news is that fluid intelligence peaks around the age of twenty and declines consistently and steadily throughout life. For example, adults in their early twenties score on average about 0.7 standard deviations above the mean of all adults, and adults in their early eighties score about 1.0 standard deviation below the mean. In other words, there is a decline of about one percentage point each year after the age of twenty. This means that those who scored in the thirtieth percentile at age twenty-five will score in the seventieth percentile at age sixty-five.

The decline in fluid intelligence appears to be related to general cognitive slowing and to reduced volume and decreased functioning of the frontal lobes. The frontal lobes are involved in higher mental functions, including planning for the future and restrain- ing emotional responses. The frontal lobes are active when we solve tasks that involve fluid intelligence. Also, the range of performance remains remarkably consistent for all age groups. While you might

---

*The next number is 16.

FIGURE 5-1

Fluid and crystallized intelligence and overall cognitive performance

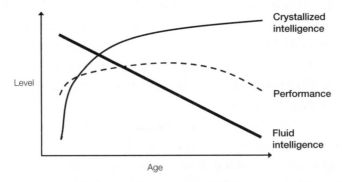

Source: Based on Sumit Agarwal, John C. Driscoll, Xavier Gabaix, and David I. Laibson, "The Age of Reason: Financial Decisions over the Life Cycle and Implications for Regulations," *Brookings Papers on Economic Activity* (Fall 2009), 51–117.

expect that the range in performance would increase with age as some people maintain high levels of performance while others suffer large declines, in fact the data show nearly constant variability for all ages.[15]

The ability to reason with numbers also tends to erode with age. For example, researchers presented subjects with the following question: if five people all have the winning numbers in the lottery and the prize is $2 million, how much will each person get? Roughly half of the subjects in their early fifties say $400,000, the official correct answer, while only 10 percent of those in their nineties do.[16]

The good news is that crystallized intelligence tends to improve with age. There is something to the idea that older people are wiser than young people because they know more. The mean scores in tests of vocabulary, synonyms, and antonyms for people aged seventy-five to ninety-seven exceeded those of subjects who were twenty-five to forty-five years old by 25 percent or more.[17] Growing knowledge compensates for a reduction in fluidity, up to a certain age. Beyond that age, aggregate cognitive performance declines.

Four economists, Sumit Agarwal, John Driscoll, Xavier Gabaix, and David Laibson, quantified the age of peak performance for financial decisions. They wanted to know at what age people get the lowest interest rates on their mortgages, auto loans, and credit cards. They also studied the age at which individuals did the best job of avoiding fees for late payments on their credit cards. They found a curve shaped like an inverted "U" to represent performance. They also found that the average age of peak performance in matters of finance is fifty-three. This age is remarkably consistent, no matter what the financial task is.

The researchers focused on the rising prevalence of dementia and other cognitive impairment in older adults in the United States. They point out that about half of the population of people aged eighty to eighty-nine and three-quarters of those ninety and older have one of those conditions.[18] David Laibson calculated that the net worth of Americans sixty-five years old and older approaches $20 trillion, so an enormous amount of wealth is controlled by individuals who have a deteriorating ability to make good decisions, either as the result of normal aging or because of cognitive impairment.[19]

As we age, the changes in fluid and crystallized intelligence appear to be consistent with peak performance in other fields as well. David Galenson, a professor of economics at the University of Chicago, has studied artistic creativity in detail. He argues that there are two types of artistic innovators and that each one peaks at a different time. The first type, the *conceptual innovator*, produces work that is novel and different from that of other artists. Although these artists tend to make detailed preparations before they start a project, they rely much less on what has come before them and more on "the desire to communicate specific ideas or emotions." Galenson identified Pablo Picasso as a classic conceptual innovator. The peak of Picasso's productivity came when he was twenty-six years old, and his pieces from that period are the most valuable of all his work.

Experimental innovators, on the other hand, do lots of research, accumulate knowledge, and rely on slow and incremental progress. They often remain unsatisfied with their final work, believing that there's always room for improvement. Galenson's prototypical experimental innovator was Paul Cézanne, who asked, "Will I ever attain the end for which I have striven so much and for so long?" Cézanne's peak of productivity came at age sixty-seven. As with Picasso's peak period, paintings from his later years are the most valuable of Cézanne's work.[20]

The two peaks of creativity, young for novel work and old for cumulative work, fit well with the patterns in fluid and crystallized intelligence. Fields where novel approaches to problems are important, including math and physics, are where young researchers have the most success.

Galenson argues that it is not the field itself that determines the age of peak intellectual performance, but rather the type of innovation the scientist or artist pursues. Still, math, physics, and poetry are fields that have been dominated by younger practitioners, while older people tend to do better in history, biology, and novel writing.[21]

Intelligence Quotient Versus Rationality Quotient: Why Smart People Do Dumb Things

Intelligence tests measure certain cognitive capabilities, but it is also clear that they fail to assess other important mental faculties that reflect cognitive skill. Perhaps the most important among these is the ability to make good decisions. Keith Stanovich, a professor of psychology at the University of Toronto, distinguishes between an individual's intelligence quotient (IQ) and rationality quotient (RQ). While many people assume that intelligence and rationality are related, Stanovich shows that these are distinct abilities. This is why we see objectively intelligent people make poor decisions. If we are considering cognitive skill, RQ is primarily what we are after. The trouble is, we haven't made very much progress in learning how to test RQ.

The attributes of RQ, as Stanovich lists them, include "adaptive behavioral acts, judicious decision making, efficient behavioral regulation, sensible goal prioritization, reflectivity, [and] the proper calibration of evidence."[22] He argues that plenty of people have adequate intelligence but an inability to think and behave rationally. The gap between IQ and RQ is the result of trouble with mental processing and limits to what we know.

To illustrate the difficulty we might have processing information, consider the following problem: Jack is looking at Anne, but Anne is looking at George. Jack is married, but George is not. Is a married person looking at an unmarried person?

(A) Yes

(B) No

(C) Cannot be determined

Take a moment to answer.

The answer is A, but more than 80 percent of people choose C. At first, the problem doesn't seem solvable because Anne's marital status is unknown. So while you know that Jack is married, you don't know Anne's status, so you can't answer the question based on that pair. For the same reason, you can't answer the question as it applies to Anne and George. So at first blush, you are stuck. As a result, most answer "Cannot be determined." But the way to solve the problem is to consider Anne's two possible marital states: married or unmarried. If she is unmarried, the answer is yes because Jack is looking at her. If she is married the answer is yes as well because she is looking at George. You can come to the correct answer only by considering all of the possibilities.

The natural tendency when solving problems is to rely on cognitive mechanisms that are fast, low in computational power, and require little concentration, rather than recruiting those mechanisms of the mind that are slow, computationally intensive, and that require effort. To use Stanovich's phrase, we are "cognitive misers."[23] Another characteristic of a cognitive miser is the tendency to reason from an egocentric point of view. This bias leads to systematic and predictable departures from rationality. The ability to avoid thinking like a cognitive miser has a correlation with IQ that is only in the range of 20 to 30 percent. So you can be smart and still make this mistake.[24] Conversely, you don't need the IQ of a genius to make good decisions.

A low RQ also stems from the issue of what we don't know. Most of us ought to learn how to think properly about problems related to probability, statistics, and the best ways to test hypotheses. Take, for example, the appropriate use of probabilities. How would you answer the following problem?

Imagine that the Zapper virus causes a serious disease that occurs in one of every thousand people. Say there is a test to diagnose the disease that always indicates correctly that a person who has the Zapper virus actually has it. Finally, imagine that the test indicates that the Zapper virus is present in 5 percent of the cases where the person does not have the virus (a false-positive rate of 5 percent). We now choose a person randomly without knowing anything about his medical history and administer the test, and the test indicates he has the Zapper virus. What is the probability, expressed as a range from 0 to 100 percent, that he actually has the Zapper virus?[25]

The most common answer is 95 percent, while the correct answer is approximately 2 percent. Sorting the various probabilities is cumbersome. People who answer incorrectly tend to overlook the first part of the setup: the disease occurs in only one person out of every thousand. You can solve this problem formally using Bayes's theorem, a formula for calculating conditional probabilities, but the more intuitive way is to translate all of the probabilities into actual numbers.[26]

Here's how to think about it. With a population of 1,000, you know that 1 person has the virus and that the infected person would test positive. You also know that if all of the other 999 people were to take the test, roughly 50 of them (5 percent of 999) would test positive. So if everyone took the test, 51 people would test positive and only 1 person would actually have the virus. So if a random person tests positive, he or she has only about a 2 percent (1 out of 51) chance of having the virus. You can learn to think this way, but it doesn't come naturally to everyone. Stanovich estimates that the correlation between IQ and success with content-related problem solving is about 25–35 percent. Again, a high IQ does not translate automatically into a high RQ.

It would be nice to have a test to measure RQ, but it doesn't yet exist, so there's no way to know how it changes with age. But we do know that older adults rely more on rules of thumb, which would suggest that the cognitive processes behind RQ decline with age. Scientists have measured cognitive reflection, the ability to manage the cognitive miser within us, for different age groups. One team of researchers found a clear deterioration in cognitive reflection with age (see figure 5-2).[27] Adults seventy-five to ninety-seven years old performed considerably worse on a test of cognitive reflection than did a group of twenty-five- to forty-five-year-olds. This result fits the same pattern as seen with other cognitive tasks,

FIGURE 5-2

Performance in tests of cognitive reflection

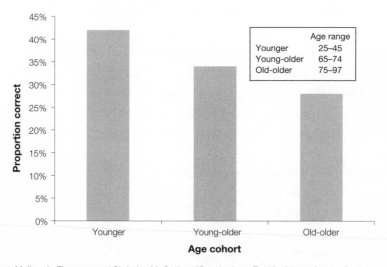

	Age range
Younger	25–45
Young-older	65–74
Old-older	75–97

Source: Melissa L. Finucane and Christina M. Gullion, "Developing a Tool for Measuring the Decision-Making Competence of Older Adults," *Psychology and Aging* 25, no. 2 (June 2010): 271–288.

but scientists must design additional tests of RQ to determine how it changes with age.

The Aging of Organizations

People lose skill with age, but so do organizations. Great sports teams, for instance, are a collection of above-average players. But even a team that stays together a long time inevitably declines because the players age and management is hard-pressed to replace them at an effective cost. One of the reasons that teams are so difficult to run is that managers must constantly replace older players with younger players. Older players tend to be known entities, which means that their value is reflected in their salary. Younger players are more difficult to assess. So sports executives are trading the known for the unknown.

Corporate performance also follows a life cycle (see figure 5-3). Performance is defined as returns—return on invested capital, or ROIC, to be more precise—in excess of the opportunity cost of capital (opportunity cost is a measure of the return you could earn doing something else with the money, given the same amount

FIGURE 5-3

Company life cycle

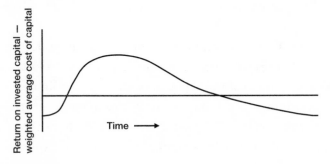

Source: Analysis by author.

of risk). Since the primary sources of capital, equity and debt, have different costs, the weighted average cost of capital (WACC) reflects the opportunity cost. Firms generally start with low returns. They see their returns rise as the industry grows and the employees acquire skill, and then drift lower as the industry matures and competitive forces take their toll. Competition plays a particularly important role in shaping the pattern of returns. Companies that earn high returns and enjoy good growth attract competitors that seek to capture some of that value for their own shareholders. As a consequence, competition serves to drive the price of goods or services down, pushing a company's economic return toward the opportunity cost of capital.[28]

Recent research shows that while some companies do sustain superior economic performance, the rate of reversion to the mean today appears to be accelerating. The research also indicates a clear link between the age of a firm and a decline in economic profitability. Not only do companies see their performance deteriorate with age, but the aging process is also happening faster because technology is changing faster and the life cycles of products are getting shorter.[29]

Managerial skill—the ability to allocate financial, human, and organizational capital—explains some fraction of corporate performance. Luck also plays a prominent role. Outcomes of strategic decisions are probabilistic by nature, and companies (like people) don't live a long time without enjoying some good luck. In the following chapter, the role of luck is examined in greater detail.

Probably the best explanation for why companies decline is that they fall prey to organizational rigidities. Companies must balance exploiting profitable markets with exploring new markets. Exploiting known markets requires optimizing processes and executing effectively, and leads to reliable, near-term success. Exploring unknown markets requires search and experimentation and offers none of the immediate benefits of exploitation.[30]

Finding the best balance between exploration and exploitation depends on the rate of change in the environment. When change comes slowly, the balance can tilt toward exploitation. When it comes quickly, an organization must dedicate more resources to exploration, since profits are quickly exhausted. In general, companies tend to lean more on exploitation, which increases efficiency and profits in the short run but makes the company rigid, a state of affairs that only grows worse with age. Similar to aging individuals, companies rely on methods and rules of thumb that worked well in the past rather than embrace novelty. Companies, too, follow an arc of skill.

Skill rises and falls as a function of age for individuals and organizations. Knowing where a person or team is on the arc is important in predicting performance. The biggest risk in giving a guy like Jayson Werth $18 million a year to play baseball for another seven years is that the management of the Washington Nationals was extrapolating from his skill near the peak of his arc of development as a player. The same risk holds for companies and other organizations.

CHAPTER 6

THE MANY SHAPES OF LUCK

CARLY HENNESSY HAD "charisma, drive, and pipes," the three things that executives in the recording industry look for in their quest to find the next Britney Spears. A native of Ireland, Hennessy caught the eye of the brass at MCA Records after she cut an album of Christmas carols and toured Europe in the cast of *Les Misérables*. In the summer of 1999, the MCA executives treated Hennessy to dinner at Spago in Beverly Hills and laid out the plan to make her a pop star. She was just sixteen years old. Over the next couple of years, the studio spent $2.2 million recording her and promoting her work, a substantial commitment for a budding star.

Hennessy recognized her good fortune. "Some people struggle," she said, "I was very, very lucky." MCA launched her album *Ultimate High* in late 2001. Despite the lofty expectations, the outcome was very, very unlucky. In the first three months, the album sold a grand total of 378 copies, earning less than $5,000. The president of MCA Records could do little more than scratch his head. How could the experts in that business have been so wrong about what seemed like a sure thing?[1]

In April 2004, the chairman of ABC Entertainment Group, Lloyd Braun, was fired because ABC's television ratings were last among the four major networks. Robert Iger, who was then president of Disney, ABC's parent company, explained the move: "I felt that given the performance, change was necessary." Iger and Braun had a strained relationship, in part because Braun felt that Iger's inaction had caused the hit show, *The Apprentice*, to slip away from ABC to its rival network NBC.

The previous summer, Braun had pitched a new show, *Lost*, based on a cross between *Cast Away*, a movie that featured Tom Hanks stranded on a desert island, and *Survivor*, a reality TV show about contestants who compete with one another in the wilderness and then vote to remove members until only one person is left. Michael Eisner, the CEO of Disney and Iger's boss, heard the pitch and rated *Lost* a 2 on a scale of 1 to 10, 1 being the worst. Eisner later called the show "terrible." Still, production was well on its way, so *Lost* was in the fall lineup even though Braun was out.[2]

Despite Eisner's dim view of the show, *Lost* was a smash success. It drew an average of 15.7 million viewers to each episode in its first season. *Lost* was the most popular show in its prime-time slot. It also won an Emmy for Outstanding Drama Series. *Lost* ran for six seasons and improved ABC's slumping ratings and profits.

The failure of Carly Hennessy and the success of *Lost* are both the result of luck. You may find that hard to accept. The very fact that Hennessy's songs went unheard and *Lost* was widely watched seems to be sufficient evidence that her songs were no good and the show was terrific. But that thinking is dead wrong and demonstrates that we vastly underestimate the role of luck in what we see happening around us. One of the main goals in this chapter is to change the way we view luck.

Gauging Luck: Independent and Dependent Outcomes

In chapter 3, I used a model based on two jars to make some simple points about the relative influence of skill and luck, outliers, and reversion to the mean. As numbers are drawn from the two jars, they form a normal, bell-shaped distribution. In most cases, and in fact in the most interesting cases, the events we see in the world are far different from a normal distribution. The success of pop songs is one example.

But there are instances where a simple model using two jars can provide a good deal of insight. One way to learn about the distribution of luck in the real world is by asking whether events are dependent on or independent of one another. *Independent* means that what happened before doesn't affect what happens next; *dependent* means the first event influences the next one. A system in which events are dependent is a system that has memory of what happened before.

If events are independent, a simple model, such as tossing a coin or picking numbers from a jar, will work. If they are dependent, as many social interactions are, then the distribution of luck is skewed. In a skewed distribution, good and bad luck are not balanced, on average. Rather, a few benefit from extremely good luck. This means that skill and success are only loosely connected. Events in such systems are not random, but they are nonetheless unpredictable.

Let's start with sports, where luck looks a lot like a bell-shaped distribution. The richest vein of research in this area relates to the *hot hand* in sports. The idea behind the hot hand is that a person who has made his last shot, say in a basketball game, is more likely than average to make his next shot. Researchers tested this belief by asking fans to consider how successful a player will be who makes 50 percent of his shots, on average, following a shot missed and a shot made. Their average estimate of success after a miss was 42 percent. After a made shot, the estimate leaped up to 61 percent. Fans believe in the hot hand. So do most players.

No one questions whether there are lucky streaks in sports. The issue is whether those streaks are simply the outcome of a random process or whether skill levels rise and fall over time. Streaks that result solely from luck tell us little about a player's skill, while streaks caused by variation in skill tell us little about luck. If the observed outcomes are consistent with what a simple model of luck predicts, then the perception of hot hands is more of a matter of psychology than of performance.[3]

Two statisticians, Jim Albert and Jay Bennett, have done a detailed analysis of streaks in baseball. They selected a baseball player who experienced both hot and cold streaks and analyzed his statistics. Todd Zeile's batting average was .280 over the part of a season they examined, but the statisticians calculated that the eight-game moving average dipped as low as .069 (cold) and peaked at .548 (hot). In their book *Curve Ball*, they offer two models to test whether variation was the result of luck or skill.

The first model is what they call "Mr. Consistent." Imagine a spinner that lands on "hit" 28 percent of the time and on "out" the rest of the time. (See figure 6-1.) Each spin represents a turn at bat, and we can keep track of the moving average of the hits and outs over time. In this model, skill is invariant. The statistical result reflects only the luck of the spinner. Because the Mr. Consistent model generates independent outcomes, this system has no memory.

The second model is what they call "Mr. Streaky." This model has two spinners: one when the player is hot and the other when the player is cold. When the player is hot, Albert and Bennett assume that his batting average is .380, exceeding his season average by .100. When the player is cold, his average is only .180. And because the player is presumed to be streaky, the model assumes that the probability of using the same spinner from one game to the next is 90 percent. So if the player is hot in one game, there's a 90 percent chance he'll be hot in the next game. The model has memory and adds variance to the player's ability. (See figure 6-2.)[4]

FIGURE 6-1

Mr. Consistent spinner model

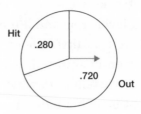

Source: Analysis by author.

FIGURE 6-2

Mr. Streaky spinner model

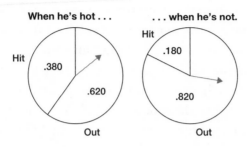

Source: Analysis by author.

FIGURE 6-3

Moving eight-game batting average for Adam Jones (2011)

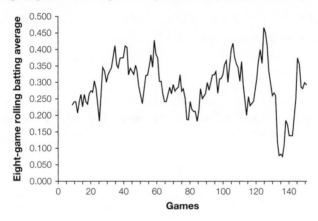

Source: Analysis by author.

I took this same approach to evaluate a baseball player for the 2011 season. Figure 6-3 shows this analysis applied to Adam Jones, an outfielder for the Baltimore Orioles. Jones was up to bat in 145 games and had a batting average of .280. The figure shows the moving average of his batting for the eight most recent games. As in the example that Albert and Bennett offered, Jones had his ups and downs. At the end of his best eight-game stretch, his moving average reached .467. But it dipped to just .074 at one point, too. The question is, which model best reflects his actual performance, Mr. Consistent or Mr. Streaky?

I ran ten thousand simulations of the Mr. Consistent and Mr. Streaky models. To compare the result of this simulation with Jones's actual batting averages, I examined the following statistics: the maximum value within the moving average minus the minimum value; the number of games in which Jones had no hits; the number of games in which he had three or more hits; the number of long streaks in which he hit above his average or in which he hit below his average; and streaks of good or bad games, a measure of how frequently he flips from being hot to cold. Table 6-1 shows a summary of these statistics, including the mean and standard deviation for the simulations.

The Mr. Consistent model, as parsimonious as it is, does a very good job of explaining Jones's results and is closer to the empirical data than Mr. Streaky on every measure except the number of games in which Jones had no hits. A simple model that assumes

TABLE 6-1

Adam Jones's results compared with the Mr. Consistent and Mr. Streaky models

	Empirical	Mr. Consistent	Mr. Streaky
Maxium-minimum	0.393	0.371	0.466
Standard deviation		0.055	0.063
Hitless games	47	41.8	45.2
Standard deviation		5.3	7.4
3+ hit games	11	10.4	13.2
Standard deviation		3.0	4.1
6 game or longer streaks (good or bad)	0	1.5	2.7
Standard deviation		1.1	1.4
Runs of good or bad games	75	70.7	64.0
Standard deviation		6.1	6.7

Source: Jim Albert and Jay Bennett, Curve Ball: Baseball, Statistics, and the Role of Chance in the Game (New York: Springer-Verlag, 2003), 111–144, and analysis by author.

each turn at bat is an independent trial captures most, but not all, of what we see.

This fits with the conclusion that Jim Albert and Jay Bennett reach—that there is some evidence for streakiness. The outcomes in athletics are not strictly independent, which makes some sense because players face varying conditions (for example, they play games at home and away, face different pitchers, and cope with injuries). There is also a modest case for clutch performance (players rising to the occasion and performing above their level of skill) and choking (players collapsing under stress and performing below their level of skill). Yet none of those effects is very strong. For practical purposes, the Mr. Consistent model approximates the relative influences of skill and luck in baseball.[5]

Michael Bar-Eli, Simcha Avugos, and Markus Raab examined the findings of more than forty papers covering baseball, basketball, bowling, darts, golf, tennis, and volleyball. While some evidence for the hot hand does exist in horseshoe pitching ("modest hot and cold spells") and bowling ("the probability of rolling a strike was not independent of previous outcomes"), they concluded that the empirical evidence for the existence of the hot hand is "considerably limited."[6]

In many cases, we do have a sense of what the distribution of numbers in the luck jar looks like. Statisticians have a name for the normal ups and downs that you should expect when the distribution of luck is known: *common-cause variation*. For example, common-cause variation can explain most of the changes in Adam Jones's batting average during the season. It also applies to the output of manufacturing processes and to winning the lottery. In economics, common-cause variation is akin to risk. Frank Knight defined risk in its economic sense as a case where "the distribution of the outcome in a group of instances is known." You don't know what the outcome will be, but you do know all of the possible outcomes. By this definition, you can quantify the risk involved in the turn of a card or the roll of a die.[7]

For sports, gambling, and some elements of business, the simple model using two jars does a very good job of explaining the events we see. The influence of luck is larger or smaller depending on where the activity falls on the luck-skill continuum, but we can understand its role over time. Yet in many other activities, luck is a much wilder influence.

Power Laws and the Mechanisms That Generate Them

Figuring out whether or not Carly Hennessy's recordings or *Lost* will be a success has little to do with estimating the amount of skill involved. While we may have a sense of the range of possible outcomes, predicting success in the world of entertainment is an inherently unpredictable pursuit. In some realms, independence and bell-shaped distributions of luck can explain much of what we see. But in activities such as the entertainment industry, success depends on social interaction. Whenever people can judge the quality of an item by several different criteria and are allowed to influence one another's choices, luck will play a huge role in determining success or failure. This led William Goldman, the screenwriter, to quip, "Nobody knows anything."[8]

For example, if one song happens to be slightly more popular than another at just the right time, it will tend to become even more popular as people influence one another. Because of that effect, known as *cumulative advantage*, two songs of equal quality, or skill, will sell in substantially different numbers. That makes it next to impossible to predict success.[9] Skill does play a role in success and failure, but it can be overwhelmed by the influence of luck. In the jar model, the range of numbers in the luck jar is vastly greater than the range of numbers in the skill jar. Let's take a more careful look at the outcomes, some of the mechanisms, and a somewhat surprising conclusion from this analysis.

The process of social influence and cumulative advantage frequently generates a distribution that is best described by a power law. Figure 6-4 shows the rank and size of the largest 275 cities in the

FIGURE 6-4

Top U.S. cities, rank and size on a logarithmic scale (based on 2010 data)

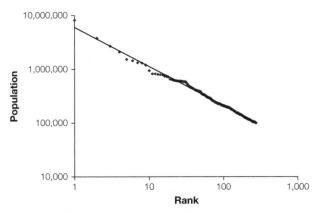

Source: United States Census Bureau and analysis by author.

United States as of 2010. The rank of the cities is on the horizontal axis, and the size of the cities is on the vertical axis. Both the horizontal and vertical axes are on logarithmic scales, which means that the percentage change between tick marks is the same (the percentage difference between 1 and 10 is the same as between 10 and 100). The data fall close to a straight line, which can be expressed with a relatively simple formula known as a *power law*. For example, the formula for the United States would be able to tell you the size of the seventh-largest city (San Antonio, Texas; population 1,325,000) as well as the seventieth (Buffalo, New York; population 260,000).

The term *power law* comes from the fact that an exponent (or power) determines the slope of the line. An astonishingly diverse range of socially driven phenomena follow power laws, including the rank and number of book sales, the rank and frequency of citations for scientific papers, the rank and number of deaths in acts of terrorism, and the rank and deaths in war.[10]

One of the key features of distributions that follow a power law is that there are very few large values and lots of small values. As a result, the idea of an "average" has no meaning. Take book sales as an illustration. Of the millions of titles available, the top ten each sell more than a million copies a year, while a million titles each sell fewer than one hundred. In this case, there is a select number of huge winners and a large number of commercial flops. The number of books that sell a million copies is so small that there is no credible way to make the argument that those authors succeed in proportion to their skill. Since skill alone clearly cannot explain power laws, we need to turn to the mechanisms that generate those lopsided outcomes.

The distinction between independent and dependent outcomes is crucial. The probability that a baseball player will get a hit is not completely independent of whether or not he got a hit during his last turn at bat. Nevertheless, over the course of a season, you can treat individual turns at bat as independent events. So the two-jar model will do a good job of representing his performance.

A path-dependent process is one in which what happens next depends on what happened before. It's a process that, in effect, has memory. These processes are very sensitive to initial conditions and lead to phenomena such as the rich getting richer and the poor getting poorer. Robert K. Merton, a renowned sociologist who taught at Columbia University, called this the *Matthew effect*, after a verse in the Gospel of Matthew: "For whosoever hath, to him shall be given, and he shall have more abundance: but whosoever hath not, from him shall be taken away even that he hath."[11]

Consider the case of two graduate students of equal ability applying for a faculty position. Say that by chance one is hired by an Ivy League university and the other gets a job at a less prestigious college. The professor at the Ivy League school may find herself with better graduate students, less teaching responsibility, superior faculty peers, and more money for research than her peer. Those advantages would lead to more academic papers, citations, and professional accolades. This accumulated edge would suggest that, at the time of retirement, one professor was more capable than the other. But the Matthew effect explains how two people can start in nearly the same place and end up worlds apart.[12] In these kinds of systems, initial conditions matter. And as time goes on, they matter more and more.

A number of mechanisms are responsible for this phenomenon. A simple one is known as *preferential attachment*. Let's say you launch a new website and want to make it as popular as possible. A logical step would be to link your site to sites that already have lots of connections to other sites, including Google or Wikipedia, rather than sites that only have a few connections. In order to get ahead, you have a preference for attaching to sites that are already well known and frequently visited. This behavior causes positive feedback: the more connections you already have, the more new connections you get. Through the process of preferential attachment, some sites gain more links and others fade into obscurity as new sites join the network. Initial differences, even modest ones, are amplified over time.[13]

Here's a very simple model of this process. Say you have a jar that is filled as follows:

5 red marbles

4 black marbles

3 yellow marbles

2 green marbles

1 blue marble

You now close your eyes and randomly select a marble. Say you pick a black one. You return the marble to the jar and then add one more black marble. The jar now contains five black marbles. The other numbers remain the same. You repeat the process of randomly selecting a marble, replacing it, and adding an extra one of a matching color. When you've done that one hundred times, the jar is full.

In the beginning, the probability of choosing any particular color matches the numbers. For instance, there's a 20 percent chance of choosing a yellow marble (3 in 15). It's easy to see how this process is path-dependent. If you select a yellow marble first, the chance of selecting a yellow marble in the second round rises to 25 percent (4 in 16). So while the distribution does give some colors a distinct advantage over others at the start, predicting the winner is difficult.

Figure 6-5 shows three runs of my computer simulation of this game. At the top, the heavy favorite, red, ran away with the game. In the middle, yellow wins and red comes in second. On the bottom is the rare occasion when blue, a distinct long shot, comes in first. You might think of the number of marbles of a particular color as a proxy for skill. More skillful balls have the greatest probability of winning, but there is no assurance that skill will win out. Luck shuffles the initial distribution in ways that are surprising.[14]

Further, once one color has established a sufficient lead, the game is basically over. Preferential attachment locks in the result. This model is vastly less complex than the real world but demonstrates how success can become detached from skill in a path-dependent process.

Critical points and phase transitions are also crucial for the Matthew effect. A *phase transition* occurs when a small incremental change leads to a large-scale effect. This is known colloquially as a *tipping point*. Put a tray of water in a freezer and it cools to the critical point, zero degrees Celsius, and then it becomes ice. A small change in temperature at a critical point leads to a substantial change from a liquid to a solid. Social systems also have critical points and phase transitions.

Mark Granovetter, a professor of sociology at Stanford University, proposed a simple model to show the importance of critical points. Imagine one hundred potential rioters milling around in a public square. Each individual has a "riot threshold," the number of rioters that person would have to see in order to join the riot. Say one person has a threshold of 0 (the instigator), one has a threshold of 1, one has a threshold of 2, and so on up to 99. This uniform distribution of thresholds creates a domino effect and ensures that a riot will happen. The instigator breaks a window with a rock, person one joins in, and then each individual piles on once the size of the riot reaches his threshold.

Now imagine the same setup with a tiny change: replace the person with a threshold of 1 with someone who has a threshold of 2. Now, the group will look virtually identical to the first one, but the riot won't happen. The media would likely call the first crowd rowdy and the second docile, but in reality the groups are nearly

FIGURE 6-5

Simple model of preferential attachment

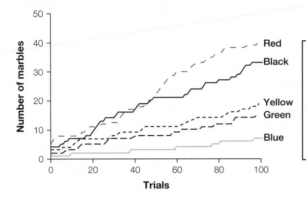

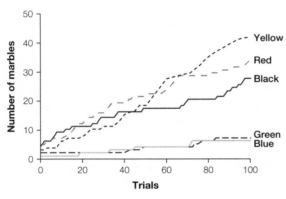

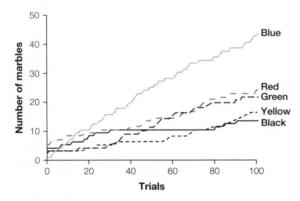

Source: Analysis by author.

indistinguishable. The minute modification in the threshold for one person is enough to make the difference between violence and peace.

As simple as this example appears, it can work with assumptions that are only modestly more realistic as a model for the adoption of innovations (the iPad), for fads (South Beach Diet), for fashions (yoga clothes), and for the spread of disease (the flu). Once an innovation reaches a certain level of popularity, its success is virtually assured. By the same token, great innovations can fail because the domino effect doesn't kick in.[15]

In economics, the lopsided outcomes are frequently the result of increasing returns and network effects. Much of conventional economic theory is based on diminishing returns. If the demand for a commodity exceeds supply, prices will rise, and whoever makes that product will earn more money. Those high profits will attract competitors, who will increase production and effectively push prices back down. This is called *negative feedback*, a mechanism that promotes stability. The strong get weaker and the weak get stronger.

In some sectors of the economy, this framework does a poor job of explaining outcomes because *positive feedback*, which promotes change, takes hold. The classic illustration is the battle to establish standards for a given technology. Examples include the duel for videotape formats between VHS and Betamax in the 1970s and BluRay versus HD DVD for high-definition optical discs more recently. These are cases of increasing returns. It's a winner-take-all game, and the standard that gains a sufficient lead goes on to dominate the market. In the mid-1970s, for instance, VHS and Betamax had roughly equal market shares. But once VHS pulled ahead, it went on to steal 90 percent of the market within a few years. The rich get richer, and the poor get poorer.[16]

The effect of increasing returns is especially pronounced when it is accompanied by high up-front costs followed by low incremental costs and by network effects, where the value of a product or service increases as more people use it. Microsoft's strength in personal computer operating systems neatly demonstrates high up-front costs, network effects, and increasing returns.

The first version of Microsoft Windows had a high up-front cost. It took substantial time and money to develop. But the cost of creating additional copies was extremely low—the price of a floppy disk, which was how software was distributed at the time. Network effects were strong for operating systems and related computer programs, because the de facto standard ensured that people could exchange files. As the standard grew in popularity, computer programmers were encouraged to develop new software for Windows, which made it even more popular. People wanted a product that was widely used because that made it more valuable to them. That resulted in what's known as *demand-side economies of scale*, where more value for the consumer leads to more demand for the software and, ultimately, more profit for the producer.

Add together the economics of software and network effects, and the result is increasing returns. Profitability soars for the winner, creating a level of success that is all out of proportion to the differences between the various products when competition began. The point of reviewing these mechanisms is to show that they are sensitive to initial conditions, frequently undergo critical transitions, and can lead to skewed results. Skill doesn't carry the day, luck does. So, effectively, these mechanisms are luck generators.[17]

Inequality *and* Unpredictability

In 1981 the late Sherwin Rosen, who was an economist at the University of Chicago, wrote a very influential paper called "The Economics of Superstars." He observed that a few superstars— "performers of first rank"—earn incomes that are vastly larger than performers with only modestly less ability. While fans may prefer the superstars to lesser performers, he argued that the difference in skill is too modest to explain the sizeable gap in pay. He suggested that technology is the primary factor that causes the phenomenon.[18]

Imagine two singers of similar ability, with one being only slightly better than the other. In the era before recording technology was developed, the singers would have earned a comparable sum from their concerts, with the superior singer perhaps earning a modest premium consistent with the difference in skill. But once recording technology was introduced, consumers would no longer have to settle for the lesser of the two and would buy the record of the better singer almost every time. So her earnings would soar relative to her rival. Despite the similarity of talent, this becomes a winner-take-all market.

In their book *The Winner-Take-All Society*, Robert Frank and Philip Cook suggest that increased competition for talent is another factor that creates outsized pay for top performers. Frank offers the example of a board of directors that must select between two candidates to become the next CEO of a company that earns $10 billion a year in profits. If one candidate can make better decisions than the other, Frank argues, the company's profits may be 3 percent higher than they would be otherwise, creating an additional $300 million in income. So even a modest difference in the abilities of the CEO candidates is worth a difference in pay that seems enormous to the rest of us. Moreover, companies today are more willing to hire a CEO from outside the company than they were a few years ago. This mobility has made CEOs even more valuable, just as free agency has increased salaries for baseball players.[19]

This line of thinking appears to be supported by two threads of analysis. The first is that a CEO earns an amount that is proportional to the size of the company where he works. Since the distribution of the size of companies follows a power law, so too do the amounts that CEOs are paid. Research also shows that pay for CEOs in the United States has grown over time in line with the market capitalizations of the largest companies. Specifically, the sixfold increase in pay from 1980 through 2003 is consistent with the sixfold increase in market capitalizations. While this story may appear to be about competition, the researchers don't rule out the effects of contagion in explaining the sharp rise in pay for CEOs. This means that in setting pay, members of the boards of directors may look at what other companies are doing and set their policies accordingly. If every company does this, then just a handful of companies over-paying their CEOs at the outset can lead to a broad increase in pay over time. The researchers show that if 10 percent of the companies want to pay their CEOs twice as much as their competitors, then compensation eventually doubles for all CEOs. So the skewed pay may be the result of contagion, not competition.[20]

We have seen that path dependence and social interaction lead to inequality. Technology and competition also contribute to this phe-nomenon. But there is a crucial assumption underlying all of these models of superstardom: that we know exactly who is most skillful.[21] That assumption, as we will see, is false. Social influence leads not just to inequality, but to a fundamental lack of predictability as well. More skill gives people an edge in attaining success, but like the red marbles that started out in the majority, that edge offers no assurance that they will end up on top.

Consider the analysis that showed that pay for CEOs is consistent with market capitalization. The same researchers tried to find dif-ferences in the skill of CEOs in the largest companies. They couldn't find much, if any. For example, their model suggests that replacing the CEO of the 250th-largest company in the United States with the CEO of the largest company, at the pay of the smaller company, would increase the market value of the smaller company by 0.016 percent. The decimal point isn't misplaced: that's basically zero.[22]

There are a variety of ways to assess skill or quality. For example, you might evaluate a song according to its rhythm, tonality, lyrical content, vocal quality, and instrumentation. Different people may have different lists or may weight those qualities in different ways. But no matter how we assess someone's skill, luck will also help to shape our opinion through social influence. So luck is not only behind the inequality of outcomes, it determines what we perceive to be skill. If a product is judged through social processes, there is an inherent lack of predictability. The process doesn't generate ran-dom results, but the specific results are unknowable before the fact.

Contrast this with a realm where you can objectively assess the results. If you want to know who is the fastest of five runners, you line them up and run a race. Since you are assessing them on one dimension—speed—the winner is the most skillful. No luck is involved.

Now say you want to select the most appropriate college for your child. You might consult the annual "Best Colleges" guide in *U.S. News & World Report*, which ranks hundreds of universities and colleges. For the 2012 guide, the team at the magazine used these variables and weights to assess national universities and liberal arts colleges:[23]

Undergraduate academic reputation	22.5%
Graduation and retention rates	20.0
Faculty resources (2010–2011 year)	20.0
Student selectivity (2010 entering class)	15.0
Financial resources	10.0
Graduation rate performance	7.5
Alumni giving	5.0
Total	100.0%

It's easy to see why this list is alluring to students and parents: it seems to provide an objective way to measure what amounts to the skill of the school. But there are two big defects with this sort of ranking. The first is that the method *U.S. News* uses largely shapes the outcome. There's no doubt that the editors strive to do the best possible job at this difficult task, but this is a one-size-fits-all approach that simply can't provide what every student and parent wants and needs. For instance, cost or geographic location may be much more important to a student than retention rates or selectivity. So the highest-ranked schools may not be the most attractive schools for your child. Harvard, Princeton, and Yale are at the top of the list for 2012 and are undoubtedly outstanding institutions. But the full ranking says as much about the approach the magazine uses as it does about the schools themselves. Unlike runners, schools offer no way for us to say that one of them is the best.

This is essential to bear in mind any time you see a ranking, or ordering, of anyone or anything that can be evaluated in different ways. The ranks reflect the methods. Unless the method the researchers use exactly matches your own criteria, which is highly unlikely, you should take the ranking with a grain of salt. The ranking of the best place to live, the best car to drive, or the best college to attend provides a simple answer that is not a good fit for the complex question it addresses. The bias produced by the method is also relevant for elections and for ranking sports teams. The winner of an election, whether for the president of the United States or for student body president, can vary depending on what method is used to count and weight votes.[24]

The second defect is that some of the variables themselves are based on perception. For instance, the variable with the highest weighting in the college ranking is undergraduate academic reputation, which U.S. News assesses primarily by surveying the presidents, provosts, and admissions officers of peer institutions. Given that these educational leaders have knowledge of only a handful of other schools, their assessments tend to follow . . . the published rankings.

Oberlin College provides an interesting case. When U.S. News first ranked colleges in the early 1980s, Oberlin ranked fifth among liberal arts colleges, in large part because of its strong reputation. But a few years later, U.S. News changed the method used in ranking the colleges. They lowered the importance given to the assessments by presidents, provosts, and admissions officers. Oberlin dropped out of the top ten. The school's ranking continued to sink, and within a decade the overall ranking was close to falling out of the top twenty-five, which U.S. News defined as the top tier of liberal arts schools. Tellingly, the assessment of Oberlin by peers dropped even as other objective measures of the school's quality remained the same. The decline in ranking, initially triggered by a methodological shift, lowered Oberlin's status in the eyes of its peers. This is a process driven by social influence.[25]

At this point, it should be clear that when the forces of social influence are at work, we get positive feedback that makes the strong get stronger and the weak get weaker. Who benefits from this process of amplification has a lot to do with luck.

But what is more unsettling is that if you can evaluate skill in many different ways (think of art, music, literature, movies, etc.), luck also manipulates our perception of quality or skill. Better products do have a higher probability of succeeding. But there is an enormous amount of latitude in sorting out who or what will do well. This explains why Carly Hennessy flopped, *Lost* won, CEOs with seemingly similar skills make disparate incomes, and Harvard receives thirty-four thousand applications for fewer than seventeen hundred spots. It's as if the luck in the luck jar reaches across and changes the distribution in the skill jar.

Living in Alternate Universes with MusicLab

In 2006, Matthew Salganik, Peter Dodds, and Duncan Watts published the findings of a remarkable study that showed just how social influence amplifies inequality and makes so much in the world unpredictable.[26] The experiment was called MusicLab, and was ostensibly about musical taste. Over fourteen thousand people came to the website the researchers established. Each had the opportunity to listen to and rate forty-eight songs from unknown bands. They could also download whatever songs they liked.

Unbeknownst to the people who participated in this experiment, when they entered the website for the first time they were randomly assigned to one of two experimental conditions—an independent condition or a condition in which social influence was at work. In the independent condition, which included 20 percent of the people, the researchers presented the songs in random order. The subjects could rate and download the songs, but they had no information about what others had done before them. By removing any social interaction, the independent condition provided a reasonable measure of quality. People were essentially voting on what they thought was good. As far as the choices others made were concerned, they were blindfolded.

The other subjects were divided into eight groups, with 10 percent of the population in each. They were free to rate and download songs, but they could also see how many people had downloaded each song before them. One version of the experiment enhanced the social effect by showing the download counts in descending order. In effect, the eight social worlds were parallel universes. They all started with the same initial condition but were left to go in any direction that social influence took them.

Salganik, Dodds, and Watts found that quality did matter. Songs that were ranked as inferior by the independent group tended to perform poorly before the other groups as well. Likewise, songs that the independent group ranked high were among the most popular in the other groups. But in the groups where social influence was at work, there was also substantial inequality. The market shares of the best songs were much higher in the social worlds than in the independent world. This is all consistent with the research on inequality done by Sherwin Rosen, Robert Frank, and Philip Cook.

In what was perhaps the most significant finding, MusicLab showed that while quality is roughly correlated with commercial success, there is little predictability with hits. Really bad songs did poorly, but an average to above-average ranking in the independent condition made a song a contender to be a smashing success. For example, "Lockdown," a song by a group called 52metro, ranked twenty-sixth in the independent condition, right in the middle of the pack. But it was the number-one hit in one of the social influence worlds and number forty in another. As one of the researchers, Matthew Salganik, notes, "It's as if luck is more important for good songs than for bad songs."

The beauty of MusicLab was that it allowed the researchers to separate these important effects. Comparing the independent world to the social world revealed exactly how social interaction created the environment in which inequality could emerge. And by running several social worlds at once, the experiment showed how hard it is to predict which songs would succeed. While its design was simple, MusicLab demonstrates exactly why we are so limited in our ability to pick hits.

Why It's So Hard to Live with the Many Shapes of Luck

At this point, you probably accept the intellectual case that it is possible for skill, or quality, to play only a minor role in commercial success. But, if you are like me, you have a hard time accepting that there isn't something just a little special about *The DaVinci Code*, *Titanic*, or the *Mona Lisa*.[27] The very fact that they are so wildly popular seems to be all the evidence you need to conclude that they have some special qualities that make them stand out above all the rest. But all three were surprises. Our minds are expert at wiping out surprises and creating order, and order dictates that these products are special.

We are very good at fooling ourselves about our own success, a phenomenon that psychologists call the *self-serving attribution bias*. It is common for us to attribute success to our own terrific skill, even in endeavors that are determined mostly by luck. Part of the explanation is that we see ourselves as capable agents. We can do things. We can make things happen. So we assume that our skill caused the success we experience. On the other hand, we readily attribute failure to external causes, including bad luck.[28]

In a paper called "Heads I Win, Tails It's Chance," Ellen Langer and Jane Roth describe an experiment in which they asked subjects to call heads or tails for a coin tossed in the air thirty times. The subjects were told whether they were right or wrong according to a preordained schedule rather than the real results. In all trials, the participants were "successful" 50 percent of the time, but some were told that they were correct frequently at the beginning of the sequence while others started with more wrong answers. Subjects who were told they were right seven out of the first eight tosses estimated their own ability to predict heads or tails as 5.7 (0 = very bad and 10 = pretty good), well above those who were told they were wrong at the beginning. In this case, initial success with random events persuaded those people to think that they had some sort of skill at predicting the way a coin would land.[29]

Likewise, when we observe the success of others, we fall victim to the *fundamental attribution error*. In this context, the error is the tendency to base our explanation of what happens on an individual's skill rather than the situation. Once we create a narrative that explains success, we tend to suppress other explanations and see what happened as inevitable. For example, while researchers have come to different conclusions about the influence CEOs have on their companies, few would deny that the perception of their importance is exaggerated. In his book *Searching for a Corporate Savior*, Rakesh Khurana, a professor of leadership development at Harvard Business School, writes, "Social psychologists have found that the construction of leader images is a process of matching leaders' characteristics with performance outcomes: outcomes, whether positive or negative, are attributed to leaders and then determine whether these leaders are viewed in a positive or negative light." This is in spite of the fact that "the CEO effect is swamped by contextual factors such as industry and macroeconomic variables."[30] The success of a company is rarely owing to the efforts of one person. It is typically the result of the work of a large number of people, as well as the environment in which they operate. Still, we tend to assign credit to individual people for collective success.

The simple models that generate the power laws that govern phenomena such as MusicLab are just that: simple models. They do provide us with some good answers and can help keep us from relying too much on intuition, but the real world is vastly more complicated than the model. Take the sizes of cities as an example. We saw that they follow a power law, and we can construct a model that generates a reliable picture of this. But any realistic discussion of how any city achieved its particular size would require analysis at multiple scales. You could start, of course, by saying the cities get larger when people move to them and that they shrink when people leave. But then you'd have to ask *why* people are coming and going. Perhaps it has to do with companies expanding or contracting. In turn, companies may grow or shrink because of macroeconomic factors, or local tax breaks, or regulations, or myriad other possibilities. There are real mechanisms that drive social influence, which are themselves difficult to identify. As a consequence, you should be very skeptical of anyone who claims to be able to predict results whenever social influence is a factor.

One final point. People who work in businesses where social influence operates are often paid for good luck, although they generally don't suffer symmetrically from bad luck. This issue, of course, is central to the outrage about the financial crisis that occurred from 2007–2009. Many finance professionals, including bankers, traders, and brokers, collected outsized pay when the markets were ascending, capitalizing on good luck. But when the financial system nearly collapsed and a number of large firms went out of business, governments had to step in to stabilize the system. The gains were privatized and the losses were socialized, leading to a palpable sense of unfairness. Paying for luck is not limited to finance. It occurs in many fields, such as music, art, and movies. Even so, we should do our best to measure and reward success properly while acknowledging luck for what it is.

CHAPTER 7

WHAT MAKES FOR A USEFUL STATISTIC?

AT A CONFERENCE HELD in the spring of 2010, I heard the CEO of a company that produces video games talk about his plans to transform his firm. Some of his proposed actions, including cutting costs and concentrating on the most profitable products, were what I expected. But his most emphatic point was something that I would not have guessed: to improve the quality of his products. The company set a goal of releasing fifteen new games with scores of 80 or better, on a scale from 0 to 100, as rated by a site called Metacritic that aggregates reviews. Further, the company was going to use those ratings of quality as part of the formula to determine how big a bonus its executives would receive.

Making high-quality products is a good thing, of course. You want your customers to be happy. But there's no evidence that the ratings from Metacritic are reliable, and, more to the point, it's not clear how well those ratings relate to the CEO's goal of creating "long-term stockholder value." Poor quality makes a company uncompetitive, but so does quality that is too high. The relationship between quality and value is not at all clear.

Consider the case of the Wallace Company, a pipe and valve distributor, which won the prestigious Malcolm Baldrige National

Quality Award in 1990, only to file for bankruptcy two years later. Although Wallace succeeded in improving its on-time product delivery rate and gaining market share, its customers were eventually unwilling to pay higher prices to offset the costs of the quality program. An executive at the company that later acquired Wallace said, "If [the effort to win the award] leads to problems by making it more expensive to operate under a number of burdensome procedures, winning the Baldrige can almost be a negative."[1]

This chapter is about what makes for a useful statistic. Few people take the time to distinguish between statistics that are truly helpful and those that are not. A sense of the relative contributions of luck and skill in shaping the outcome of our efforts is essential to understanding how valuable a statistic is likely to be.

Useful statistics have two features. First, they are *persistent*, which means what happens in the present is similar to what happened in the past. If the job you do is predominantly a matter of skill, you can expect to be able to repeat your performance reliably. If you measured the performance of a trained sprinter on two consecutive days, you would expect to see similar times. In statistics, this persistence is called *reliability*. If luck is more important, then you would expect the reliability to be low. The test for reliability, or persistence, measures the same quantity over different periods of time.[2]

Good statistics are also *predictive* of the goal you seek. Let's say that we keep track of the percentage of shots that a player makes in a basketball game, and the goal of the team is to score points when playing offense. We see that, all things being equal, the higher percentage of shots a player makes, the more points he produces. Statisticians call this *validity* and would say that it is valid to conclude that the higher the percentage of shots a player makes, the more points he will score. This is an obvious case, of course, but not all relationships between cause and effect are as clear. The test for predictive value compares two measurements: in this case, the percentage of shots made and points scored.

Statisticians assess persistence and predictive value by examining the *coefficient of correlation*, a measure of the degree of linear relationship between two variables in a pair of distributions. The coefficient of correlation, r, can fall in the range of 1.00 to −1.00. If $r = 1.00$, then the plot of each point from both distributions falls exactly on a straight line. The values in each distribution need not correspond exactly, but the differences between the points in the two distributions are identical. If $r = -1.00$, then there is a perfect inverse correlation, where increases in one variable accompany decreases in the other variable.[3] Most of the correlations examined in this chapter are positive.

Here's an example of how to interpret r. Let's consider the correlation between runs scored in baseball and the percentage of games that a major league team wins, which is relatively high ($r = .75$). This says that if a team ranks one standard deviation above average in the number of runs it scores, it will rank 0.75 standard deviations above average in the number of games it wins. So the coefficient of correlation provides practical information about the relationship between scoring runs and winning games.[4]

The process of determining which statistics are useful begins with a definition of your objective: What do you want to use the statistics for? In sports, the object is to win the game. In investing, it is making money; or to put it more technically, generating risk-adjusted returns in excess of some benchmark over time. Knowing your objective is important because it's hard to chart a course without knowing the destination. Next, you have to determine what factors contribute to achieving your objective. To do so, you have to translate a theory of cause and effect into quantities that you can observe and measure. This allows you to assess how skill, measured as high persistence, translates into your objective, measured as high predictive value.[5]

It is now easy to see why a shareholder may have some concern about the CEO's emphasis on high quality. You can assess video games by judging many different elements and characteristics, so a measure of quality from period to period is likely to be unreliable. More significantly, it's very difficult to prove a cause-and-effect relationship between high-quality games and the stated objective, "to create long-term stockholder value." As the case of the Wallace Company shows, both too little and too much quality can be bad for a company's financial performance and, consequently, its value.

We will now take a tour through the worlds of sports, business, and investing and examine the statistics that people commonly use in those pursuits. The goal is to see how well the statistics hold up to the tests of persistence and predictability. Because high skill is associated with high correlations for persistence and predictability, correlations allow us to infer a great deal about the nature of the activity.

Baseball Statistics and the *Moneyball* Insight

Jim Albert, the professor of math and statistics whom we met in chapter 6, presents an analysis of batting average, the most common statistic used to measure the performance of hitters in baseball. He starts by analyzing the various things that can happen when a player steps up to the plate (see figure 7-1). Batting average is the ratio of

FIGURE 7-1

Analysis of hitting in baseball

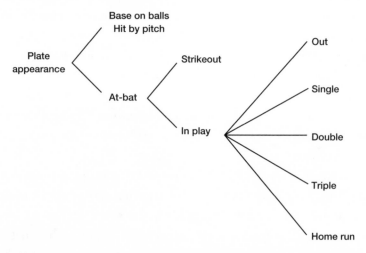

Source: Analysis by the author based on Jim Albert, "A Batting Average: Does It Represent Ability or Luck?" working paper, April 17, 2004, http://bayes.bgsu.edu/papers/paper_bavg.pdf.

hits (singles, doubles, triples, or home runs) to at-bats. But there are many other statistics you can use to analyze the skill of a hitter. One is called "on-base percentage." It is roughly defined as the number of times a hitter is walked to first base, plus the number of hits he gets, divided by the number of plate appearances. Another statistic is called the "strikeout rate." That is the number of times he strikes out divided by plate appearances. Albert wanted to know which statistics were the result of skill and which were the result of luck.[6] In short, he wanted to know which ones were persistent.

He reasoned that a good way to test this was to compare two years of hitting data. If a statistic accurately measures a player's skill, you would expect the values to be similar from one season to the next. On the other hand, if the statistic varies a great deal from year to year, you can assume that luck plays a large role in that outcome.

Figure 7-2 shows scatter plots for three hitting statistics: batting average, on-base percentage, and strikeout rate. What is clear is that both batting average ($r = .37$) and on-base percentage ($r = .44$) have a decent correlation from year to year. But luck plays a size-able role in those outcomes.

Strikeout rate, the image on the right, is highly correlated from year to year ($r = .77$) and is a very good indicator of a batter's skill. The plot on the far left is much more scattered than the one on the

FIGURE 7-2

Scatter plots for three hitting statistics (2010 and 2011 seasons for players with 100 or more at-bats)

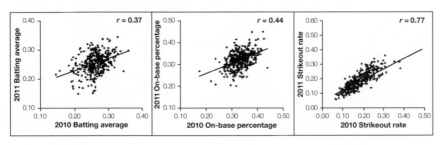

Source: Analysis by author.

far right, indicating that the former is more random and the latter is more a result of skill. These correlations make intuitive sense. There are many factors that determine whether a ball lands for a hit when a batter puts it into play, including where and how well the ball was hit, the quality of the defense, the field, and the weather. Strikeout rates reflect a duel between the pitcher and batter, and the umpire is the only other meaningful variable that weighs on the outcome.

Figure 7-3 shows the coefficient of correlations for eight batting statistics, using data from the 2010 and 2011 seasons in Major League Baseball. I included all players with one hundred or more at-bats, which includes a sample of about 340 players. The analysis shows that a few statistics are very strong measures of skill, including

FIGURE 7-3

Ranking of hitting statistics by coefficient of correlation (2010 and 2011 seasons for players with 100 or more at-bats)

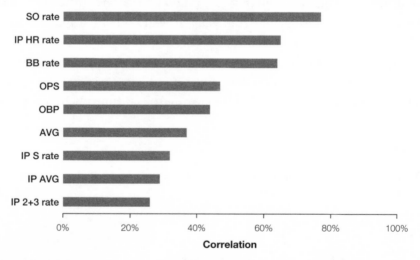

Source: Analysis by author.
Definitions: SO rate: Strikeout rate (strikeouts/plate appearances); IP HR rate: In-play home run rate (home runs/[at-bats - strikeouts]); BB rate: Base-on-ball rate (base on balls/plate appearances); OPS: On-base percentage + Slugging (on-base percentage + slugging percentage); OBP: On-base percentage ([hits + base on balls + hit by pitch]/[at-bats + base on balls + hit by pitch + sacrifice flies]); AVG: Batting average (hits/at-bats); IP S rate: In-play single rate (singles/[at-bats - strikeouts]); IP AVG: In-play average (hits/[at-bats - strikeouts]); IP 2+3: In-play doubles and triples rate (doubles + triples/[at-bats - strikeouts]).

strikeout rate, home run rate, and base-on-ball rate (how frequently a player is walked). Measures such as batting average, singles, and doubles are subject to the powerful influence of luck.

It is worth reiterating a point that I have made a number of times: to get the same signal, you need a larger sample size when lots of luck is involved than you do when skill dominates. For example, you can get a good idea of how skilled a player is in terms of his strikeout rate by recording one hundred at-bats. If you want to measure the skill involved in what's known as his "batting average for balls in play," you need to record eleven hundred at-bats.[7] (This number is the percentage of times a batter gets a hit, excluding home runs, for balls in play.)

In their book *Stumbling on Wins*, David Berri and Martin Schmidt calculated the persistence of statistics for football, basketball, and ice hockey. In hockey, for instance, the coefficient of correlation for shots on goal each minute is strong from year to year ($r = .89$) while the percentage of shots that score is moderate ($r = .63$), and plus-minus, a measure of how many goals a team scores versus how many goals a team gives up when a specific player is on the ice, is relatively low ($r = .32$).[8] In general, the more a statistic relies on the interaction of teammates, the lower the coefficient of correlation.

Now that we have calculated the persistence of the statistics used in baseball, we turn to their value in predicting who will win. Since the goal is to measure offense, we'll focus on runs scored. To win over time, the overarching objective, a team must consistently score more runs (offense) than it gives up (defense). The number of runs a team gives up is suitable for analyzing defense.

Figure 7-4 shows the correlations among the three statistics in figure 7-2 (batting average, on-base percentage, and strikeout rate) and how many runs a team gets. There are only thirty data points for each chart, because the charts measure teams, not individual players. The coefficient of correlation indicates that on-base percentage has a strong relationship with runs per game ($r = .92$).

FIGURE 7-4

Correlations between three statistics and runs per game (team level, 2011 season)

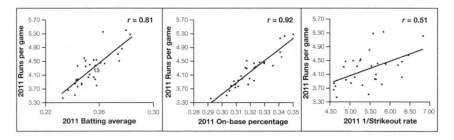

Source: Analysis by author.

Batting average has a weaker relationship (r = .81). And the inverse of the strikeout rate (higher numbers mean fewer strikeouts) has the weakest relationship (r = .51). As you can see, the plot on the right is the most scattered and therefore the most random.

Having checked the statistics for persistence and predictive value, we can now plot them on a chart that has the luck-skill continuum as the horizontal axis and the predictive value on the vertical axis. (See figure 7-5.) The most telling statistics fall into the top right quadrant, indicating that they are not only persistent, but they can be used to predict the number of runs a team will score. Measures that fall into the lower left quadrant are the least useful, because they are inconsistent from period to period and don't correlate strongly with winning.

This analysis highlights one of the key themes of *Moneyball*, the best-selling book by Michael Lewis that describes how the Oakland A's built a winning baseball team on the cheap by finding players whose skills were underpriced. The common way to assess players, Lewis wrote, was to look at their five tools: the ability to run, throw, field, hit, and hit with power. When managers "talked about scoring runs, they tended to focus on team batting average." The A's realized that the percentage of times a player got on base was much better at predicting how many runs a player would score and that "a player's ability to get on base—especially when he got on base in

FIGURE 7-5

Scatter plots for three hitting statistics (2010 and 2011 seasons for players with 100 or more at-bats)

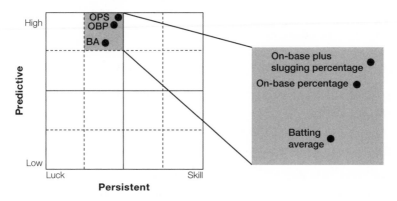

Source: Analysis by author.

unspectacular ways—tended to be dramatically underpriced in relation to other abilities."[9]

A glance at figure 7-5 shows why the A's approach could work. The coefficient of correlation for on-base percentage, .44, is higher than that for batting average at .37. The higher level of persistence tells us that the number of times a player gets on base will tell us more about his skill than his batting average will. A look at the value of this statistic in predicting what will happen tells an even clearer story. The number of times players get on base has a .92 correlation with the number of runs the team will score, making batting average look relatively poor by comparison.

In truth, the A's were doing much more sophisticated analysis than a simple trade-off between batting average and on-base percentage. In fact, among other statistics, the A's were using a refined version of on-base percentage called on-base plus slugging, or OPS, which is the sum of on-base percentage and slugging percentage. *Slugging percentage* is the total number of bases divided by at-bats. For example, a single is worth one base, a double is worth two bases, and so on. The persistence and predictive value of OPS is even greater than that of on-base percentage. But the point is that the A's looked beyond conventional statistics to find the most useful ones in an effort to win more cost-effectively than other teams.

The idea of on-base percentage was by no means new. Branch Rickey, an innovative baseball executive best known for breaking the color barrier by signing Jackie Robinson in the 1940s, wrote about on-base percentage (he called it "on base average") in an article published by *Life* magazine in 1954.[10] Bill James, who started writing about baseball in the late 1970s, recognized the importance of getting on base for scoring runs. Most baseball executives did not embrace the statistical approach to untangling skill and luck, but rather chose to rely on their intuition. James wrote, "Baseball men, living from day to day in the clutch of carefully metered chance occurrences, have developed an entire bestiary of imagined causes to tie together and thus make sense of patterns that are in truth entirely accidental."[11]

Decision makers in sports, as in other fields, have historically developed rules of thumb for how to assess players and implement strategies on the field. In many cases, these rules of thumb are consistent with what the statistics say—great hitters and pitchers stand out in both cases. But most executives have been slow to apply statistical analysis that focuses on persistence and predictive value, thereby missing the true causes of winning. As we will see, this failure is not unique to sports.

Business Statistics: Going with the Crowd and Making It Up

While professional baseball is a business, many players, fans, and managers view it first and foremost as a game. But the goal of a corporation seems much clearer. The most widely accepted objective is to maximize the value of the company's shares. Practically speaking, this means that each dollar that a company invests should create more than one dollar in value.[12] With that in mind, the next step is figuring out what to measure to find the actual causes of success.

Companies generally measure both financial and nonfinancial values. We can figure out which financial measures are most popular by finding out how executives are paid and listening to what executives say are the most the important measures. As it turns out, the answer is the same in either case: earnings per share (EPS).

A survey of executive compensation by Frederic W. Cook & Co. found that EPS is the most popular measure of performance, used by about half of all companies.[13] Researchers at Stanford Business School independently came to the same conclusion.[14] Companies are also consistent in saying that's what they measure to determine their performance. A survey of four hundred financial executives by John Graham, Campbell Harvey, and Shiva Rajgopal, professors of finance, found that nearly two-thirds of companies placed earnings first in a ranking of the "three most important measures reported to outsiders." Sales and the growth of sales also rated highly for measuring performance and for communicating externally.[15]

The immediate question to ask is whether the growth of EPS serves the objective of creating value for shareholders. The answer is: it depends. The growth of earnings and the creation of value can go together, but it is also possible to deliver higher EPS while destroying value.[16] Indeed, the survey by Graham, Harvey, and Rajgopal found "the majority of companies are willing to sacrifice long-run economic value to deliver short-run earnings," a result they deem to be "shocking."[17] Theory tells us that the causal relationship between the growth of EPS and the creation of value is tenuous at best.

Let's examine the persistence of EPS and the growth of sales. Figure 7-6 shows the coefficient of correlation for growth of EPS for more than three hundred large, nonfinancial companies in the United States. The compounded annual growth rates from 2005 to 2007 are compared with the rates from 2008 to 2010. The correlation is negative and relatively weak ($r = -.13$). The correlation for the growth of sales is somewhat higher ($r = .28$). This is consistent with large-scale studies by academics showing low persistence for the

FIGURE 7-6

Scatter plots for EPS and growth of sales (2008–2010 versus 2005–2007)

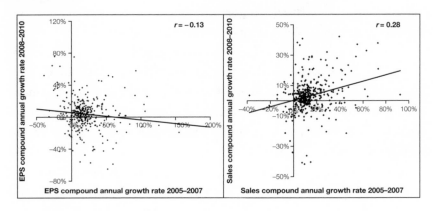

Source: Analysis by author.

growth of earnings and higher persistence for the growth of sales. In addition, the rates of growth for earnings rapidly revert to the mean, which is what you would expect to see when luck plays a large role in the process.[18]

Figure 7-7 shows the correlations that indicate the value of these measures in making predictions. The dependent variable, represented on the vertical axis, is the total return to shareholders for each company's stock less the total return for the S&P 500. Adjusted earnings show a reasonably good correlation ($r = .37$). This analysis shows that if you can forecast the rate of earnings growth, you can earn relatively attractive returns, even considering the important caveat that not all growth in earnings creates value. The problem is that forecasting earnings is difficult because of the lack of persistence.[19]

The growth of sales involves a different trade-off. While more persistent than the growth of EPS, the growth of sales has a weaker correlation with relative total returns to shareholders ($r = .27$). So the two most popular measures of performance have limited value. This should come as no surprise, given that the movement of stock prices over time reflects changes in expectations. Naturally, a company's performance helps shape those expectations, but

FIGURE 7-7

Correlations between EPS and sales growth and total shareholder returns relative to the S&P 500 (2008–2010)

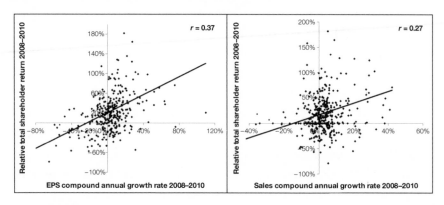

Source: Analysis by author.

fundamentals and expectations can get out of step with each other. For that reason, thoughtful executives and investors strive to understand the expectations that are reflected in the price of a stock and seek to determine whether those expectations are reasonable.

As we saw with the example of the company that produces video games, companies also use nonfinancial measures of performance. These include the quality of a product, safety in the workplace, loyalty of customers, how satisfied employees are with their jobs, and whether or not a customer would be willing to promote a given product. It is also common for these measures to have a big influence on what an executive earns, which introduces the risk that executives might choose to measure what makes them look good.

Christopher Ittner and David Larcker wrote in the *Harvard Business Review* that "most companies have made little attempt to identify areas of nonfinancial performance that might advance their chosen strategy. Nor have they demonstrated a cause-and-effect link between improvements in those nonfinancial areas and in cash flow, profit, or stock price." Ittner and Larcker's survey of 157 companies showed that more than 70 percent of them failed to demonstrate that the measures they've chosen actually cause the effects they're seeking in their companies. And more than three-quarters of the companies in the survey made no effort to demonstrate that what they're measuring has any effect on what the company earns. The researchers suggest that at least 70 percent of the companies they surveyed didn't consider a nonfinancial measure's persistence (the authors called it *reliability*) and predictive value (which they called *validity*).

But the news is not all bad. The two professors of accounting did find that those few companies that bothered to measure a non-financial quantity and took the trouble to verify that it had some real effect earned a lot more money than companies that didn't take those steps.[20] In other words, you can use nonfinancial measures to improve your performance.

Sadly, the most popular measurements companies use to track and communicate their own performance don't exert much influence in how much value those companies create for shareholders. Carelessly chosen nonfinancial measures are even worse. Too many companies select statistics for their ubiquity rather than their utility. Thoughtful executives clearly state their governing objective. They then try to identify the causes that reliably lead to that objective. That persistence suggests that skill is exerting more influence than luck. Enlightened executives will actually draw maps that allow them to understand, track, and manage the cause-and-effect relationships that determine the value of the company and its stock.

Investing: Past Returns Are No Guarantee of Future Returns

The business of investing is filled with institutional practitioners who are smart and motivated. As we have already seen, the industry is highly competitive, and reversion to the mean is a strong force. That it is difficult for fund managers to deliver returns in excess of the market, adjusted for risk, is a testament to the efficiency of the market. The idea behind efficiency is that the prices of assets reveal all known information. This is not strictly true, and markets are notorious for going to extremes. But only a small percentage of investors have shown an ability to systematically beat the market over time. It's not that investors lack skill, it's the paradox of skill: as investors have become more sophisticated and the dissemination of information has gotten cheaper and quicker over time, the variation in skill has narrowed and luck has become more important.[21]

Because investing involves so much luck in the short term, it would stand to reason that short-term success or failure is not a reliable test of skill. But all of us effortlessly find causes for the effects we see, and making money appears to be clear evidence that the investment manager knew what he was doing. Investing is a field where this fallacy is very costly.

Academics have studied in great detail how people decide where and when to invest. The general story, for both individuals and institutions, is that they tend to invest in managers or assets that have done well and pull their money from managers or assets that have done poorly. Institutions, which include pension funds and endowments, are run by trained professionals who are generally well versed in the workings of financial markets. Even so, they show the tendency to focus on recent outcomes in the same way that individuals who are presumably less sophisticated do.[22]

So rather than looking at a measure that is correlated with a desired outcome, most investors look directly at the outcome. Figure 7-8 shows the poor correlation ($r = -.15$) between risk-adjusted excess returns for the period 2005–2007 and 2008–2010 for almost fifteen hundred mutual funds. Each fund's returns are compared with those of the index that it uses as its primary benchmark. (Finance professionals represent excess return with the Greek letter α. Since more risk is generally related to more reward, α measures the excess returns considering the risk that the investment manager assumed.) The lack of correlation is consistent with the paradox of skill and the strong reversion to the mean in the practice of investing.

FIGURE 7-8

Correlation between excess returns (2008–2010 and 2005–2007)

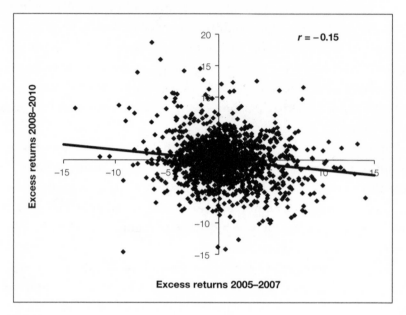

Source: Analysis by author.

Individual investors who do not have access to the sophisticated analytical tools that professionals use tend to rely on rating agencies to guide their decisions. The best-known of these agencies is Morningstar, Inc., which rates mutual funds on a five-star scale. Researchers who have studied initial ratings and changes in those ratings report that investors put more money than normal into funds that receive positive ratings or upgrades of their ratings, and withdraw money from funds with low ratings or downgrades of ratings.[23]

The star rating system is a forced normal distribution based on prior, risk-adjusted returns. For example, the top 10 percent of funds earn a rating of five stars, the next 22.5 percent four stars, and the middle 35 percent three stars, the following 22.5 percent two stars, and the bottom 10 percent one star. Morningstar weights the results according to the longevity of the fund, so the full track record of a fund with a long history has a greater weight than its recent performance. The star system is not really a measure that leads to making money; it tells you what the past performance of the fund looks like.[24]

I examined the correlation between the Morningstar rating at the end of 2007 and the end of 2010 for more than four hundred mutual funds to determine how much the ratings change over time. The correlation was moderate ($r = .29$), which makes sense because many funds start as three-star funds and remain there. Furthermore, there is strong reversion to the mean. Fewer than half of the five-star and one-star funds keep their rating from one year to the next, while a majority of three-star funds do.[25] The closer a fund is to average, the more likely it is to remain the same.

The main question is whether Morningstar ratings can help you to predict anything. I compared excess returns for the three years ending in 2010 with the Morningstar ratings for the funds at the end of 2007. Consistent with figure 7-8, I found a poor correlation ($r = -.10$). The primary reason individuals and institutions invest in a fund is that they like the way it performed in the past. But those figures give little information about what the fund will do in the next three years.

I also examined expenses associated with mutual funds. The investor earns a mutual fund's gross returns minus fees and other costs. Lower expenses lead to higher returns all else equal. Indeed, the ratio of expenses to assets under management from any given period is highly correlated with the ratio from the next period. The expense ratio for 2010 had a very significant correlation ($r = .91$) with that of 2007. Unfortunately, I also found that the ratio of expenses to assets did not correlate with subsequent returns. The correlation between the ratio for 2007 and excess returns for 2008–2010 was essentially zero ($r = 0.01$).

The search for a satisfactory statistic in investing may appear futile; indeed, I will make the case later in chapter 8 that a focus on an investor's process is more useful than dwelling on past outcomes. But there is a statistic in investing, called *active share*, that is worth considering. Developed by two economists, Martijn Cremers and Antti Petajisto, active share measures the fraction of a portfolio that is different from the benchmark index. The measure has a range from 0 percent, which means the fund is identical to the benchmark, to 100 percent, meaning that the fund is completely different from the benchmark. Funds with low active share have portfolios that look similar to the index and are derisively labeled "closet indexers." Because of the fees they charge, closet indexers consistently deliver returns below that of the benchmark, but not by a wide margin. Funds with high active share distinguish their results from the benchmark either through selecting different stocks or by overweighting and underweighting industries relative to the benchmark.[26]

Because active share essentially represents the policy chosen by the fund manager, it comes as little surprise that it has a high correlation from period to period. Figure 7-9 shows that the correlation from 2007 to 2010 is very high ($r = .86$). The figure also shows that the correlation between active share (2007) and subsequent excess returns (2008–2010) is respectable ($r = .27$). That correlation is not impressive in most activities but stands out in the world of

FIGURE 7-9

Analysis of active share: persistence and predictive value

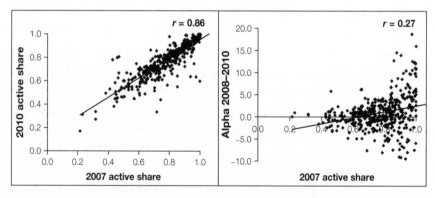

Source: Analysis by author.

investing. The right panel of figure 7-9 shows that while funds with high active share do well on balance, there is a great deal of variability. Cremers and Petajisto further refine the analysis by introducing tracking error, which measures how closely a portfolio tracks the index it uses as a benchmark. They find that funds with high active share but moderate tracking error generate excess returns, adjusted for risk, that are better than those funds with high active share and high tracking error.

Investing is a highly competitive activity, which means that randomness plays a large role in determining results. While there is evidence of skill, only a small percentage of investors are skillful, and an assessment of their short-term results will not reveal their ability. Most people want to invest their money with a manager who has done well in the past. But that's no indication of what he'll do in the future. In investing, as in other activities that are heavily probabilistic, process trumps outcomes.

Comparing Across Domains

A useful statistic is one that is persistent over time and that helps you to make predictions. Those qualities are measured through their correlation with the outcome you desire. These two measurements allow us to analyze activities as diverse as sports, business, and investing on a similar basis. Figure 7-10 suggests that statistics in sports are often more persistent and predictive than those in business and investing.

Figure 7-10 requires a few more words. It is important to acknowledge that the time periods, and hence the sizes of the samples, are different for these activities. The common thread is that I selected the time period that I felt best matched the one used by the people in each profession. For example, in sports the natural length of time is a season. For business and investing, most professionals use a three-year period.

FIGURE 7-10

Various activities placed according to persistence and predictive value

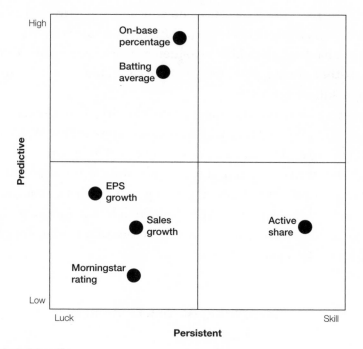

Source: Analysis by author.

The message that correlation does not equal causality is also relevant. A theory is an explanation of cause and effect, and statistics is a means to test theories. The process of identifying your objectives and thoughtfully considering what factors lead to those objectives is essential. As we saw, companies often fail to go through these steps before adopting nonfinancial measures.

Finally, while skill is persistent, it is not always the case that persistence reveals skill. A careful consideration of what elements of performance are within the command of an individual or a sports team is essential. For instance, active share is something that is clearly under a portfolio manager's control, assuming no external constraints. On the other hand, success by means of the Matthew effect—the rich get richer—is consistent but is largely the result of luck.[27]

Statistics are widely used in a range of fields. But rarely do the people who use statistics stop and ask how useful they really are. The simple test of persistence and predictive value goes a long way in judging how practical a measure is likely to be.

CHAPTER 8

BUILDING SKILL

T'S NOT UNUSUAL FOR ACADEMICS to collaborate on research. But a paper published in 2009 entitled "Conditions for Expertise" paired a truly odd couple.[1] One author was Daniel Kahneman, probably the world's preeminent psychologist, who developed what is known as the *heuristics and biases* approach to understanding decision making, research that shows that people generally make decisions quickly and intuitively, leading to predictable mistakes. Those who accept this idea regard experts with skepticism, and they focus on the flaws in intuitive judgment. Kahneman's best-selling book *Thinking, Fast and Slow* describes the work that supports this point of view.[2]

The other author was Gary Klein, a psychologist known for his study of naturalistic decision making. Klein studied the successes of expert intuition in fields including firefighting, military combat, and medicine, and sought to describe and analyze how experts decide so well. Naturalistic decision making celebrates experts and dwells on the strengths of intuitive judgment. Klein wrote a book called *Sources of Power* that documents the richness of expertise.[3]

The subtitle of the article, "A Failure to Disagree," hints at their conclusion. Although they approached the question of expertise from opposite points of view, they agreed that expertise is valid under relatively narrow conditions: you can become an expert if cause and effect are clear and consistent in what you do (the condition of validity), and if you practice intensely and are guided by accurate feedback.[4]

The approach you take to developing skill depends on where an activity lies on the luck-skill continuum. For activities that take place in environments that are stable and in which luck plays a small role, deliberate practice improves skill. Under those conditions, people can develop true expertise. For example, if you practice playing the violin, the music you produce will sound consistently better over time. If you want to learn to type well, you can follow a formula, set aside time each day to practice, and actually see your mistakes disappear on the page. You get instant and reliable feedback, and the more you practice, the faster you get and the fewer mistakes you make.

When activities are more influenced by luck, you won't get that kind of feedback, at least in the short term. What you do is not connected strongly to the result. So the best approach is to focus on the process you're using. If you practice playing poker, as you develop your skill, what you win will still fluctuate, because the game is partly determined by luck. But as you gain expertise, you are more likely to win over time.

Most jobs have elements that combine tasks that are familiar with those that are unfamiliar. In those situations, checklists can help a lot in improving your skill. In most cases, checklists don't contain anything that you don't already know. They just ensure that you actually perform all the tasks you're supposed to perform. Furthermore, whenever there are distractions, checklists help direct and manage your attention. It's surprising how many fields there are in which checklists could help but are not used.

The topic of skill and expertise has received a lot of attention in the popular press in recent years, but it's not clear that the attention has improved the quality of our thinking regarding how we gain skill. Few authors have been careful to specify the conditions under which deliberate practice is useful, and many seem to accept the notion that hard work can overcome any innate differences between individuals. But the main problem remains that people use their intuition in situations where they shouldn't.

Take investing as an example. Investing involves a great deal of luck, which we know from the low degree of persistence in the results and from the absence of experts who can consistently forecast where markets are going. Investing is a field with low validity and unclear feedback. While there is evidence that a small percentage of practitioners are skillful, it's a field where training your intuition is virtually impossible because the conditions change too much. Yet many investors rely on their intuition to make decisions. A survey of more than 250 seasoned investors found that almost two-thirds of them agree with the statement, "As a forecasting/recommendation task becomes more complex and difficult, I tend to rely more on judgment and less on formal, quantitative analysis."[5] In the face of complexity, investors default to a simpler and more intuitive mode. Daniel Kahneman calls this *substitution*. He explains, "The target question is the assessment you intend to produce. The heuristic question is the simpler question that you answer instead."[6] We fight complexity with simplicity.

So to understand where intuition works and where it doesn't, let's examine deliberate practice, which is relevant for activities in which you can improve skill, develop expertise, and hone intuition.

Deliberate Practice: Structure, Hard Work, and All About Feedback

Kahneman suggests that it is useful to consider two systems of decision making. System 1, the experiential system, "operates automatically and quickly, with little or no effort and no sense of voluntary control." System 2, the analytical system, "allocates attention to the effortful mental activities that demand it, including complex computations." System 1 is difficult to modify or direct, while you can deliberately engage System 2. The distinction between these two systems of thinking is useful in considering how deliberate practice can shape performance.

Kahneman explains how the two systems typically interact:

Systems 1 and 2 are both active whenever you are awake. System 1 runs automatically and System 2 is normally in a comfortable low-effort mode, in which only a fraction of its capacity is engaged. System 1 continuously generates suggestions for System 2: impressions, intuitions, intentions, and feelings. If endorsed by System 2, impressions and intuitions turn into beliefs, and impulses turn into voluntary actions. When all goes smoothly, which is most of the time, System 2 adopts the suggestions of System 1 with little or no modification. You generally believe your impressions and act on your desires, and that is fine—usually.[7]

Here's where deliberate practice comes in. You can become an expert by using deliberate practice to train your System 1. You become an expert when you learn to perform unconsciously and free your attention for higher-level thinking. This is why a chess master can effortlessly assess the relative strength of positions on the board. It is also how a champion tennis player knows how to return a specific shot without thinking. Because of their intense and carefully guided training, experts perceive patterns automatically, solve problems rapidly, and respond with actions that are complete and correct, all while a novice would still be trying to analyze the situation using System 2.[8]

Deliberate practice and the concept of expertise apply only near the skill side of the luck-skill continuum. You can train System 1 only for activities that are stable and linear. As noted in chapter 4, *stable* means the rules of the game don't change, and *linear* means that cause and effect are clear and consistent. A chessboard, for instance, always has 64 squares arranged in 8 columns and 8 rows with alternating colors of black and white. The pieces always move in the same fashion. And when you make a mistake, you lose pieces.

In a linear system, a particular cause always has the same effect. The interaction of balls on a billiards table is a good example. If you know the basics of the cause, including the velocity of the ball that's in motion, the mass of the ball that it hits, and the angle of the collision between the two, you can predict the effect with great accuracy. Contrast that with the stock market. Some of the moves the market makes are clearly the result of important information. For example, the S&P 500 declined 4.9 percent on the first day of trading following the terrorist attacks on September 11, 2001. However, a remarkable number of the big moves appear unrelated to new information. The press always likes to point to some clear cause on days when the market makes big moves. But as economists studying the issue have found, those causes don't really have any significance. They just make good copy.[9] Because cause and effect are not linear in markets, there's no reliable way to train your System 1 to anticipate prices. Deliberate practice is powerful in domains where it applies, including chess, music, and sports. But acknowledging its limits is crucial. A number of the popular books that celebrate deliberate practice fail to distinguish between when it works and when it doesn't.[10]

Deliberate practice begins with a coach or teacher who designs the curriculum specifically to improve performance.[11] A teacher can identify the skills that are essential for a particular pursuit, allowing the student to concentrate on mastering those skills in order to improve performance. Most of us do not practice according to a deliberately designed curriculum. If you attend a practice for a youth sports team, for instance, you will frequently see a lack of structure. The children do drills that have little or no connection to the skills required to excel during a real game. They practice casually and rarely test the limits of their skills. Done correctly, deliberate practice demands performance that is just outside of your comfort zone so that there's a constant sense of being challenged without feeling overwhelmed.

Once you have an appropriate routine, deliberate practice requires an enormous amount of time and effort. Consider the case of Apollo Robbins, who is one of the world's greatest pickpockets. During his show, Robbins invites a guest on stage, tells him that he's going to take various items from him, and then does so in front of a large audience. (He gives everything back, which is why he's known as "the gentleman thief.") He is a master at managing the attention of others, which is essential for succeeding at sleight of hand. Robbins honed his skills at Caesar's Magical Empire in Las Vegas, where he entertained people waiting in line to see the main show. By his estimate, Robbins stole from about 25 guests each hour, for 5 hours a night, 5 nights a week, for 5 consecutive years. He worked for more than 6,000 hours refining his skills. He'll tell you that most of his moves are now automatic. Key to his expertise is this: he doesn't even have to think about it. He trained his System 1 through years of repetition. He'll also tell you that his best moves were really hard to learn and took hours of dedicated practice to master.

There is little fun in deliberate practice. Anders Ericsson, the psychologist most closely associated with the theory of deliberate practice, writes that it "is not inherently enjoyable," and that individuals do it because of "its instrumental value in improving performance."[12] Progress requires a great deal of focus and concentration, which is difficult to achieve and sustain. Indeed, individuals who practice more than one thousand hours a year run the risk of exhaustion. One reason that deliberate practice is so taxing is that it compels you to stay in the cognitive stage, constantly thinking about and improving your results, rather than allowing you to slip into the automatic stage, where performance becomes habitual and fluid. The combination of structure and effort are the key to advancing beyond plateaus in performance. And as Kahneman points out, our natural tendency is to rely on the easy, automatic routines of System 1 and avoid the effortful actions of System 2. Our minds are naturally lazy.

Feedback is the glue that holds together the elements of deliberate practice. Your performance improves only if you receive accurate and timely feedback. Elite performers often use coaches for that purpose. A strong link between cause and effect is essential, of course, and when it is difficult to get quality feedback, deliberate practice is less effective.

Atul Gawande is a surgeon at Brigham and Women's Hospital in Boston, a staff writer for *The New Yorker* magazine, and an associate professor at Harvard Medical School. Gawande underwent exhaustive training to become a surgeon and, like other doctors, was left on his own to ply his craft once he finished school. For the first few years of his practice, he noticed that his performance in the operating room improved steadily. Then it reached a plateau. He was doing extremely well but wondered whether hiring a coach could improve his performance even more.

For his coach, Gawande enlisted Robert Osteen, a retired surgeon under whom he had trained. The first operation that Osteen observed went flawlessly from Gawande's point of view. But later, in the lounge, Osteen told Gawande that he hadn't positioned and draped the patient as well as he could have, his elbows were too high during the procedure, and the operating light had drifted from the wound. As accomplished as Gawande was, the unusual step of bringing in a coach allowed him to hear feedback that improved his performance. The experience prompted him to write an article asking why coaches aren't used more widely in other fields, including teaching.[13]

There is no reason to doubt that deliberate practice is essential to acquiring skill in pursuits that are near the skill side of the continuum. But some popular books that discuss deliberate practice leave their readers with false impressions. One of these is the idea that achieving expertise in anything requires 10,000 hours of deliberate practice. It is reasonable to say that experts require 10,000 hours of practice on average, but there is a great deal of variation in the true figures. For example, one study found that the amount of practice required to achieve the level of chess master ranged from 3,000 to 23,600 hours. The overall average was 6,700 hours. Achieving expertise requires an enormous amount of effort, but the sum of 10,000 hours is not set in stone.[14]

Another misleading idea is that innate talent plays no role in determining performance. This view holds that expert performance is a function only of the amount of deliberate practice. Recent research does not support a claim that strong. Zach Hambrick and Betsy Meinz, professors of psychology at Michigan State University, examined how factors other than deliberate practice influenced performance. They write, "The available evidence *does not* justify the claim that basic abilities are always unimportant for skilled performance: There is now good evidence that basic abilities predict success in a wide range of complex tasks, from chess to music, even among skilled performers." Hard work explains a great deal, but not everything.[15]

A related claim is that there is a threshold of intelligence that individuals must reach in order to achieve high performance in cognitive realms (typically an intelligence quotient of 120, roughly the top 10 percent of the population) but that anything beyond that threshold does not confer any advantage.[16] But researchers have shown that variation among young adolescents within the top 1 percent of the population in cognitive ability leads to differences in how well they do in school and how well they do even years later at work. For instance, children who scored in the 99.9th percentile on the math section of the SAT Reasoning Test at age thirteen were eighteen times more likely to earn a PhD in math or science than children who scored in the 99.1st percentile.[17] In activities that are largely a matter of skill, basic ability counts.

If you want to do something that requires skill, you have to practice. The emphasis for young people seeking to improve should be on hard work that is properly structured. There is no substitute for effort and grit. For this reason, parents, teachers, and coaches should encourage children on the basis of their effort and not a sense of innate ability.[18] That said, the claim that talent plays no role in how well people do is not supported by the facts. High performance combines a dash of basic ability with lots of perspiration. The result is a well-trained System 1 and expertise.

Checklists: A Structured Way to Manage Attention

Most jobs combine tasks that are procedural with tasks or situations that are novel.[19] Medicine is a good example. A doctor may use a set of guidelines to prepare a patient for surgery, and then proceed without knowing what complications he or she may face during the operation. The problem is that most doctors allocate the bulk of their attention to the surgery itself and pay less attention to the procedural part of their job. As a result, they sometimes improperly handle the part of the treatment controlled by a set of rules and thereby put the patient's health at risk. The problem is not that the doctors don't know how to do the procedural tasks; it's that their attention is elsewhere.

Peter Pronovost is an anesthesiologist and critical-care specialist at Johns Hopkins Hospital. Pronovost had noticed that about forty thousand people in the United States died each year from infections caused by central line catheters—intravenous tubes placed in patients as part of their treatment. These deaths typically showed up as "complications" from surgery, but were completely preventable. Yet the number of people dying from these infections was equal to the number of women dying from breast cancer each year. Pronovost was able to get doctors to use a simple checklist when installing central line catheters and thereby saved hundreds of millions of dollars and thousands of lives, more than "any laboratory scientist in the past decade," as Atul Gawande wrote in *The New Yorker*.[20]

A checklist is a series of steps that must be carried out accurately and on time. Where cause and effect can be clearly established, checklists have been widely embraced. Examples include aviation and construction. Airplane pilots, for instance, use checklists universally and with great benefit. Checklists ensure that the pilots follow all procedures precisely and unfailingly.

Checklists are highly effective but underutilized in jobs that combine probabilistic tasks with tasks that follow a set of rules or set procedures. Here's the reason: professionals in these fields think of themselves as practicing a craft and actually find it demeaning to resort to a checklist. They think they have the knowledge to do the job and do not need any aids. They are wrong, and their attitude is costly.

Physicians put 5 million intravenous tubes into patients each year, so Pronovost knew that he needed to create a simple and pragmatic checklist if he wanted doctors to use it. The Centers for Disease Control offered guidelines about installing central line catheters in a scholarly, 120-page document, but the report was too long and too ambiguous to be of practical use. So Pronovost collaborated with colleagues and came up with a checklist with five simple steps:

1. Wash your hands using soap or alcohol;

2. Wear sterile gloves, hat, mask, and gown and cover the patient with sterile drapes;

3. Avoid placing the tube in the groin, if possible;

4. Clean the insertion site with antiseptic solution;

5. Remove the tubes when they are no longer needed.

Pronovost distributed the checklist to the surgical intensive care unit and asked the nurses to note the rate at which the doctors fulfilled all five steps. The compliance rate was only 38 percent, a fact that shocked and deeply dismayed Pronovost. The doctors needlessly exposed almost two out of three patients to the risk of infection. He quickly realized that a major part of the problem was that the supplies were scattered in different places, requiring doctors and nurses to gather gloves, masks, drapes, and tubes from various locations. He created a "central line cart" so that everything a doctor would need was readily available in one place. Compliance rose to 70 percent, which was better than before but still far from the goal of total adherence. He had no doubt that the doctors wanted to take excellent care of their patients and that they could readily enumerate the items on the checklist if asked. The problem was that the physicians simply didn't focus on the mundane tasks.

So Pronovost took the unusual step of placing the nurses in charge of compliance. Hospitals, like many other organizations, are hierarchical, and doctors are at the top of the heap. But Pronovost sat down with the staff and explained what he was trying to achieve and why it was so important. At first, the doctors saw it as an effort to undermine their authority, while the nurses worried that it would open them up to criticism. But Pronovost convinced all parties to try the new approach. Within a year, the rate of infection dropped nearly to zero.[21]

Pronovost's work on checklists was noticed by Atul Gawande, eventually prompting him to write a book called *The Checklist Manifesto*. In the book, Gawande looks at the use of checklists in various fields and provides some guidelines on how to write ones that are effective. Specifically, it is essential to involve the people who are doing the work.[22] For example, Pronovost started with the Centers for Disease Control's long and academic discussion of procedures but soon realized that thoughtful practitioners would have to play a central part in creating the actual checklist. Involving users from the beginning also helps to mitigate potential cultural conflict.

Because checklists have been used the longest and most reliably in aviation, Gawande spent time with Daniel Boorman, an engineer at Boeing. Boeing is among the largest airplane manufacturers in the world, and Boorman has lots of experience creating checklists for pilots.[23] Boorman advises that a checklist should be short. The rule of thumb is that it should be five to nine items and fit on one page, although the exact length depends on the context. Further, the language should be simple, exact, and familiar to the users. The checklist must also be free of distracting colors and graphics, and use a typeface that is easy to read. A good checklist also prompts communication among coworkers. These items encourage team members to try to identify, prevent, or solve problems. Finally, those who are going to use the checklist should test and refine it as necessary. Checklists are living documents that evolve.[24]

Boorman describes two types of checklists: DO-CONFIRM and READ-DO. With DO-CONFIRM checklists, pilots do their jobs from memory but pause from time to time to ensure that everything is complete and has been done properly. This checklist might say "Flaps . . . Set" and "Briefing . . . Completed." These checklists make sure pilots adhere to normal procedures.

READ-DO checklists typically deal with an emergency or an abnormal situation. In these cases, the pilot is likely to be unfamiliar with the situation, so the READ-DO checklist offers a recipe for action. The main virtue of a READ-DO checklist is that it allows the pilot to focus on concrete steps to address the problem. For example, if the warning light on a Boeing 747 for "Door FWD Cargo" goes on, indicating that the front cargo door is open, a READ-DO checklist would direct the pilot's decisions: "Lower cabin pressure partially. Descend to the safest altitude or 8,000 feet, whichever is higher. Put the air outflow switches on manual and push them in for 30 seconds to release the remaining pressure." READ-DO checklists prescribe correct actions under stressful conditions when it's easy to forget things and make mistakes.[25]

As his checklists have been rolled out to hospitals around the world, Peter Pronovost has come to realize that there are three essential elements to making a checklist successful. The first step is to make the checklist itself practical and useful. Next, the culture of the organization has to support the use of checklists. The introduction of a checklist usually confronts an attitude of "I know what I'm doing, leave me alone." But the fact is, the proper use of checklists improves performance without demanding a higher level of skill. The doctors in Pronovost's unit were world-class. Their knowledge and skill were not lacking. Their errors were the result of their attitude, which in turn caused them to overlook the obvious. If you look carefully at Pronovost's checklist, you'll see that what he's proposing is not much more than what Joseph Lister proposed in the 1800s: clean conditions eliminate infection.

The final element is collecting and analyzing data properly. Pronovost helped disseminate checklists to hospitals throughout the state of New Jersey. But those hospitals didn't collect and report the effect of using checklists properly. So while the state claimed some success from the program, Pronovost was unwilling to endorse the data. He said, "Our team has learned from experience that reliable data collection is what separates mumbo jumbo from science, hope from reality. We viewed quality improvement as a science—and scientific experiments demand robust and correct data."[26] Accurate data form the foundation for high-quality feedback.

Most of us don't spend time dwelling on our errors. But if we did, we could create checklists that would eliminate those errors. To adopt a checklist is to embrace humility and admit our own fallibility. None of us can flawlessly cope with a complex world. A grocery list is a checklist that we use in a very low-risk environment. Why not use one when the stakes are high as well?

When Success Is Probabilistic, Focus on Process

The beauty of deliberate practice and checklists is that cause and effect are clear. You can tell when you're right and when you're wrong. When doctors followed the checklist for inserting intravenous tubes, for instance, the rate of infections dropped to near zero. But when your undertaking involves a dose of luck, the link between cause and effect is broken. In the short term, even when you do everything right, the outcome of your effort can be bad. Moreover, you can succeed even when you do everything wrong. Pretend that you are in a casino playing blackjack and that you are dealt a 17. Staying with that hand offers the highest probability of winning. But if you ask for a hit and the dealer reveals a 4, you get 21. You win. That's an example of a bad process and a good outcome. You did something stupid and got lucky. Do it enough times, and you're certain to lose.

We can take the blackjack example a little further. Let's say I wanted to assess whether you are a competent blackjack player.

One approach would be to give you $1,000 and let you play for an evening. At the end of the night, I would count the money and judge your skill. But what you win or lose in a single night is mostly a matter of luck. If I kept track over weeks or months, I might get a better sense of your skill. But even though there is an element of skill in blackjack, so much of the game is influenced by luck that it takes a long time for skill to make a difference in how much you win.

Another strategy would be to give you the money and then look over your shoulder and compare the correct strategy for playing blackjack to the way you actually play the game. Basic strategy in blackjack dictates when you should request a card and when you should stick with the hand you're dealt. (For example, you always stand when you have 17, but if you have 16, you take another card only if the dealer has 7 or higher.) That strategy ensures that you will lose the least amount of money to the house in the long term. If I saw that you played according to basic strategy, I could be confident that you were going to hold your own, at least within the limits of the house advantage. In other words, in a pursuit such as blackjack, where luck is very important, you have to adopt a process that you can trust and not worry so much about the outcome of each hand or even each session of play. Your only chance of winning is to adhere to the rules that you know work. Your skill can't change the odds, it can only be applied to make sure that you play the cards properly.

Whether you're managing a sports team, running a business, or investing in stocks, a skillful process will tend to have three parts: analysis, psychology, and the influences exerted by your organization. Coming up with a process that accommodates any one of these isn't easy. Being good at all three is rare. We'll look at each part and use the process of investing as an example throughout.

Analysis

First the analytical part. Find a stock that you think is worth more than the current price. Value is what you think it's worth. Price is what people are paying (or receiving) today. For a company, the value today is equal to the present value of its future cash flows. Taking the present value of future cash flows acknowledges that a dollar today is worth more than a dollar in the future. The price you have to pay for the stock today represents what you have to give up to gain that value at some point in the future. Your process, in short, is to buy stocks at a price that is less than your appraisal of the value of that cash flow in the future. The goal is to get more than you pay for.

Horse racing is a vivid metaphor because you can easily interpret value and price. The value is how fast a horse will run and price is the odds on the tote board. Unlike stocks, where the expectations are implicit in the price, the odds at the track explicitly express the chances that a horse will win. As any serious handicapper knows, the only way you can make money is by finding a discrepancy between the performance of the horse and the odds.[27] There are no good or bad horses, just correctly or incorrectly priced ones. This principle holds across all probabilistic domains: again, the goal is to get more than you pay for.

To begin your analysis, you need to identify the real causes of success, such as supply and demand, economic profit, and sustainable competitive advantage. For this purpose, markets can provide a window on the world. So if you see a discrepancy between what a stock ought to be worth and what people are paying, you need to develop a theory about why price and value have diverged. What's going on in the world that's making people pay more or less for the stock? Your analytical edge is embodied in your theory of what determines the fundamentals and why the price is wrong.

Your edge should also include what Benjamin Graham, the father of security analysis, called a *margin of safety*. You have a margin of safety when you buy a stock at a price that is substantially less than its value. As Graham noted, the margin of safety "is available for absorbing the effect of miscalculations or worse than average luck." The size of the gap between price and value tells you how big your margin of safety is. As Graham says, the margin of safety goes down as the price goes up.[28] In other words, make your margin of safety as large as possible.

Finding a discrepancy between value and price is only part of your analysis. Next, you have to build a portfolio that takes advantage of the opportunities. There are two common mistakes you can make when building a portfolio. The first is a failure to match how much of each stock you buy with the attractiveness of the opportunity. In theory, you should allocate more of the portfolio to the most attractive stocks and less to the stocks that are not quite as good. In some settings, a mathematical formula can help work out precisely how much you should bet given your perceived edge.[29] While this is difficult in practice for most money managers, the main idea remains: the best stocks deserve the most capital. In many portfolios, the percentage represented by each stock (known as weightings) doesn't match the attractiveness of the stocks.

At the opposite end of the spectrum is a mistake called *overbetting*. An investment manager who's watching her edge dwindle may attempt to boost her returns by using debt. For example, assume you buy a stock at $100 that you think is worth $110. If it reaches that price, you will make 10 percent on your investment. If you want to get an even higher return, you could borrow another $100 at a 5 percent interest rate. Now you buy $200 worth of the stock. If it goes to $220, you make 15 percent on your money (you pay back the $100 loan plus $5 in interest and are left with $15/$100). Overbetting occurs when the size of an investment is too large for the opportunity that it represents and therefore introduces the possibility of failure.

Using debt does enhance returns assuming the trade goes as expected. But debt can also lead to buying too much and can be ultimately disastrous in cases when the stock does poorly. Long-Term Capital Management, a hedge fund, provides one of the best-documented cases of overbetting.[30] At the height of its borrowing and betting, LTCM enjoyed returns of more than 40 percent. But through a variety of complex factors, it went on to lose $4.6 billion in not quite four months in 1998. The fund had vanished by the year 2000.

Those in the United States who used huge mortgages to buy homes in 2005–2007 made effectively the same mistake. As home prices declined, these owners soon owed more than the value of their homes. A sound analysis involves doing enough research to correctly estimate the value of your edge, as well as to estimate how much of a given stock you should buy.

Psychology

The second part of a skillful process is psychological. This part deals with Kahneman and Tversky's work on biases. These include over-confidence, anchoring, confirmation, and relying on what is most recent. Kahneman and Tversky emphasize that these biases arise automatically and are therefore very difficult to overcome.[31]

For example, when making a prediction, people tend to give disproportionate weight to whatever has happened most recently. In investing, there is a strong tendency to buy stocks that have done well or to place bets on a money manager who seems to have a hot hand. This is just as true for professional money managers as it is for everyone else. Individual investors consistently earn returns that are 50–75 percent of those of the market as a result of bad timing.

Kahneman and Tversky also developed the idea of *prospect theory*, or how people make decisions when they are uncertain about gains and losses. Prospect theory reveals behavior that is at odds with classical economic theory.[32] Compensation provides a good example of the difference between these two theories. Ideally, you should consider your salary for a new job in the context of your aggregate wealth rather than comparing it with what other employees are making. But, of course, few of us do that. In one study, researchers asked people which new employee was happier, the person making $36,000 in a firm where the average starting salary is $40,000 or the one making $34,000 in a firm where the average starting salary is $30,000. Eighty percent of the respondents said the employee earning $34,000 would be happier.[33]

In investing, the reference point is what you paid for a stock. When you buy a stock at $30, for instance, you effectively open a mental account. You have a gain if the stock rises above $30 and a loss if it drops below that price. Rather than viewing the value of the stock in the context of a larger portfolio, the natural tendency is to consider each stock relative to its reference point.

Loss aversion is another feature of prospect theory. We suffer roughly two times more from a loss than we enjoy a gain of the same size. The combination of the reference point and loss aversion leads investors to hold on to losing stocks and sell winners, because it is painful to take losses.[34]

Because good decisions can have bad outcomes, not everyone has a temperament that is well suited to making decisions about activities that involve luck. But Seth Klarman has the right temperament. He's the founder and president of a highly successful hedge fund called the Baupost Group. Klarman has a wonderful line: "Value investing is at its core the marriage of a contrarian streak and a calculator."[35] He's saying that you have to be different from others and focus on gaps between price and value. This idea extends well beyond the world of investing.

When most people come to believe the same thing, large gaps open up between price and value. That's what happened during the dot-com euphoria of the late 1990s and during the spring of 2009, when despondency established the low point for the market. The first part of Klarman's line properly emphasizes the importance of being willing to go against the crowd. Most people know that it is more comfortable to be part of the crowd than to be alone. But it's also hard to distinguish yourself if you're doing the same thing as everyone else.

Skillful investors heed Benjamin Graham's advice: "Have the courage of your knowledge and experience. If you have formed a conclusion from the facts and if you know your judgment is sound, act on it—even though others may hesitate or differ."[36] However, Klarman correctly observes that it is insufficient to be a contrarian because sometimes the consensus is right. The goal is to be a contrarian when it allows you to gain an edge, and the calculator helps you ensure a margin of safety.

Constraints

The third part of the process of skill addresses organizational and institutional constraints. The most important job is to manage *agency costs*, or the costs that arise because the money manager (the agent) may have interests that differ from those of the investor (the principal).[37] For example, mutual fund managers who are paid fees based on assets under management may place more emphasis on increasing those assets than on delivering excess returns. They might, for example, aggressively market products that have been successful recently, launch new products in hot areas, and manage portfolios to look similar to their benchmarks.

Charles Ellis, the founder of Greenwich Associates, made this point when he distinguished between the profession and business of investing.[38] The profession is about managing portfolios so as to maximize long-term returns, while the business is about generating earnings as an investment firm. Naturally, a vibrant business is essential to support the profession. But when a manager emphasizes the business at the expense of the profession, the investor in the fund is not well served. Rather, a manager should concentrate on finding stocks that are underpriced and building sensible, balanced portfolios. This requires going against the consensus and being willing to appear very different from the pack.

John Maynard Keynes, the renowned economist and investor, wrote about this in *The General Theory of Employment, Interest, and Money*, published in 1936. He discusses the conduct of a long-term investor: "For it is in the essence of his behaviour that he should be eccentric, unconventional and rash in the eyes of the average opinion. If he is successful, that will only confirm the general belief in his rashness; and if in the short run he is unsuccessful, which is very likely, he will not receive much mercy. Worldly wisdom teaches that it is better for reputation to fail conventionally than to succeed unconventionally."[39]

As Keynes suggests, the risk of getting fired for straying too far from convention is also important. As a result, in careers where skill involves developing a process and then following it, professionals will often strive to be different enough to succeed but not so different as to be considered unconventional. The reason is that decision makers are often inappropriately judged by how well they do in the short term. A person who makes a conventional decision that turns out to be wrong can fall back on the argument that the decision was standard practice, even if uninspired, and hence the outcome was unavoidable. A person who makes a correct but unconventional decision that ends badly is exposed to criticism and the risk of being fired.

In investing, the trend toward conformity is clear. For example, portfolios today look more like their benchmarks than they did thirty years ago. The average active share, a measure of how different a mutual fund portfolio is compared to its benchmark, has fallen from 75 percent in 1980 to about 60 percent in 2010 in the United States. Leaders in sports as well as in business fear straying too far from convention, even in cases where the convention isn't all that great.[40]

Because all three parts of a skillful process are difficult, they stand in the way of achieving good performance. Some organizations can succeed in one or two of those areas, but very few can master all three. This fits with the conclusion of our analysis of skill and luck in investing: different people have different abilities, but only a handful of investors can surmount the analytical, psychological, and organizational hurdles. The same is true in both sports and business.

Match the Technique to the Situation

Whether or not you can improve your skill depends a great deal on where the activity lies on the luck-skill continuum. In cases where there is a clear relationship between cause and effect, and in activities that are stable and linear, deliberate practice is the only path to improvement. Expertise exists, and you can reliably develop your intuition by training your System 1 so that the decisions you make take place smoothly and automatically. Checklists can be useful when you need to perform tasks accurately and consistently (DO-CONFIRM). They can also guide decisions when unusual circumstances arise (READ-DO). Near the skill side of the continuum, the quality of your performance provides dependable feedback on your progress when you're trying to improve your skill.

If an activity involves luck, then how well you do in the short run doesn't tell you much about your skill, because you can do everything right and still fail, or you can do everything wrong and succeed. For activities near the luck side of the continuum, a good process is the surest path to success in the long run.

Accurate feedback is essential no matter where you are on the continuum. Improving your skill means constantly looking for ways to change your behavior, either because what you're doing is wrong or because there's a slightly better way of doing it. This is true whether you are a basketball player shooting free throws, a doctor performing surgery, an executive making acquisitions, or an investor buying stocks. No matter what your profession or level of expertise, the chances are very good that accurate feedback can improve your performance.

CHAPTER 9

DEALING WITH LUCK

SPAIN HAS HAD A NATIONAL LOTTERY since 1763. The most coveted prizes are awarded in the days before Christmas. The first prize, known as El Gordo ("the fat one"), paid out €4 million in 2011. In the mid-1970s, a man hunted for a lottery ticket with the last two digits ending in 48. He found a ticket, bought it, and then won the lottery. When asked why he was so intent on finding that number, he replied, "I dreamed of the number 7 for seven straight nights. And 7 times 7 is 48."[1]

This chapter is about coping with luck. The first approach deals with reducing the advantage of a skilled opponent if you are the underdog and improving your advantage if you are the favorite. The second approach involves reducing the influence of luck by more effectively tying cause to effect. Finally, it is critical to understand the limits of what you can understand. The strategy here is to learn how to define your limits and cope with events that have small and incomputable probabilities, but very large consequences.

What Colonel Blotto Can Teach You About Coping with Luck

The biblical story of David and Goliath is perhaps the most famous battle between the strong and the weak. The Philistines and

Israelites drew a battle line in the Valley of Elah, with each group standing on a mountain. Goliath, a Philistine, was reportedly taller than six and a half feet and wore a bronze helmet, full armor, and wielded a massive spear. Goliath's armor alone weighed 125 pounds. Goliath made the Israelites a bold offer: Send any man to fight me and the winner can enslave the troops of the loser. That challenge scared the heck out of the Israelites.

David was a young shepherd who was the last of eight sons, and three of his brothers were among the men of Israel. David's father sent him to the battlefront to provide supplies to his brothers. David heard Goliath's challenge and asked what was in it for the man who killed Goliath. When informed that the man who killed Goliath would receive great riches and would marry the king's daughter, he thought it sounded like a pretty good deal. David reasoned that he had killed lions and bears that had tried to prey on the lambs in his flock, so slaying Goliath wouldn't be so much of a stretch.

Saul, the leader of the men of Israel, gave David a helmet, a full suit of armor, and a sword. The idea was that David would fight Goliath on the giant's terms. The younger and weaker David didn't like the sound of that. He left the gear behind and entered the field of battle with his shepherd's staff, five smooth stones that he'd collected from a creek, and a slingshot. The two combatants faced off and exchanged threats. Then David did something no one could have anticipated. He loaded his trusty slingshot, flung a stone at Goliath, and hit him square in the forehead. Goliath fell dead on the spot.[2]

The essential point of this story is that David did not engage in hand-to-hand combat as Goliath expected. He saw that getting close to the giant would be suicidal. So he changed his strategy. The lesson of David's success and Goliath's failure is even more general. When competing one-on-one, follow two simple rules: If you are the favorite, simplify the game. If you are the underdog, make it more complicated. David's chance of success going toe-to-toe with Goliath would have been very slim. But by competing in a different way, he shifted the odds in his favor.

Colonel Blotto

The game called Colonel Blotto is a useful model for quantifying and understanding these rules.[3] In Colonel Blotto, two players distribute imaginary soldiers across a given number of battlefields. If you allocate twelve soldiers to a given battlefield, and I send eleven, then you win. The player with the greater number always wins, and the player who wins the most battles overall is the victor. A simple version of the game has players A and B allocating one hundred soldiers to three battlefields. Each player's goal is to employ a strategy that creates favorable mismatches. (See figure 9-1.)

Colonel Blotto is a zero-sum game in which one player's loss is the other's gain. As long as you avoid bad strategies, such as putting all your soldiers on one battlefield, the game resembles Rock-Paper-Scissors. As a consequence, we can't really tell what the best strategies are for simple versions of Colonel Blotto.

FIGURE 9-1

Simple example of the Colonel Blotto game

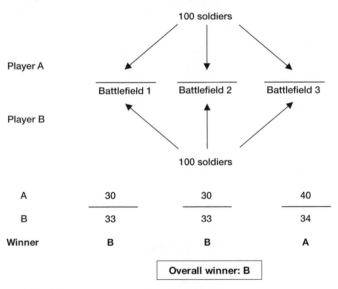

	Battlefield 1	Battlefield 2	Battlefield 3
A	30	30	40
B	33	33	34
Winner	B	B	A

Overall winner: B

Source: Analysis by author.

But as you add more battlefields and soldiers, the game starts to get interesting. For example, you can assume that one side has more soldiers than the other, creating a favorite and an underdog. Or you can give the players ten battlefields. In fact, in most zero-sum strategic interactions, resources are rarely equal and there are many battlefields.[4]

Let's start by examining what happens when the players don't have the same number of soldiers. In a game with three battlefields, a player with 25 percent more soldiers will win 60 percent of the battles. A player with an army twice as large as his opponent's will win 78 percent of the time. While luck still exerts an influence, the bigger army has a decisive advantage. This analysis is what lies behind the first rule. If you are the stronger player, simplify the game and go toe-to-toe. The larger your army, the more likely you are to win.

If the two armies are the same size, then adding battlefields doesn't change how many times each side wins. But when one player has more soldiers than the other, the stronger player's advantage goes down as the number of battlefields goes up. For example, in a game with fifteen battlefields, the weaker player's chance of winning is nearly three times higher than it is in a game with nine.

The strategic implication is clear. Before the game begins, the weaker player should attempt to add battlefields. This forces the stronger player to spread his soldiers more thinly and increases the chances that the weak player can pull off an upset simply by getting lucky. The underdog improves his standing by placing larger numbers of soldiers on battlefields where, by chance, his opponent has placed smaller numbers of soldiers. Remember, the score is based on battlefields won, not on the number of soldiers defeated. Hence the second rule: If you are the weaker player, try to complicate the game by adding battlefields, or new points of competition.[5]

Adding Battlefields

Sports offer a good illustration of this point. KC Joyner, an analyst at ESPN, separates football coaches into two groups: ones who work hard to recruit the best players and ones who spend their time developing winning strategies. A coach who assembles the most talented players can keep the game plan simple and attempt to overwhelm opponents with pure strength and skill. The other type of coach worries less about attracting the finest players and instead works on outsmarting opponents with innovative game plans.[6]

Mike Leach, who coached football at Texas Tech for the ten years ending in 2009, is an example of the second type of coach. He won more than 70 percent of his games in the latter part of his career despite playing in a tough conference. The team's success was particularly remarkable since few of his players were considered first-rate by professional scouts.

Leach took his comparatively weak team and complicated the game against a stronger opponent. He designed a large number of formations so that the opponents couldn't predict what they'd see on the field in any given play. By creating new matchups, his formations changed the geometry of the game and forced opponents to change their defensive strategies. For example, opposing defensive linemen were frequently forced to drop back to cover receivers. Leach explained that "defensive linemen really aren't much good at covering receivers. They aren't built to run around that much. And when they do, you have a bunch of people on the other team doing things they don't have much experience doing." By adding battlefields to the game, Leach diluted the advantage of the stronger teams.[7]

Colonel Blotto also has parallels to business. One illustration is the theory of disruptive innovation developed by Clayton Christensen at Harvard Business School. Christensen studies why great companies with smart managements and substantial resources consistently lose to companies with simpler, cheaper, and inferior products. He calls these upstarts "disruptors" and distinguishes between what he calls sustaining and disruptive innovation.[8]

Sustaining innovation involves steadily improving a product that already exists. Those improvements can be substantial, but the key is that they build on the existing business model. Think of going from a mom-and-pop bookstore to a superstore with tens of thousands of books and a coffee shop. The superstore may be bigger, but it's built on the same basic business model.

You can think of sustaining innovations as putting more soldiers on the same set of battlefields. Christensen's work shows that when a new company comes along and tries to beat the leading company at its own game by introducing another version of the same product, the attempt will fail. Years ago, Kodak, then the leader in selling film for cameras, tried to get into the business of selling batteries. Despite its leading market share in film and its clout with retailers, Kodak never made a dime on batteries. Duracell and Energizer, which sold most of the batteries in the United States, were motivated to defend their turf and had lots of resources at their disposal to do so. It was as if David had agreed to engage in toe-to-toe combat with Goliath.

When disruptors succeed, they approach the market using a completely new business model. A disruptor can introduce a product at the low end of the market that is neither profitable for the big guys nor in demand from their customers. For example, Japanese automobile manufacturers, including Toyota and Honda, entered the market in the 1970s with cars that were small and cheap. The Big Three auto manufacturers just laughed. It wasn't a credible threat. The leading companies tend to leave the low end and aim for the bigger profits at the high end of the market. They get blindsided when the disruptors gradually improve their product and stealthily move upward in the marketplace. If they do so successfully, they will eventually begin stealing customers from the big guys and will do so at a lower cost. Think of the ascent of Lexus (a brand owned by Toyota) versus Cadillac.

An example that Christensen likes to use involves the steel industry. Mini-mills melt scrap steel, so they are a small fraction of the size of the integrated mills that make steel in blast furnaces. Because the integrated mills controlled the whole process, they started with the substantial advantage of producing steel of high quality. The mini-mills launched their simpler and cheaper model in the 1970s. At first, their vastly inferior quality relegated them to making rebar, the bars that reinforce concrete. This is the cheapest and least valuable market for steel. The integrated mills left the low-profit market for rebar to the mini-mills, and in fact their profit margins improved as a result. For a time. But the mini-mills rapidly improved their ability to make better and better steel, allowing them to move up and start to compete in markets that had more value. That process continued over time until the mini-mills were shouldering into the high end of the market for steel, undercutting the integrated mills and destroying their profitability.[9]

In the case of steel, the product is the same but the processes and business models are different. But disruptors may also introduce new products that were previously unavailable to a segment of the population. Christensen's theory predicts that existing companies tend to ignore these new products because the new business model is so different from what the established companies are used to. The history of the personal computer is a good case study. Until the mid-1970s, computers were large machines that only a handful of trained people knew how operate. But that changed in the late 1970s and early 1980s when Apple, Atari, Commodore, and IBM introduced PCs. At that time, minicomputers stood between the giant mainframes of IBM and the small personal computers. They were midsized computers suitable for educational institutions and medium-sized businesses. These manufacturers occupied the perfect spot and had the perfect talent and know-how to enter the market for personal computers.

Yet a number of the leading manufacturers of minicomputers did nothing. Data General, Digital Equipment Corporation, and Wang completely misunderstood the market. They either failed to launch their own product or offered computers that were too sophisticated and didn't do what the customers wanted. They essentially ceded the market to the upstarts. As PCs improved, they eventually edged out the minicomputers. Data General, Digital Equipment Corporation, and Wang all merged or went out of business, and minicomputers, for all practical purposes, were swallowed up by PCs.

Whether the disruptor's strategy is based on a low-end segment of the market or on a new product, the existing companies, which are initially stronger, typically fail to compete in a way that allows them to beat weaker challengers. They effectively concede defeat in parts of the market, which is equivalent to additional battlefields, allowing the disruptors to build up their resources. And because products tend to improve over time, the disruptors eventually use their superior business model to make enough money to beat the incumbents at their own game.[10]

One of the strengths of the theory of disruptive innovation is that it allows us to make predictions. In his book *The Innovator's Manifesto*, Michael Raynor shares the story of a young lawyer named Thomas Thurston who was steeped in the theory of disruptive innovation. Thurston had the unique opportunity to review forty-eight of the business proposals that Intel's New Business Initiatives group considered over the ten years ending in 2007. Without knowing how each business fared, he used this theory to predict which ones would succeed or fail.

Thurston created a simple decision tree. If the innovation was sustaining and launched by an incumbent, he predicted it would succeed. If it was sustaining and launched by a new company, he predicted it would fail. If it was a disruptive innovation but was part of the parent company's structure rather than being in an autonomous unit, he predicted it would fail. Only a disruptive innovation that was autonomous had a chance of success. When he compared his predictions with what actually happened, he found that he had been right for about forty-five of the forty-eight business proposals. His predictions were 94 percent accurate. This sounds impressive until you consider that only about 10 percent of new businesses succeed, so predicting failure for every one will make your guesses 90 percent accurate. So Raynor used statistical tests to look carefully at

Thurston's predictions and found that it was very unlikely that he succeeded by luck alone.[11]

Strong and Weak Nations

The theory of disruptive innovation fits well with Colonel Blotto. Another field where the game provides useful comparisons is war between strong and weak actors, generally nations. While Colonel Blotto sheds light on both business and war, there's a thread of research that studies war through the theory of disruptive innovation.[12]

In his book *How the Weak Win Wars*, Ivan Arreguín-Toft, a professor of international relations at Boston University, analyzed roughly two hundred wars that took place between weak and strong opponents between 1800 to 2003. He called those wars *asymmetric conflicts*. He considered a war asymmetric if the stronger nation's resources—the size of its armed forces and population—exceeded those of the weaker country by a factor of ten or more. Surprisingly, the stronger country prevailed just 72 percent of the time. Since this analysis included only wars where the asymmetry in resources was large, the success of the weaker players is even more remarkable.

In addition, Arreguín-Toft found that the weaker nations have been winning at a rising rate over the past two centuries. For instance, weak countries prevailed in just 12 percent of the wars from 1800 to 1849, but the rate exceeded 50 percent from 1950 to 1999. Further, the weak saw their percentage of victories rise in each half-century from 1800 to 1999.

After reviewing and dismissing a number of possible explanations for these findings, Arreguín-Toft concluded that he could explain the facts by analyzing two different strategies. Specifically, when the strong and weak nations go toe-to-toe, the weak lose roughly 80 percent of the time because "there is nothing to mediate or deflect a strong player's power advantage." When the weak nations choose a different strategy, increasing the number of battlefields, they lose less than 40 percent of the time "because the weak refuse to engage where the strong actor has a power advantage."[13] Weak nations have been winning more conflicts over the years because they see and imitate the successful strategies of others and have come to the realization that refusing to fight on the strong country's terms improves their chances of victory.[14]

Nearly 80 percent of the losers in asymmetric wars never switch strategies. Part of the reason combatants don't switch is that when training and equipment are developed for one strategy, it's often costly to shift to another. Leaders or organizational traditions also stand in the way of adopting new strategies. This type of inertia often prevents an organization from pursuing the strategy that offers the best chance of winning.

The two rules that emerge from playing Colonel Blotto make sense when you think about them, but surprisingly they are often ignored. While there is no way to change luck, the main goal is to increase or decrease the relative importance of skill in a toe-to-toe conflict, depending on whether you're the stronger or weaker opponent. We will never know how David would have fared against Goliath if he had fought with a sword and armor instead of a stone and slingshot. But our experience with Colonel Blotto suggests that Goliath's skill would have overwhelmed the shepherd boy.

Teasing Out Causality Through Little Bets

When it came time to pick a title for my last book, my editor and I were at odds. On the basis of a colleague's recommendation, I favored *Think Twice* because it is active, alliterative, and accurately captures the content. My editor was understandably lukewarm on the title because just a few months earlier, the publisher had released a book called *Think Again* and preferred to avoid confusion. She suggested a number of titles, none of which grabbed me. I asked her how she came up with her list, and she admitted that she thought of interesting titles, asked others in the office which ones they liked, and ranked them accordingly. Reasonable enough. But the process was very informal, and there was no explicit effort to figure out which title was best.

The goal of coming up with a catchy title is to get someone to purchase the book. If a prospective reader likes a title, then she might be more likely to open the book and take a look, and that would increase the likelihood that she'd buy it. As we saw in the discussion of the shape of luck, there are many factors that go in to book sales beyond the title. All things being equal, though, a good title is better than a bad one.

So I took matters into my own hands and set up a tournament. I used a service from Amazon.com called Mechanical Turk. The site allows you to offer micropayments to people willing to complete a "human intelligence task," often a question that needs an answer. I asked my editor for her favorite seven titles and added *Think Twice*, paired them randomly, and offered turkers $0.10 to "select the best title for a book." The titles that won each round moved on to the next round, just as in a sports tournament. In the end, *Think Twice* prevailed (otherwise, I wouldn't be telling this story), followed by *Perfectly Preventable Errors*, *Ways of Our Errors*, and *Counter Your Intuition*. Hundreds of people from around the world participated in the tournament by voting, and the whole project cost only a couple of hundred dollars.

The point of the story is that we can do a better job of figuring out cause and effect than we do.[15] The basic idea is very simple. Let's say you want to know whether an advertising campaign is effective. You run the ad for a selected group, called the experimental group. You don't run the ad for a statistically similar group, called the control group. You then compare the purchases the members of the two groups make. If the experimental group bought a sufficiently different amount of the product you advertised than the control group did, you have a reason to believe that the advertising caused the difference. You can run these experiments on a small scale so that failure is not too costly, and then increase the size of the bets only when an advertisement has proved that it can sell your product.[16]

Randall Lewis and David Reiley, scientists at Yahoo! Research, ran such an experiment for a large U.S. retailer on yahoo.com. The scientists created a sample of 1.6 million people and assigned 1.3 million to the experimental group and the other 300,000 to the control group. The experimental group was exposed to two advertising campaigns on Yahoo! in the fall of 2007, and most of the people saw the ads. They tracked what the people bought to measure the effects of the advertising.

Lewis and Reiley found that users exposed to the ads bought about 5 percent more than the people in the control group, and the researchers estimated that the increase in revenues from the advertising campaign was seven times the cost of running the online ads. They also observed that the people who saw more ads bought more often and spent more money. So the advertising seemed to have worked.

But here's an even more interesting point: The usual practice in advertising is to run an ad and watch what happens to sales. If the researchers had done that, they would have concluded that their ad didn't work, because overall sales actually happened to go down during the period they studied. By taking sufficient care to isolate the influence of the advertising, Lewis and Reiley were able to show that the experimental group bought more than they would have had they not seen the ads.[17]

In his book *Everything Is Obvious*, Duncan Watts suggests that we shift our way of thinking. Tradition in the ad business dictates that we "predict and control"; that is, we try to predict how people will respond to an advertisement or product. Watts suggests that instead, we "measure and react"; that is, we do carefully controlled experiments and let our actions be guided by the results. He argues that advertising should be viewed as an ongoing process of learning and that companies should use control groups whenever possible to pinpoint cause and effect.[18] Technology is rapidly enabling this shift, and companies are increasingly employing these methods. But practices in many fields remain entrenched in the old ways.

Even parts of the political process have warmed to the controlled experiment. Dave Carney is among the first strategists to understand the importance of doing experiments for political campaigns. Working for President George H. W. Bush's reelection campaign in 1992, Carney used a small amount of money to test a mailing campaign. The test worked. Even though the party brass refused to let him spend more money on the approach, he realized then that he could improve on the old methods and manage campaigns much more scientifically.[19]

Fourteen years later, Carney ran Rick Perry's race for governor of Texas and made the unprecedented move of hiring four political scientists to create randomized trials for the campaign. The scientists tested the importance of mailings, phone calls, television ads, and appearances by the candidate, all using the gold standard of scientific testing: randomized trials. They paired cities according to demographic and socioeconomic attributes and then randomly assigned television ads. So, for instance, the campaign might run ads in Amarillo but not in Abilene. They then did surveys to measure the impact of their actions.

They found that the ads did improve the candidate's standing. Advertising volume is measured using gross rating points (GRPs), where one GRP is equal to 1 percent of the viewing population. Perry's relative standing increased nearly five percentage points in the markets that had one thousand GRPs, which is equivalent to a person in the population seeing an ad ten times on average, the biggest blast of advertising that they did. The scientists also tested radio ads, which were less effective.

The experiment's most provocative finding was that the benefits of advertising decay rapidly. The benefit during the week the ads ran was strong and statistically significant. But it grew smaller and statistically equivocal by a week later. It essentially vanished after the second week. The scientists posited that the short-term bump in favorable ratings might be attributable to priming effects, where the advertising provides a stimulus that encourages favorable responses to a survey. By running these experiments, the political scientists could start the process of "measure and react," versus the standard "predict and control" model that prevails in politics.[20]

Randomness and luck are the result of insufficient information—an inability to pinpoint cause and effect. Controlled experiments can be a quick and effective way to improve our understanding of cause and effect. This approach reiterates a broader point: whenever you evaluate results, ask if you have considered the outcomes that would come from a proper null model, the simplest model that might explain the result. For example, I teach a class called Security Analysis at Columbia Business School. On the first day of class each year, I put the students through an exercise. I toss a coin four times and everyone calls heads or tails. Most years, a few students get all four right. I toss the coin again and have them call it. In the most recent exercise, one student called the coin correctly six times in a row. One conclusion we could draw from this is that the student is really good at calling coins. But the null model says that it was just the result of chance, and indeed, it was what we should expect from a random system. This is why randomized trials lead to much more reliable findings than observational studies do.

How to Live in a World That We Do Not Understand

Chapter 1 introduced Nassim Taleb's useful method for figuring out where statistical analysis works and where it doesn't. He sets out a 2×2 matrix, in which the rows distinguish between activities that have extreme outcomes and those that have more clustered outcomes, and the columns capture simple and complex payoffs. He shows that statistical methods work in the first quadrant (simple payoffs and clustered outcomes), the second quadrant (complex payoffs and clustered outcomes), and the third quadrant (simple payoffs and extreme outcomes). But statistical methods fail in the fourth quadrant (complex payoffs and extreme outcomes). We can take positive steps to untangle skill and luck in the first three quadrants, but face a more complex task in dealing with the *black swans* of the fourth quadrant—events of small and incomputable probability that have significant consequences.

The good news is that a great deal of what we care about is in the first three quadrants, and there are methods to cope with events in the fourth quadrant. Taleb doesn't seem very interested in the first three quadrants—understandably so because the problems are reasonably tractable. Sports, for instance, seem to hold no interest for him. In his book of aphorisms, *The Bed of Procrustes*, he writes: "Sports are commoditized and, alas, prostituted randomness."[21] I don't know exactly what that means, but it leads me to believe that watching a ball game is not among Taleb's favorite pastimes.

One of my main points is that most people have trouble untangling skill and luck even in cases where it is possible to do so. But it is still important to acknowledge the limits of the methods at our disposal, and Taleb's work effectively illustrates that point. Let's look at the nature of the fourth quadrant in an effort to understand why we get fooled by it and what we can do about that.

The fourth quadrant is the world of black swans. Taleb argues that having no theory or model of events in the fourth quadrant is preferable to having a theory or model, because the errors we make are huge and often lead to bad results. In practice, we try to use policy and models to manage a part of the world that defies control and understanding.[22] In a paper coauthored with Mark Blyth, Taleb argues that efforts by political leaders and economic policy makers to stabilize the economic system by inhibiting fluctuations actually create fragility and even greater vulnerability to extreme events.[23]

This fragility explains why it is so easy to be fooled by economic, social, and political events in the fourth quadrant. Take the profits for banks in the United States for the years preceding the financial crisis of 2007–2009. The picture would show steady and growing profits. But the crisis, in one fell swoop, led to extreme losses that wiped out a substantial percentage of the gains from previous years. For instance, Citigroup suffered losses in 2008 that were more than one-quarter of the cumulative profits the company had made during the previous seven years. Figure 9-2 shows this pattern of small gains punctuated by a substantial loss. Leaders feel good when the payoffs are positive and have a tendency to extrapolate past success into the future. But, as Taleb emphasizes, it can take a long time for a series of data in the fourth quadrant to reveal its properties.

Moral hazard refers to a person or organization taking an action on behalf of others without suffering the consequences if the outcome is bad. Take the case of MF Global, a large financial broker of derivatives. Through 2010 and 2011, the firm's chairman and CEO, Jon Corzine, directed an investment in European sovereign debt that peaked at more than $6 billion. The basic trade was simple: borrow money at a relatively low rate, buy sovereign debt yielding a

FIGURE 9-2

Small gains and large losses in the fourth quadrant

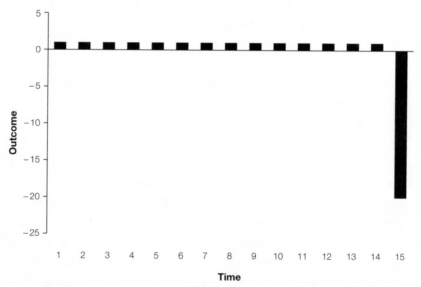

Source: Based on Nassim Nicholas Taleb, "Antifragility, Robustness, and Fragility Inside the 'Black Swan' Domain," SSRN working paper, February 2011.

higher rate, and book the difference as a profit. But this trade relied on steady access to money. Indeed, the firm was forced to declare bankruptcy in the fall of 2011 when concerns about the fiscal condition in Europe caused the lenders to get nervous and refuse to do business with MF Global on the same terms. Further, after inspecting the books, regulators found that $1.6 billion of funds belonging to clients were missing. Had the bet on the bonds turned out well, it is likely that Corzine, the former CEO of Goldman Sachs, would have profited handsomely. But after busting the company, Corzine remains wealthy, though the episode has sullied his reputation, and he is likely to face a slew of lawsuits.[24]

In dealing with events in the fourth quadrant, Taleb recommends that we avoid optimization and allow for redundancy. You can optimize your behavior to serve a specific goal in a stable system. For example, swimming strokes have been improved and refined to maximize the swimmer's speed. This works because the basic relationship between the swimmer and the water is sufficiently constant over time. But optimization in a changing system is a setup for failure. If you are an animal that evolved in a cold climate, you might die if the climate becomes too warm.

Because optimization works well in some systems, there is a temptation to optimize in the fourth quadrant during times of relative stability. In building a portfolio of investments, for example, optimization would mean getting the highest return you can for a given level of risk. You might decide to borrow money to make more money. But if the market tanks, you'll be wiped out quickly. One way to think about this is to ask under what conditions experts can predict well. We know that experts don't do so well when it comes to many political, economic, and social events. Where expert predictions are poor, optimization is a bad idea, because you can get locked in to one approach and can't adjust to change.

There are two kinds of payoffs in the fourth quadrant. In the first kind, shocks and mistakes lead to painful losses. This is what Taleb suggests avoiding, because the small gains over time do not compensate for the infrequent but sizeable losses. Here's an illustration. A financial option is the right, but not the obligation, to buy or sell some asset. Say a share of a security that represents a stock market index is selling at a price of $1,000. You can sell an option, called a *put*, which grants the buyer the right to sell you a share at the price of $800 at any point within the next three months. From your point of view, the probability of the index going down 20 percent or more in three months is very low, so you are willing to sell this option for a small sum—perhaps $1. Indeed, if you do this over and over, you will collect a modest but steady income. But in the very rare event that the market drops more than 20 percent, you will suffer a loss because you are on the hook to buy the share at $800. Figure 9-2 is an illustration of this type of payoff. People and institutions making these kinds of trades commonly do so with borrowed money and rely on models that are unable to reflect the probability or magnitude of their potential losses. They don't understand that they're in black swan territory, and so they get blindsided.

If the seller of an option is exposed to frequent small gains and infrequent but large losses, the buyer of that same option must have the opposite payoff. The buyer loses a little over and over and then has a very large gain. Figure 9-3 shows this payoff. Taleb's message is that if you are dealing with events in the fourth quadrant, you should seek payoffs that are equivalent to buying options, even though they have a small but steady cost and you don't know if or when you will get a big payoff.[25]

When it comes to managing luck, Taleb has two very useful messages. The first is to understand the limits of your knowledge about events that have probabilities that you can't compute and consequences that are significant. In other words, know what you don't know. The second is to take steps to make sure that whatever exposure you do have in the fourth quadrant is the result of buying, or acquiring, options and not the result of selling options. Selling options is the more profitable strategy most of the time. But you do not define your ultimate success by the frequency of gains, but rather by how much you make when you are right versus how much you lose when you are wrong.

FIGURE 9-3

Small losses and large gains in the fourth quadrant

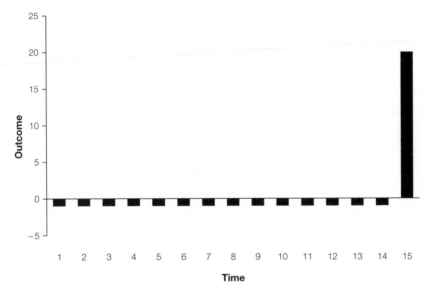

Source: Based on Nassim Nicholas Taleb, "Antifragility, Robustness, and Fragility Inside the 'Black Swan' Domain," SSRN working paper, February 2011.

Learning to Live with Luck

By definition, luck is something that no one can control. But there are ways that you can manage it more effectively. The main lesson from Colonel Blotto is that in competitive interactions, the strong should seek to simplify to emphasize their advantage in skill and the weak should try to add randomness to dilute the stronger player's advantage. This approach has proved useful in sports, business, and war, and yet many people fail to use it because of tradition, a lack of awareness, or because they are afraid of damaging their careers by doing something different and then failing.

In some cases, it is helpful for you to consider luck as equivalent to a lack of knowledge. In particular, in an activity dominated by luck, the relationship between cause and effect is difficult to discern. But organizations can now get a clearer sense of cause and effect than they had before through a combination of applied scientific methods and technology, thereby reducing the role of luck. Researchers can get a better understanding of how cause and effect interact through experiments that use both a control group and an experimental group. Scientists can now carry out experiments on a much larger and more cost effective scale because of new technology. That in turn is leading to large improvements in efficiency.

Statistical methods are of great value in measuring a wide range of activities. But understanding the limitations of models is as important as applying them properly. Nassim Taleb has developed a useful map that shows the limits within which we can apply statistics usefully. Specifically, he suggests that in the fourth quadrant, an area characterized by complex payoffs and extreme outcomes, we're better off using no model than using a faulty one. The key is to sidestep activities that have small gains and large losses and to gain exposure to payoffs that have small costs but large gains.

CHAPTER 10

REVERSION TO THE MEAN

FRANCIS GALTON, a cousin of Charles Darwin, was a polymath who was particularly fond of counting things. He gathered and analyzed a huge amount of data in his life, and through a process of inquiry and investigation, figured out how reversion to the mean works while counting sweet peas in the late 1800s.[1]

Reversion to the mean says that an event that is not average will be followed by an event that is closer to the average. Let's return to the example of Charlie, the student introduced in chapter 1. The teacher assigned Charlie to memorize one hundred facts, he learned eighty of them, and the test consisted of regurgitating twenty of the hundred facts that the teacher selected at random. Say Charlie took the test and received a score of 95 percent. You would reasonably interpret that score as the combination of skill (the student knew 80 percent of the information) and good luck (the teacher selected facts that he happened to know). In reality, we don't know the relative contributions of skill and luck. But an exceptional score suggests a high degree of luck. This is consistent with the model, introduced in chapter 3, that combines the draws from a skill jar and a luck jar and shows that outstanding outcomes combine great skill and great luck.

Assume that Charlie's skill remains constant and that the next test has a similar setup. We would expect his score to be closer to his skill, because we can assume that the good luck from the last test is transitory. The skill remains, but the good luck, on average, will not be present. There's no reason to believe that Charlie will have bad luck on the second test just because he had good luck on the first one. He may even have better luck. On average, though, luck will play no role at all. The more times he takes the test, the closer his cumulative average score will be to 80, the number that represents his absolute skill. So going from good skill and good luck to good skill alone is an example of reversion to the mean. The more general principle is that whenever there is an imperfect correlation between two scores, in this case from one test to the next, you will have reversion to the mean.[2]

Naturally, the effect is strongest at the extremes. If a student gets a bad grade on the first test as the result of poor skill and bad luck, he can only stay at the same level or go up. Similarly, a student who scores 100 percent on the first test can't get better. He can only score 100 or lower. While it is reasonable to predict that scores at the extremes will revert to the mean, there is no way to predict the outcome of a specific test. Some students will do poorly and continue to do so or may even see their scores go lower. Other students who are scoring high might keep it up or even improve.

A classic example of reversion to the mean is the relationship between how tall parents and their children are. Karl Pearson, a mathematician who was a protégé of Galton's, as well as his biographer, examined the stature of more than one thousand pairs of fathers and sons. The coefficient of correlation, r, between the stature of the fathers and the sons is about .50. The stature of a child is determined in part by heredity and in part by environmental factors, including health and nutrition.

Reversion to the mean tells us that very tall fathers are likely to have tall sons, but that the stature of the sons will be closer to the average of all sons than the statures of the fathers were to the average of all fathers. Figure 10-1, which is based on Pearson's data, shows this fact displayed graphically. Take the upper right corner of the figure as an example. It shows that the tallest fathers are about

FIGURE 10-1

Reversion to the mean in height from father to son

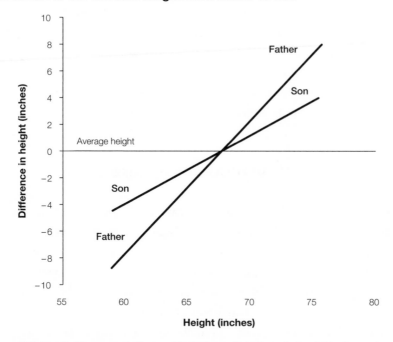

Source: Data from Karl Pearson and Alice Lee, "On the Laws of Inheritance in Man: I. Inheritance of Physical Characters," *Biometrika* 2, no. 4 (November 1903): 357–462. The presentation of the chart is based on Francis Galton, "Regression Towards Mediocrity in Hereditary Stature," *Journal of the Anthropological Institute* 15 (1886): 246–263.

eight inches above average. Their sons, however, are only about four inches above average. Likewise, short fathers are likely to have short sons, but again, the stature of the sons will be closer to the average of all sons than the statures of the fathers were to the average of all fathers. You can see that by looking at the bottom left corner of the figure.[3]

Reversion to the mean is an idea that most people believe they understand. Certainly, the example with the relative stature of fathers and sons does not surprise anyone. Yet the concept is actually very hard to grasp and even harder to employ in making decisions. Specifically, reversion to the mean creates three illusions. The first is the illusion of *cause and effect*. Our natural inclination is to look for what is causing a given measurement to regress toward the mean, an exercise that is frequently fruitless. There is also the illusion of *feedback*, which makes it seem like favorable feedback leads to worse results and unfavorable feedback leads to better results. Finally, there's the illusion of *declining variance*, the idea that reversion to the mean implies that everything we can measure converges on the same average value over time. Even famous and well-trained economists have made this last mistake.

Mean Reversion Mistakes

One of the themes of this book is that we have a difficult time untangling skill and luck because of our basic desire to find cause and effect in every situation, whether or not that view represents reality. Reversion to the mean is a statistical artifact that produces an itch that our causal minds yearn to scratch. When skill remains constant, we see reversion to the mean because of the randomness (luck from an individual's viewpoint) in the activity. There is no cause, so there is nothing to explain.

Daniel Kahneman shares an example to make this point. He suggests that you can start a lively conversation at a party by asking people to explain the following true statement:

Highly intelligent women tend to marry men who are less intelligent than they are.

He points out that your spontaneous tendency is to interpret the statement in terms of cause and effect. Your mind will search for the reasons that a woman might want, or need, to find a spouse who is less intelligent than she is. You might even search your memory for a couple that fits the description, and find a plausible explanation for their circumstances. Kahneman then introduces a second statement:

The correlation between the intelligence scores of spouses is less than perfect.

Although true, this statement is trivial and not very interesting. But its meaning is actually identical to the first statement. In the first case, your mind naturally searches for a cause, while the second case comes across as dry, dull, and obvious. The illusion of cause and effect arises when people try to assign significance to an instance of reversion to the mean, when in reality they are simply seeing a lack of correlation.[4]

If the case for the lack of causality is not yet cinched in your mind, consider that reversion to the mean works whether you go forward or backward in time. Tall fathers are likely to have tall sons, but the stature of the sons will be closer to the average stature of all sons. It's also true that tall sons are likely to have tall fathers, but the stature of the fathers will be closer to the average stature of all fathers. Now, it is clear that tall sons can't cause shorter fathers. But reversion to the mean tells us that the statement is true nonetheless. It happens without the need of a cause.

Also related to causality is the illusion of feedback. The idea is that you think that the feedback, or treatment, you provided after one outcome caused the change in performance for the second outcome, rather than acknowledging that the change was the result of reversion to the mean. Here's a simple example. Your son comes home with an awful grade on his math test. You sternly voice your displeasure, threaten to take away his beloved video games, and order him to work harder. How will he do on his next test? Reversion to the mean says that on average he will do better no matter what you say. But the natural reaction is to assume that your talk caused his improvement.

We can generalize this point. If you encourage your child when he makes a good grade, you can expect his grades to go down on average, not up. You might be tempted to believe that encouragement causes him to slack off, and therefore that encouragement is a bad idea. But reversion to the mean says that you should expect his grades to revert to the mean no matter what you say. As we have seen, you might also be tempted to conclude that negative feedback improves outcomes when reversion to the mean explains the phenomenon more simply. The main lesson is to address your feedback to the part of the outcome that is within control and forget about the rest.

This illusion often confuses doctors. In clinical practice, they commonly measure weight, cholesterol concentration, and blood pressure to see if you have a disease or the risk factors associated with it. Doctors are likely to treat you if they find an extreme value for any of those variables—high blood pressure, for instance. They'll give you a drug to try to bring your blood pressure closer to the mean. Here again, we know that the entire population of people with high blood pressure during their first visit will see on average a moderation in blood pressure on their second visit, whether individual people are treated or not. Because of errors in measurement and biological variation, the correlation between two blood pressure tests for the same person is not perfect. So there will be reversion to the mean no matter what the treatment. Naturally, the tendency is to assume that the treatment worked and caused the reduction in blood pressure, and in some cases this might be true in part. But the illusion of feedback will persuasively suggest that the treatment was the cause and lower blood pressure was the effect.[5]

Galton called his famous paper on reversion to the mean "Regression Towards Mediocrity in Hereditary Stature." The title itself conjures an image of everything moving toward the average, with the variation in the numbers shrinking. This is the illusion of declining variance. But that's not at all what happens. Reversion to the mean occurs even when the statistical properties of the distributions of the first and second outcomes are the same. Change, in the form of reversion to the mean, and no change, in the form of stable distributions, can occur at the same time, setting a trap for faulty analysis.

Recall the clear pattern of reversion to the mean in figure 10-1. Because the tallest and shortest sons are closer to the average than their fathers, you might be tempted to conclude that there is a decline in variance. Now take a look at figure 10-2, which uses

FIGURE 10-2

The distribution of heights for fathers and sons

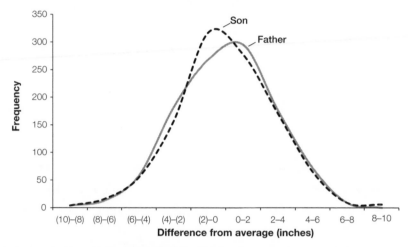

Source: Data from Karl Pearson and Alice Lee, "On the Laws of Inheritance in Man: I. Inheritance of Physical Characters," *Biometrika* 2, no. 4 (November 1903): 357–462.

the same data. While the distributions vary a little at the top, you can see that the tails appear remarkably similar. The coefficient of variation, the standard deviation divided by the mean, is nearly identical for the two distributions. In other words, the heights of the sons are not clustered closer to the average than they are for the fathers. Indeed, an equally valid presentation of the data shows a move away from mediocrity toward increasing variation.[6]

You can reconcile change and no change by recognizing that luck reshuffles the heights on the distribution. Think back to the model of the skill and luck jars in chapter 3. If the distributions within the jars don't change from one draw to the next, the aggregate distributions will be similar over time, but the extremes will revert to the mean from one period to the next. Let's say you scored well on a test as the result of average skill and above-average luck. On the next test, you may not have good luck and your score will migrate toward the average. But another average student will have good luck, filling the spot on the distribution that you vacated.

One principle of competitive markets is that excess returns get competed away. A company will attract competition if it earns a 20 percent return on invested capital and has a 10 percent opportunity cost of capital (a measure of the minimum required return, or what you'd expect to earn if you were doing something else with the money). A competitor with the same opportunity cost may be willing to sell the product or service at a lower price and accept a 15 percent return on invested capital. Since that return is still above the opportunity cost, another competitor may be willing to lower its price and accept a 12 percent return. And so on. Eventually, in theory, all of the competitors will earn nothing more than the opportunity cost of capital. This process sounds a lot like reversion to the mean, with the mean being the opportunity cost of capital.

In 1933, a statistician at Northwestern University named Horace Secrist wrote a book called *The Triumph of Mediocrity in Business*. The book is 468 pages long, and includes 140 tables and more than 100 charts. Secrist's work was meticulous, and his conclusion was consistent with the principle of competitive markets: "Mediocrity tends to prevail in the conduct of competitive business." He was also aware of the contributions of Galton, and used Galton's terminology to express his conclusion, "Both expenses and profits approach the mean or, to use Sir Francis Galton's expression, 'regress to type.'" He explains, "In the market in the presence of competition, heterogeneity gives way to homogeneity. Both advantageous and disadvantageous conditions are continuously being dissipated— equalization is in process."[7]

Figure 10-3 shows a contemporary version of the type of chart Secrist created. You can see how the median spread between the return on invested capital and cost of capital reverts to the mean for a sample of more than a thousand companies, broken into quintiles, over a decade ending in 2010. While returns don't collapse all the way back to the cost of capital, or "equalization" using Secrist's term, the dispersion at the end of the period is much smaller than that at the beginning of the period.

FIGURE 10-3

Corporate returns on invested capital revert to the mean (2000–2010)

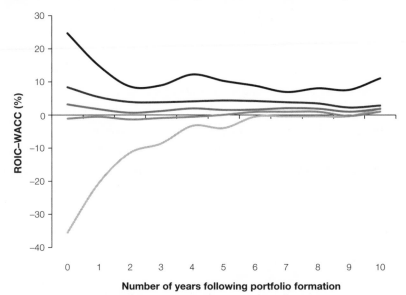

Number of years following portfolio formation

ROIC = Return on invested capital
WACC = Weighted average cost of capital
Source: Analysis by author.

Secrist's conclusion that results converge to the mean is a famous example of falling for the illusion of declining variance. As we have already seen, reversion to the mean does not imply that results will cluster closer to the average. As long as return on invested capital is not perfectly correlated with itself from year to year, you will see reversion to the mean. The coefficient of variation—the standard deviation divided by the mean—shows that the distribution of corporate performance, measured by return on invested capital, has been fairly consistent over time.

This mistake is sufficiently common among prominent economists that it prompted Milton Friedman, who won the Nobel Memorial Prize in Economics in 1976, to write an essay on the topic. In reference to a book by well-known economists and its reviewer, he wrote: "I find it surprising that the reviewer and the authors, all of whom are distinguished economists, thoroughly conversant with modern statistical methods, should have failed to recognize that they were guilty of the regression fallacy."[8]

None of this is to say that results cannot exhibit a decline in variance over time. A declining variance is the key idea behind the paradox of skill. But just because you observe reversion to the mean, that doesn't suggest that outcomes are converging toward the average. You must be careful to distinguish between a change of the system and change within the system. Those are easy to conflate.

Francis Galton figured out that correlation and reversion to the mean are two takes on the same concept. This is an essential insight for sorting out skill and luck. The coefficient of correlation between two variables determines the rate of reversion to the mean and provides valuable guidance for forecasting.

Base Rates, Persistence, and *c*

We are now ready to bring together a few of the ideas we've been considering so that we can see how to make practical use of reversion to the mean. The first idea comes from the paper, "On the Psychology of Prediction," published in 1973 by Daniel Kahneman and Amos Tversky. They said that there are three types of information that are relevant for a statistical prediction: the prior information, or base rate; the specific evidence about the individual case; and the expected accuracy of the prediction. The trick is determining how to weight the information.[9]

To answer that question, we can examine the idea of persistence, which we measure through a coefficient of correlation. High correlations are generally consistent with skill and allow for more accurate predictions. Low correlations are indicative of more luck and make specific predictions less accurate. Recall that the most useful statistics are persistent and predictive. That means the next outcome looks like (is highly correlated with) the previous one.

And it often means that you can control what happens next (high correlation between what you want and what you get through your effort).

Combining the ideas of weighting the information (How much does it count?) and persistence (Will you see the same results again?) gives you specific guidance in judging what the next result is likely to be. In cases where the correlations are low, reversion to the mean is very powerful. Indeed, the best estimate of the next outcome is in many cases the base rate, which is simply the average of the distribution. Yet this is not how most people make their decisions. Rather than assuming strong reversion, they generally act as if good news predicts good news and bad news predicts bad.

The world of investing provides clear examples of this failure to regress outcomes sufficiently. There is a strong tendency in the investment business to buy what has done well and to sell what has done poorly. That behavior is so prevalent that a pair of professors call it the *dumb money* effect. These professors of finance calculate that buying high and selling low costs investors 1 percent of their returns each year, a sizeable sum.[10] Importantly, this behavior is not limited to individuals. There is evidence that institutional investors do the same thing. One study estimated that institutional investors have forgone over $170 billion in value over a couple of decades as a result of the dumb money effect.[11]

The next piece of specific guidance is simpler. When correlations are high between the action you take and the result you get, you need not revert very much, and you can rely more on the specific evidence about the individual case. The best estimate of the next outcome is the current outcome. This works when skill is the primary influence at work. Tennis matches and foot races are examples. And, as we saw with batters in baseball, some outcomes within an activity may be easier to predict than others. For baseball players, strikeout rate (strikeouts divided by plate appearances) reflects the interaction solely between the pitcher and hitter and is mostly determined by skill. As a result, it has a high correlation between cause and effect. Many more factors affect batting average (hits divided by at-bats), including weather, fielding, and minute differences in how the bat hits the ball. Batting average has a much lower correlation with skill than strikeout rate, and is therefore less predictable.

The shrinkage factor, c, is the final idea that allows us to put the concept of reversion to the mean into practice. Chapter 3 discussed the James-Stein estimator. Here's the equation to estimate true skill:[12]

$$z = \bar{y} + c\left(y - \bar{y}\right)$$

In plain language, the formula says:

Estimated true skill = Grand average +
shrinkage factor (observed average – grand average)

The value of c has a range of zero to 1.0, where zero implies complete reversion to the mean and 1.0 implies no reversion to the mean at all. So c tells us how much we should revert, and to what mean we should revert. Galton's insight was that correlation and reversion to the mean are two elements of the same concept. We can turn that insight into an instrument of mathematical analysis through a simple equation: $c = r$. I have found that c only approximates r, but for practical purposes the idea still works. A high correlation suggests weak reversion to the mean. A low correlation suggests strong reversion to the mean. If you have an understanding of r, you have taken a big step in recognizing what value for c will give you the best estimate.[13]

This equation is very useful, but there are a number of important caveats that you need to consider, lest you apply the formula naively. The most obvious hazard is that correlations are not stable in many fields. Correlations happen to be consistent for the stature of fathers and sons or the strikeout rate of hitters in baseball, but in other realms they move around. This sets up a potential trap, especially for those who bet that correlations will remain high and that predictability will be good as a result. In stable and linear activities, correlations will tend to be consistent over time. But in unstable and nonlinear activities, relying on past correlations won't work in the long run.

It is also worth reiterating that skill isn't constant in most pursuits. As we saw in chapter 5, skill tends to rise and fall in the shape of an arc. You may show the same amount of skill over a short period of time, but the longer the amount of time you consider, the more you need to account for the rise and fall of skill.

Related to this point is the importance of the sample you decide to measure. Your ability to assess skill rises as you gather more information. Small samples are notoriously unreliable. So make sure your sample is large enough so that you can draw reliable conclusions. All things being equal, small samples require you to allow for more reversion to the mean than big samples do.

Finally, a reminder that when you estimate true skill, you must keep in mind that you are doing just that: *estimating*. You can't calculate an exact and objective answer. This is another case of being aware of the limitations of the tools. Broadly speaking, though, the research shows that people fail to revert their predictions sufficiently to the mean. So having a basis for making predictions will put you ahead of the game.

Why Your Team Is Not as Good (or Bad) as You Think

Here is a case study to solidify some of these concepts. I learned this approach from Tom Tango and Phil Birnbaum, two excellent sabermetricians.[14] I applied the method to the records of all of the teams in Major League Baseball for the 2011 season. The goal of the analysis is to figure out how much you need to revert the actual record of wins and losses to have a good estimate of a team's true skill. (The appendix presents this analysis in detail.)

In effect, the analytical process attempts to eliminate the role that luck plays and get a clear look at skill. This may seem somewhat different from using reversion to the mean to make a prediction. But it's a similar exercise, because by removing luck we allow skill to move to the fore. We also know that if skill doesn't change from one period to the next (a big *if*), we will get a correlation, r, close to 1.0. And a high coefficient of correlation tells us that we don't have to adjust our estimates very much toward the mean. So this approach can tell us a great deal.

The first step is to estimate the shrinkage factor, c, basing it on the results of all of the teams for the entire season of 162 games. Tango's equation gives an answer that is similar to what the James-Stein estimator provides.[15] The details of the calculation are a little messy, so I relegated them to the appendix. But using either equation, the shrinkage factor, c, comes out to about 0.7. In practical terms, this says that if you want to estimate a team's true skill, you combine 0.7 parts of the team's actual record with 0.3 parts of a .500 record. Let's say your favorite team went 97–65, for a .599 winning percentage. To estimate your team's true skill, you take the sum of 0.7 × .599 and 0.3 × .500 to find a true winning percentage of .568. This means that the best estimate of your team's true skill is a 92–70 record, and that luck contributed about five wins. Let me stress again that we don't *know* this is right. Maybe your team's skill suggested 100 wins and the team was unlucky. But what we do know from reversion to the mean is that it's much more likely that the teams that won the most games had the benefit of luck and that the teams that lost the most had bad luck.

Tango's way of estimating a team's true skill takes a different approach with the same effect. He adds a specific number of games, at a .500 record, to the team's actual record of wins and losses. His calculation shows that the appropriate number for a full Major League Baseball season is 74 games.[16] So if your team goes 97–65, you add 37 wins and 37 losses to the overall record, making it 134–102, for a winning percentage of .568. You get the same answer.

But here's the neat part of Tango's approach: it turns out that 74 games at a .500 win percentage is the right number to add to *any* number of games played in Major League Baseball to get an estimate of true skill. Say your favorite team stumbles out of the blocks and wins just 2 of its first 10 games. The team's winning percentage would be a dismal .200, but this approach would add 37 wins and 37 losses for a 39–45 record, a winning percentage of .464. That's still not great but it gives you a more realistic assessment of the team's actual skill.

This is a Bayesian approach, which starts with a prior probability and updates the probability in light of new information.[17] In this case, 74 games of .500 ball defines the prior probability and additional games provide new information. Winning or losing the first game, or even the first bunch of games, does little to move the prior probability. But as the season progresses, the model assigns more weight to the new information until the weighting stops at 30 percent prior and 70 percent new information, the team's actual win-loss record.

You can calculate the shrinkage factor, c, at any point during the Major League Baseball season with a simple equation:

$$c = \frac{n}{74 + n}$$

where n equals the number of games played. The value for c rises as the team works through its schedule, stopping at about 0.7. A rising shrinkage factor tells you that the approach is placing increasing weight on the new information. So now you have a method to moderate your enthusiasm or despondency after your team has played only a few games in a new season.

Consistent with the theme of this book, you can expect that there is less reversion to the mean for a sport like basketball, which involves little luck, than baseball, which involves a lot of luck. And that is indeed the case. For one season in the National Basketball Association, the value of c is close to 0.9, and you can set your prior probability with only 11 games of .500 results. Each game in the NBA has a lot more information than a game in professional baseball.

Avoiding the Trap

A final note. For reversion to the mean to be relevant, there has to be some sense of the mean, or average. For distributions that follow a power law, where there are a few extremely large values and lots of small values, there is no meaning in the idea of an average. For instance, if you collected the stature of one hundred men in your neighborhood, you could readily calculate an average. If Bill Gates moved in and you added him to your calculation, the average wouldn't change much. Gates is about average when it comes to stature. But even if he were taller or shorter than average, he wouldn't be tall enough or short enough to move the average much.

Now say you collected the net worth data for one hundred of your neighbors and calculated the average. Adding Bill Gates, whose net worth is likely many multiples of all of your neighbors combined, would lead to a huge increase in the average. With outcomes so skewed, there is no sensible way to assess an average. So reversion to the mean applies where the average has some meaning. Many, but not all, activities fit this description.

Reversion to the mean is a trap that ensnares a lot of people, from individual investors buying a hot mutual fund to learned economists who misinterpret their findings. The concept creates some tricky illusions related to causality, the effect of feedback, and shrinking variance. But, simply stated, the biggest hazard is that decision makers have a tendency to insufficiently regress outcomes to the mean.

The lesson of this chapter is that effective forecasts require you to consider carefully where you are on the luck-skill continuum, estimate an appropriate shrinkage factor, and incorporate reversion to the mean into your decision. Even the simple and approximate equation $c \approx r$, which says that the appropriate shrinkage factor is roughly equal to the correlation between two outcomes, can get you into the right frame of mind.

CHAPTER 11

THE ART OF GOOD GUESSWORK

IN MICHAEL LEWIS'S BOOK *Moneyball*, there is a scene in which the scouts and front office executives of the Oakland A's gather to determine which players to select in the 2002 draft. The scouts are ex-players who have been around the game their whole lives. They rely on their experience and their senses to tell them which players will succeed. In many cases they are spot on. But they also fall prey to biases. The executives relied more heavily on the use of statistics to assess the players. The statistics don't care what the player looks like. Billy Beane, the general manager, was fond of saying "we're not selling jeans here." They care only about his performance. While dramatized by Lewis, the point was that the traditional scouting approach overvalued some attributes and undervalued others. The scouts for all the other teams were using those old and inefficient methods. So the goal of the Oakland A's managers, with their statistical analysis, was to uncover those inefficiencies and take advantage of them.

Looking back over this book, it is now pretty clear why untangling skill and luck is so difficult. The first obstacle to learning is psychological. The way most of us learn about the world is by experiencing it. Our senses take in what's going on around us, and our minds process the inputs into a coherent story. But we know from the work of psychologists that our minds frequently use shortcuts.

These shortcuts are marvelous time savers, and serve us well most of the time. But they also induce biases that are consistent and predictable.

Perhaps the largest impediment to thinking clearly about skill and luck is our innate desire to identify cause and effect. While most of us are comfortable acknowledging that luck plays a role in what we do, we have difficulty assessing its role after the fact. Once something has occurred and we can put together a story to explain it, it starts to seem like the outcome was predestined. Statistics don't appeal to our need to understand cause and effect, which is why they are so frequently ignored or misinterpreted. Stories, on the other hand, are a rich means to communicate precisely because they emphasize cause and effect.

Other psychological tricks we play on ourselves include the recency bias and sample size bias. The recency bias says that we weight recent information more heavily than a body of past evidence. As a result, we tend to overrate players who have done well recently even if they did poorly in the past. Sample size bias is related. The natural tendency is to extract more meaning from small samples than the data warrant. Psychologists who study these biases can teach us a great deal about why we struggle to sort out skill and luck.

Another barrier to clear thinking is an analytical one. Once we have a basic grasp of the issues, we still need analytical processes to place activities on the luck-skill continuum, to draw the arc of skill, to measure the impact of luck, and to develop useful statistics. In most cases, the tools of analysis are intellectually accessible. Some grounding in basic statistics is especially helpful. A final part of this analysis is an understanding of where these methods don't apply. There is risk in underutilizing analytical methods, but there is also risk in misapplying them. Careful thinking about skill and luck considers both risks.

The last obstacle to overcome is a procedural one. We have to figure out what to do if these ideas make sense. The important insight is that sorting out skill and luck leads to specific suggestions for action. For instance, the best way to improve skill is to some degree contingent on where an activity lies on the luck-skill continuum.

Deliberate practice works when skill dominates, while a focus on process and probability is appropriate when luck is the greater force. Further, an appreciation for reversion to the mean allows us to make a more thoughtful assessment of what will happen next.

Horace Barlow, a neuroscientist and the great-grandson of Charles Darwin, defines intelligence as "the art of good guesswork." More specifically, he suggests that good guesswork "is the capacity to detect new, non-chance, associations."[1] I like this definition because it fits so well with the theme of untangling skill and luck in order to think about outcomes—past, present, and future. But note that Barlow emphasizes that good guesswork means avoiding being fooled by chance. Barlow writes, "Associations discovered must be genuine ones and not due to chance. The mind that seizes on any random coincidence and sees it as a sign of an important permanent association will not guess right and is not conceded to be intelligent, though it may be at times entertaining."[2] Just so.

Here are ten suggestions to improve the art of good guesswork in a world that combines skill and luck.

1. Understand where you are on the luck-skill continuum

At this point, the benefit of placing an activity on the continuum should be evident. The challenge is that, with the exception of the extremes—all luck/no skill and no luck/all skill—we are not very good at placing activities intuitively. As a case in point, I sent an informal request to my colleagues to rank a number of sports according to the relative contributions of skill and luck. More than twenty people responded, and the aggregate of the guesses had the general ranking right. But many of the individual judgments were far off of the mark, and even the consensus misplaced some sports. Given that sports is a field that is relatively straightforward to measure, you can imagine the difficulty in characterizing more complex activities, such as business and investing.

When an activity is near the all-skill side of the continuum, you can predict reasonably well. The main issue to consider is the rate at which skill changes. A related point is that a useful statistic is one that is persistent, which means the current outcome is highly correlated with the previous outcome. At the opposite side of the continuum, prediction is very difficult. In cases where there's a drop of skill in a sea of luck, you need a very large sample to detect the influence of skill.

The location of an activity on the continuum provides guidance on how much reversion to the mean is necessary in making your predictions. High correlations imply limited reversion to the mean; the best estimate for the next outcome is something close to the previous one. Low correlations require substantial reversion to the mean, and the most logical guess for the next outcome is the average. Psychologists have demonstrated that we typically fail to regress to the mean as much as we should.

Finally, the luck-skill continuum will give you some sense of when you are most likely to get fooled by randomness. The basic challenge is that our minds naturally assign causes to all that we see, whether an event is the result of skill or luck. A positive outcome on the skill side of the continuum should clearly be chalked up to good skill, but our minds are lazy enough to attribute a good result on the luck side to skill as well. (This generally doesn't apply to pure luck activities, including the lottery, although even there you hear explanations using causal attribution.) A good example is an investor who succeeds in the short run in spite of a poor investment process. The success itself will look like skill to the investor and plenty of others. Whenever randomness explains a result as well as or better than skill does, we are at risk of being fooled.

2. Assess sample size, significance, and swans

In 1971, Amos Tversky and Daniel Kahneman wrote an influential paper called, "Belief in the Law of Small Numbers." They suggested that for small samples, people have "strong intuitions" that are "wrong in fundamental respects," a shortcoming "shared by naïve subjects and by trained scientists."[3] The flaw, simply stated, is that we have a tendency to believe that a small sample of a population is representative of the whole population.

As we saw in chapter 3, we must always consider outcomes in the context of the size of the sample, because the outcomes from a small sample can deviate meaningfully from the larger population. This leads to faulty thinking. Take an example from sports. In *The Book*, Tom Tango, Mitchel Lichtman, and Andrew Dolphin discuss the interactions between batter and pitcher in baseball.[4] A specific batter may face a given pitcher twenty times and enjoy fantastic success—a terrific batting average, lots of power, and few strikeouts. Alternatively, a pitcher might seem to shut down a batter, striking him out or otherwise keeping him off base in a high percentage of their encounters. Announcers love to point out the statistics that suggest that one player really has the other one figured out. And managers rely on these kinds of numbers to decide which player to put in the game.

By now, we know that we shouldn't place too much weight on such a small sample of interactions as this, because the extremes in performance are more readily explained by normal variability than by some special gift of one player or the other. Tango, Lichtman, and Dolphin tested this by gathering the most pronounced successes of hitters and pitchers over a few seasons and comparing them with what happened in a subsequent season when the same two players faced each other. In other words, the researchers wanted to know what made for a better prediction: the small sample of lopsided results where one player dominated, or the large sample of how a player performed when compared with all competitors. They found, conclusively, that a player's overall performance was a much better predictor of specific interactions between hitters and pitchers than the exceptional outcomes from the past.[5]

When reporting a statistic, always list the size of the sample and keep it in mind when assessing the value of that statistic. As shown in chapter 3, we need a large sample if we are close to the luck side of the continuum, whereas a smaller sample will do if we are near the skill side. Let's use another example from baseball. Statisticians have asked at what point a hitting or pitching statistic has "stabilized." They define *stabilization* as the size of the sample necessary to predict one-half of the future variation (where $r = .50$). So at the point of stabilization, good guesswork would weight the player's data and the overall average equally. Stated differently, the point of stabilization is the size of sample that allows us to predict one statistic as well as another.[6]

Strikeout rate, which is mostly skill, stabilizes at about one hundred at-bats, about one-fifth of a season. Batting average on balls in play, a measure of whether a hitter records a hit if he bats a fair ball onto the field, is largely a matter of luck and stabilizes at about eleven hundred—almost two and a half seasons. Most statistics about hitting fall between those two extremes. The point is that the sizes of the samples you need are not all created equally, a fact that we often fail to acknowledge.

Then there is the issue of what exactly the statistics from the sample are telling us. One problem is trying to identify the source of success by sampling teams (or companies or investors) that have won. In business, for example, we may create a sample of all of the companies that selected a risky strategy and won, and neglect to take into account the companies that embraced the same strategy and failed. The narrow sample of winners creates a biased view of the strategy's virtue.

Another problem is distinguishing between statistical and economic significance. There are research findings that qualify as statistically significant that are essentially meaningless in a practical sense. Part of the issue is semantics; the word *significant* carries weight with most of us. But to a statistician, the term *significant* has a different meaning. In a paper called "The Standard Error of Regressions," Deirdre McCloskey and Stephen Ziliak discuss how the use of the word *significant* as jargon in the practice of statistics can be misleading.[7]

During the 1980s and 1990s, McCloskey and Ziliak, themselves economists, analyzed more than three hundred papers that used statistical tests and were published in the prestigious journal *American Economic Review*. They found that about three-fourths of the papers failed to distinguish between statistical and economic significance. For example, say the correlation between a father and son's income is found to be about 0.2. A new estimate may find a correlation, 0.20000000001, which is statistically significant but of no economic significance. Results that are statistically significant may be more readily published by leading journals and be more attractive to the media, but they may have no practical value. They don't help in the art of guesswork. As McCloskey and Ziliak implore, "Tell me the oomph of your coefficient; and do not confuse it with merely statistical significance."[8]

Nassim Taleb calls the fourth quadrant the realm of black swans, where there are complex payoffs and extreme outcomes. A classic pattern is a long string of small gains punctuated by a huge loss. In trading, for instance, a strategy may deliver profits that appear to be steady. This consistency may even encourage the trader to borrow money to enhance his modest gains. A long string of success, however, can lull the trader into thinking that he or she has a foolproof strategy until—*thud!*—the strategy leads to a large loss. A small sample in the fourth quadrant rarely gives an indication of the extreme outcomes that lie in wait.

3. Always consider a null hypothesis

You should always compare outcomes to what a simple model would generate. It takes some mental discipline to do this. Henny Youngman, the comedian known for his one-liners, had it right. Whenever someone asked, "How's your wife?" he'd reply, "Compared to what?"

Work by Andrew Mauboussin and Sam Arbesman offers an example of this approach.[9] They were interested in understanding the potential role of skill in determining results for mutual funds. They decided to focus on streaks, defined as successive years in which a fund generates a return better than the S&P 500.

The analysis proceeded in two steps. First, they analyzed the empirical record of streaks from 1962–2008, capturing more than 5,500 mutual funds. Based on a calendar year, they found that there were 206 streaks of five years, 119 streaks of six years, 75 streaks of seven years, 23 streaks of eight years, and 28 streaks of nine years (see the left side of table 11-1). These results, however, have no context. A streak of nine years appears impressive, for instance, but there's no way to know if it's simply the product of luck.

The second step of the analysis was to create a null model. Their model assumed that the probability that a given fund would beat the S&P 500 was equal to the fraction of funds that were active in that year and that also beat the index. For example, 52 percent of the funds outperformed the S&P 500 in 1993, so the null model assigned the same percentage probability that any fund would beat the market in that year. They then simulated the outcomes ten thousand times. The simulation tells us what we would expect by chance if the world were played over and over given the empirical parameters.

TABLE 11-1

Comparing empirical results with a null model: mutual fund streaks

Streak length	Empirical frequency	Null model frequency	Standard deviation in model
5	206	146.9	11.8
6	119	53.6	7.2
7	75	21.4	4.6
8	23	7.6	2.8
9	28	3.0	1.6

Source: Andrew Mauboussin and Sam Arbesman, "Differentiating Skill and Luck in Financial Markets with Streaks," *SSRN working paper*, February 3, 2011.

The researchers found that there were many more streaks in the empirical data than the null model generated. For instance, while 206 funds had streaks of five years, the null model estimated that only about 147 funds would attain that feat by chance alone. As table 11-1 shows, there were also more streaks of up to nine years than the model suggested. The null model provides context for interpreting actual events, answering the question, "Compared to what?" In this case, the results suggest that it is unlikely that luck alone can explain the empirical outcome.

Gary Loveman, the CEO of Caesar's Entertainment, likes to say there are three things that can get you fired from the casino company: stealing, sexual harassment, and running an experiment without a control group.[10] The difference between actual outcomes and outcomes defined only by luck provide a concrete way to quantify the contribution of skill.

4. Think carefully about feedback and rewards

Everybody wants to do better, no matter what the activity. An athlete wants to perform better, a musician wants an improved sound, a corporate executive wants to have a successful product and make a healthy profit. Doctors want their patients to be well, and TV producers want hit shows. The keys to improving performance include high-quality feedback and proper rewards.

As chapter 8 demonstrated, deliberate practice is essential to improving your performance in activities where luck plays a weak role. In reality, only a small percentage of people achieve expertise through deliberate practice. One reason is that many of us hit performance plateaus and are satisfied to stay there. We could improve our ability to drive a car, for instance, if we made a concerted effort to do so. But we're generally satisfied with our level of performance. There are simply a lot of situations where good enough is good enough. And there are even situations where good enough is better than best. We could, for example, work hard and become as good as the competitors at the Indy 500. But if we were that good, we'd probably be pretty frustrated driving in traffic. But for some activities, deliberate practice is called for if we want to reach for success.

Deliberate practice requires individuals to work just beyond their true ability. Deliberate practice also requires lots of timely and accurate feedback. It is hard work. It is tedious. The fact is that few of us are surrounded by coaches who can deliver a proper program with feedback, and we are not generally motivated to commit thousands of hours to mastering a given skill. Still, we need to keep the notion of deliberate practice in mind, whether we're coaching our child's sports team or training corporate executives. The core ideas of tailored practice, high-quality feedback, and hard work apply broadly.

In activities where luck plays a strong role, the focus must be on process. Where skill dominates, performance is a dependable barometer of progress. But where luck is a stronger force, the link between process and outcome is broken. A good process can lead to a bad outcome some percentage of the time, and a bad process can lead to a good outcome. Since a good process offers the highest probability of a good outcome *over time*, the emphasis has to be on process.

As we have already seen, the investment industry struggles with this point. Long-term outcomes certainly do give insight about an investment manager's skill, but in the short term the relationship between process and outcome is extremely unreliable. Yet the evidence shows that managers who do well in the short run get more money to manage and those who fare poorly lose assets, irrespective of the quality of their processes. Ideally, we would like to avoid rewarding outcomes in an environment that has lots of luck.

Rewards, a form of feedback, have gone awry in a number of areas. Perhaps no area is as noteworthy as what executives get paid to run companies. A vigorous market for mergers and acquisitions in the 1980s woke up many corporate managers and boards, focusing them on creating value. As a consequence, there was a watershed change in the way that executives were paid. Whereas only 1 percent of a

CEO's pay was tied to the stock price in 1985, 60 percent of pay was tied to it by 2005.[11] This might seem like a favorable development on the surface, and certainly a focus on more judicious capital is welcome. The problem is that stock options for employees became the primary means of paying executives.

As noted in chapter 9, stock options give the employee the right, but not the obligation, to purchase the company's stock at a set price (typically the price of the stock at the time of the grant). The options typically vest over a period of three to five years, and expire after ten years. So the employee benefits if the stock goes up but doesn't lose if the stock goes down. This would appear to provide the employee with an incentive to boost the stock price, a laudable goal if done properly. What's wrong with a stock option is that the payoff, or reward, reflects an enormous amount of randomness. A change in the price of a stock combines a set of expectations for the company's financial performance in the future and lots of variables that are outside of the company's control, including interest rates, the rate of general economic growth, regulations, the appetite for risk of investors, and so forth. Or, using our terminology, changes in prices are the result of some skill but also a great deal of luck.

The system of rewarding executives has no way to distinguish between skill and luck: a rising market benefits all companies, including the laggards, while a falling market penalizes all companies, including the leaders. In an article on executive pay, Alfred Rappaport, a retired professor at Northwestern's graduate school of business, noted that for the ten-year period ending in 1997, each of the top hundred largest public companies in the United States had a positive total return to shareholders. As he points out, that led to "huge gains from options for below-average performers."[12] In the first decade of the 2000s, a poor stock market meant that there were no gains from options for many above-average performers. The rewards were too detached from skill and the owners of stock options were paid, or not paid, primarily on factors beyond their control.

There is a way to deal with this that doesn't throw out the idea of rewarding people with stock options. To begin with, companies can index the price at which employees can exercise the options to a market index or a basket of stocks of an appropriate peer group. This takes a large step toward removing the randomness because the exercise price would rise when the market benefited from good luck and would drop when there was bad luck. In addition, the payoff of the options can cover a longer time period. Just as a larger sample helps to detect skill in an activity where lots of luck is involved, a longer period of time reduces the role of the market's vagaries. But not too many companies have tried these approaches.

Finally, here's an observation on compensation at many corporations. When employees are at lower levels within the organization, their pay tends to be modest relative to that of the executives, but their success tends to be based largely on skill. Managers can evaluate the results of an accounts receivable clerk, an entry-level salesperson, or a junior accountant reasonably well. Employees at the top of the organization are undoubtedly more skillful than their junior colleagues. But they make a lot more money and their success relies a great deal more on luck. Whether it's the success of a new strategy or remuneration based on stock, big bucks get paid for big luck. For many companies, skill determines the small stakes and luck determines the large stakes.

5. Make use of counterfactuals

One case for learning history is to gain some insight about how the future might unfold. The difficulty with this is that we see only the path that the world followed, while events could have taken many different turns. Once we know what happened, hindsight bias naturally envelops us. This is a bias that allows us to forget how unpredictable the world looked beforehand. So we come up with reasons to explain the outcomes that appear as if they were inevitable.

One way to avoid hindsight bias is to engage in *counterfactual thinking*, a careful consideration of what could have happened but didn't. If we accept that x played a role in causing y, then we have to consider how events would have unfolded had x not happened.

History is largely a narrative of cause and effect. After the fact, those connections appear as hardened fact, so we have to make a distinct effort to consider how things could have turned out differently. As Philip Tetlock and his colleagues argue, it is healthy to maintain some equilibrium "between factual and counterfactual methods of framing our questions about what had to be and what could have been."[13]

MusicLab, the experiment discussed in chapter 6, should give pause to anyone who believes that the world as we know it is the only one that could be. The experiment explicitly set up alternate social worlds and let them run in parallel. The results showed that there was no way to predict either which song would be the top hit or how successful it would be. The conditions of that experiment were vastly simpler than the real world, where it is easy to imagine that an even greater number of forces are directly causing the effects we see.

To maintain an open mind about the future, it is very useful to keep an open mind about the past. We need to work hard to fend off our natural tendency to view what happened as having been inevitable. Our minds simply want to explain what happened and close the case, but the world followed but one path among many possible ones. If we do the Rain Dance and it rains, then to the human brain, it looks like the dance caused the rain. In the more rational part of our brain, we know it's not true. Yet we dance on.

6. Develop aids to guide and improve your skill

We can hone our intuitions if we practice intently in environments that remain stable and linear. By and large, however, our guesswork isn't better because we rely on our intuition in the wrong situations.

Different activities require different methods of improving skill. Let's go across the luck-skill continuum from left to right.

First, the luck side of the continuum. Here skill still exerts a small influence but luck is stronger; the actions we take will succeed with some probability. There is no sure thing because of the power of luck. Examples include executing a corporate strategy (remember Sony's MiniDisc) or buying an apparently undervalued stock. In these situations, the focus must be on process. Good processes must be well grounded analytically, psychologically, and organization-ally. The analytical part requires finding a discrepancy between value and price that gives you an edge. For a company, this might be the ability to offer a product cheaper than the competition's. For a sports team manager it may be identifying a player who has skills that the market undervalues. For an investor, it's buying a stream of future cash flows for less than they are worth.

The psychological requirement means learning about the common biases that plague all of us and developing techniques to mitigate them. Making good decisions sometimes requires taking the time and effort to overcome our intuitions. For instance, we tend to be overcon-fident in our ability to make predictions. So we have to slow down and make sure that we are considering alternatives—not just what *did* happen but what *might have* happened—in a sufficiently wide range.

The final requirement is organizational, and it is often the result of a conflict between a principal and the agent acting on the prin-cipal's behalf. An executive, for example, is an agent for the share-holder (the principal). Excessive perquisites or compensation are examples of costs that hurt the shareholder but benefit the execu-tive. The goal of a good process is to minimize these costs by aligning the interests of the principals and agents. One way to do that is to make the agents, in this case the executives, into principals by giv-ing them a large chunk of stock. As both an agent and principal, the executive will have less motivation to make decisions that cost the owners.

Now let's consider the middle of the continuum. Tasks in this region combine the procedural with the novel. This is where a checklist can be very useful.[14] A doctor caring for a patient has to deal with the patient's primary ailment as well as attend to details such as inserting intravenous tubes. A checklist reduces the risk of missing a step and reminds a physician to follow accepted procedures and protocols. Physicians who introduced checklists for surgery in eight hospitals around the world claimed a sharp drop in complications, infections, and in-hospital death rates.[15]

A checklist is also helpful in a stressful situation. Emergencies make it harder to think clearly and act appropriately because the chemicals of stress actually disrupt the functioning of the frontal lobes, the seat of reason. A READ-DO checklist provides a recipe for action that lets you take concrete steps to address the problem, even when you're not thinking clearly. A friend at a prominent hedge fund told me that his firm has developed a checklist for responding when a company suddenly announces bad news. While the stocks of those companies always go down at first, sometimes the drop is nothing more than an opportunity to buy more shares. At other times it's best to sell the position. The checklist helps the employees keep their heads cool as they decide which is the better decision.

Dr. Peter Pronovost has done more to promote checklists in medicine than anyone else. If you're going to introduce a checklist, he emphasizes, you have to be careful. First, you have to design a good checklist. You have to introduce it to an accepting culture. And you have to accurately measure its effects. The checklist itself has to be useful and is best developed by the people who are going to use it. You may have to spend time converting the unbelievers. In many professions, there is the perception that a checklist suggests that you don't know what you're doing and have to be reminded. You have to overcome that resistance.[16] Checklists have never been shown to hurt performance in any field, and they have helped results in a great many instances. Finally, organizations that are serious about improving their performance must honestly and precisely measure how well their actions turn out. Measurement provides the basis for the feedback that allows for the continual improvement of skill.

At the right side of the continuum, the key to improvement is deliberate practice. In many cases, a coach or instructor creates the structure for this practice. Good coaches are valuable because of their deep knowledge of the skill and an outsider's ability to see and critique a student's performance. We all use coaches or teachers when we're beginning. But once we've developed some expertise, we go it alone. It can seem almost demeaning to ask for advice. Even so, we can all benefit from coaching, no matter how good we think we are.

That's because feedback is the single most powerful way to improve skill. The fact is most of us have what Philip Tetlock calls "belief system defenses," which conjure up ways to defend our choices and preserve our self images. Being truly open to feedback is difficult because it implies change—something we would prefer to avoid.[17] One simple and inexpensive technique for getting feedback is to keep a journal that tracks your decisions. Whenever you make a decision, write down what you decided, how you came to that decision, and what you expect to happen. Then, when the results of that decision are clear, write them down and compare them with what you thought would happen. The journal won't lie. You'll see when you're wrong. Change your behavior accordingly.

7. Have a plan for strategic interactions

Skill and luck are relevant to determining the winner in a one-on-one competition. The essential issue is how to get them to work in your favor whether you are the favorite or the underdog. If you are the stronger player, simplify the interaction to emphasize your skill. If you are the underdog, complicate the game to introduce more luck into the outcome. Underdogs that successfully increase the influence of luck will also increase their chance of winning. Take war as an example. Weaker combatants won a higher percentage of wars in the twentieth century than the nineteenth century because they learned not to go toe-to-toe with their stronger foe. Instead, they pursued alternative strategies and tactics, including those of guerrilla warfare.

Professor Clayton Christensen's theory of disruptive innovation shows how companies that are initially weaker overcome their more formidable competitors. One of his insights is that the stronger companies initially concede part of the market to the weaker companies or ignore them altogether.[18] The stronger companies allow the disruptors to win small battles, which allows to disruptors to improve their products and make money. The money makes them stronger and allows them to creep up into the richer parts of the market that their competitors inhabit. Eventually, the disruptors beat the bigger firms at their own game. Christensen's work shows that challengers almost never succeed by taking on the established companies in their core markets. The larger companies are simply too strong and too motivated. But they are often too smug to admit that a small, upstart firm could pose a threat. And therein lies the advantage for the little guy.

8. Make reversion to the mean work for you

We are all in the business of forecasting. Understanding and using the phenomenon of reversion to the mean is essential in making sound predictions. On one level, reversion to the mean is bland. It arises every time the correlation between two variables is not perfect. If a class of students takes one test this week and one test next week, the highest scorers this week are apt to have lower scores next week. The coefficient of correlation between the scores is less than 1.0, so there will be reversion to the mean. That very blandness makes the idea so difficult to understand. Reversion to the mean requires no cause, and humans are innately driven to find causes, even where they don't exist. So it is essential to take some time to understand *why* reversion to the mean happens, to what degree it happens, and what exactly the mean is.

Our most common mistake is simply failing to account for this influence at all when making predictions about what's going to happen in the future. Daniel Kahneman gives an example: Julie is a senior ₑe who read fluently when she was four years old. Estimate ₐade point average (GPA). Kahneman suggests that a common ₛwer is 3.7 (out of 4.0), well above average. The reason, of course, is ₜhat we naturally assume that since she was precocious, she would do well in college. But, in fact, there is little correlation between reading at a young age and how well we do in college. So a more reasonable estimate of Julie's GPA would be much closer to the average of her class. Even if she was precocious as a child, her performance as time goes on reverts to the mean: she becomes more like the average kid.[19]

Reversion to the mean is most pronounced at the extremes, so the first lesson is to recognize that when you see extremely good or bad results, they are unlikely to continue that way. This doesn't mean that good results will necessarily be followed by bad results, or vice versa, but rather that the next thing that happens will probably be closer to the average of all things that happen.

Perhaps the most important idea is that the rate of reversion to the mean relates to the coefficient of correlation. If the correlation between two variables is 1.0, there is no reversion to the mean. If the correlation is 0, the best guess about what the next outcome will be is simply the average. In other words, when there's no correlation between what you do and what happens, you'll see total reversion to the mean. That's why there's always a small expected loss when you play roulette, whether you've just lost or won chips. Simply having a sense of the correlations for various events can help guide us in making predictions.

9. Develop useful statistics

We are bombarded with statistics every day. It is also easy to accept that not all statistics are of equal value. The goal is to develop and use only the statistics that are persistent and predictive. *Persistent* means that the same thing, or nearly the same thing, happens over and over. Statistics that measure skilled activities are persistent. If a sniper hits the target 99 percent of the time, then you can feel pretty safe predicting that he's going to hit it the next time he shoots. Statistics that measure random activities are not persistent. *Predictive* means that the quantity you are measuring leads to the outcome you want. So knowing the sniper's rate of success tells you that he'll almost certainly accomplish his mission.

Hitting in baseball is another good example. Both teams want to generate as many runs as possible in an effort to win. On-base percentage correlates strongly with how many runs the team scores. That percentage is also a reasonably persistent statistic, since it is a good measure of the skill of hitters. In contrast, batting average has a weaker correlation with how many runs a team scores. In other words, it's less predictive. And since it reflects more luck, it is also less persistent. So we can conclude that a team's on-base percentage is the better statistic to use in predicting how a team's offense is going to do. You don't have to do any calculations to grasp this idea.

Seems like common sense, right? Yet it's shocking how often companies use statistics that have nothing to do with their own strategy or even the broader goal of making money. Furthermore, companies use those statistics to determine how much money their executives make. The old saying is, "What gets measured, gets managed." If we measure the wrong things, we will not achieve our goals.

If we measure how persistent and predictive a statistic is, we can plot different activities on the same matrix for comparison. This allows us to visually assess the trade-offs between persistence and predictability and to grasp the inherent value of statistics in various pursuits. For example, we can compare the growth of earnings per share to batting average in baseball. Such comparisons provide context so that we can understand the usefulness of a given statistic.

10. Know your limitations

The ideas and tools we've been contemplating in this book provide us with concrete ways to approach the vexing difficulties of untangling skill and luck. But it is very important to approach the task with a healthy sense of humility. Even as we take steps in the right direction, there's a great deal we don't know and can't know.

Context makes a huge difference. In many of the examples throughout this book, there have been clear conclusions:

- Skill explains 90 percent of the performance of professional basketball teams over a season.

- The growth of earnings per share is better correlated with total returns to shareholders than the growth of sales is.

- Tall fathers have sons who are tall but closer to the average stature of all sons.

In many situations, however, the context makes predicting more difficult. Mutual funds may beat the market only 40 percent of the time over long periods, but if a manager's style is in vogue, she might have a considerably higher probability of success. Further, the size of the sample you take and the length of time over which you measure are essential elements of making a prediction. And of course, you have to be using valid data. So it's important to balance the statistics and the context.

Another source of limitation is that things change. The rules of a game may evolve, a new regulation may be instituted, or the behavior of a crowd might go from wise to mad. In environments that are stable, we can develop our skills and make sound predictions. But the more things change, the less weight we can place on the past. Placement on the luck-skill continuum helps guide this thinking, but managing change is difficult nonetheless.

Finally, there is a realm where statistical methods don't apply. We can define the attributes of this realm—complex payoff and extreme outcomes—and learn to cope with it. But we must be careful to avoid using methods that are not suited to the task. Most of the big blowups in finance are a consequence of naively applying statistical methods to the world of black swans.

The goal of untangling skill and luck is to get better at the art of guessing well. Almost everyone acknowledges that everything in life combines skill and luck. But few of us are able to figure out the contribution that each makes to how well we achieve our goals. The aim of this book is to allow us to think clearly about skill and luck and to provide some analytical methods to untangle the two. We want to get better at the art of good guesswork.

TWO METHODS FOR CALCULATING THE AMOUNT OF REVERSION TO THE MEAN

Method 1

This method comes from Tom Tango (applied to Major League Baseball, 2011):

1. Calculate the standard deviation (observed) of winning percentage for all teams:

   Standard deviation (observed) = 0.070524

2. Calculate the standard deviation of luck ($p = .500$ and $n = 162$):

   $$\text{Standard deviation (luck)} = \sqrt{p*\left(\frac{1-p}{n}\right)} = 0.039284$$

3. Calculate the variance for observed winning percentage and for luck winning percentage:

   Variance (observed) = Standard deviation (observed)^2
   = 0.004974

   Variance (luck) = Standard deviation (luck)^2 = 0.001543

4. Calculate the variance of skill:

   Variance (observed) = variance (skill) + variance (luck)

   Variance (skill) = variance (luck) − variance (observed)

   Variance (skill) = 0.00343

5. Calculate the standard deviation of skill:

   Standard deviation (skill) = variance (skill)$^{\frac{1}{2}}$ = 0.05857

6. Find the number of games for which the standard deviation (skill) equals the standard deviation (luck):

   Standard deviation (skill) = 0.05857

   Standard deviation (luck) = 0.05852 when n = 73 games

7. Calculate c as full season games/full season games + reversion to the mean adjustment:

   $c = 162/162 + 73$
   $c = 0.69$

For a team that went 100–62, a .617 winning percentage, the estimated true winning percentage is:

Estimated true winning percentage = .500 + c (win percentage − .500)
$$= .500 + .69 (.617 - .500)$$
$$= .581$$

That estimated true winning percentage suggests a record of 94–68.

Method 2

This method calculates the James-Stein estimator.
   The equation is as follows:

Estimated true average = Grand average +
shrinking factor (observed average − grand average)

Estimated true winning percentage = .500 + c (win percentage − .500)

$$c = 1 - \frac{(k-3)\sigma^2}{\Sigma(y-\bar{y})^2}$$

where:

$$\sigma = \sqrt{\bar{y}\frac{(1-\bar{y})}{N}}$$

and

$$\bar{y} = .500$$

$$N = 162$$

so

$$\sigma = \sqrt{.500\frac{.500}{162}}$$

$$\sigma = 0.039284$$

$$\sigma^2 = 0.001543$$

and

$$k = 30$$

$$\Sigma(y-\bar{y})^2 = 0.1442$$

so

$$c = 1 - \frac{(30-3)(0.001543)}{0.1442}$$

$$c = 1 - \frac{0.0417}{0.1442}$$

$$c = 1 - 0.2892$$

$$c = 0.71$$

For a team that went 100–62, a .617 winning percentage, the estimated true winning percentage is:

Estimated true winning percentage = .500 + c (win percentage − .500)
$$= .500 + .71 \ (.617 - .500)$$
$$= .583$$

That estimated true winning percentage suggests a record of 94–68.

Calculation of the Sum of the Squared Differences Between the Win–Loss Percentage of Each Team and the League Average of 0.500

TABLE A-1

	2011 Team win–loss	Team win–loss vs. average	Team win–loss vs. average squared
Arizona Diamondbacks	58.0%	8.0%	0.6%
Atlanta Braves	54.9%	4.9%	0.2%
Baltimore Orioles	42.6%	−7.4%	0.5%
Boston Red Sox	55.6%	5.6%	0.3%
Chicago Cubs	43.8%	−6.2%	0.4%
Chicago White Sox	48.8%	−1.2%	0.0%
Cincinnati Reds	48.8%	−1.2%	0.0%
Cleveland Indians	49.4%	−0.6%	0.0%
Colorado Rockies	45.1%	−4.9%	0.2%
Detroit Tigers	58.6%	8.6%	0.7%
Florida Marlins	44.4%	−5.6%	0.3%
Houston Astros	34.6%	−15.4%	2.4%
Kansas City Royals	43.8%	−6.2%	0.4%
Anaheim Angels	53.1%	3.1%	0.1%
Los Angeles Dodgers	50.9%	0.9%	0.0%
Milwaukee Brewers	59.3%	9.3%	0.9%

	2011 Team win–loss	Team win–loss vs. average	Team win–loss vs. average squared
Minnesota Twins	38.9%	−11.1%	1.2%
New York Mets	47.5%	−2.5%	0.1%
New York Yankees	59.9%	9.9%	1.0%
Oakland A's	45.7%	−4.3%	0.2%
Philadelphia Phillies	63.0%	13.0%	1.7%
Pittsburgh Pirates	44.4%	−5.6%	0.3%
San Diego Padres	43.8%	−6.2%	0.4%
San Francisco Giants	53.1%	3.1%	0.1%
Seattle Mariners	41.4%	−8.6%	0.7%
St. Louis Cardinals	55.6%	5.6%	0.3%
Tampa Bay Devils	56.2%	6.2%	0.4%
Texas Rangers	59.3%	9.3%	0.9%
Toronto Blue Jays	50.0%	0.0%	0.0%
Washington Nationals	49.7%	−0.3%	0.0%
Standard deviation	0.070524	$\Sigma(y-\bar{y})^2 =$	0.1442

NOTES

Introduction — Sorting the Sources of Success

1. Jennifer 8. Lee, *The Fortune Cookie Chronicles: Adventures in the World of Chinese Food* (New York: Twelve, 2008); Jennifer 8. Lee, "Who Needs Giacomo? Bet on a Fortune Cookie," *New York Times*, May 11, 2005; and Michelle Garcia, "Fortune Cookie Has Got Their Numbers," *Washington Post*, May 12, 2005.

2. Gary Belsky, "A Checkered Career: Marion Tinsley Hasn't Met a Man or Machine That Can Beat Him at His Game," *Sports Illustrated*, December 28, 1992.

3. Jonathan Schaeffer, "Marion Tinsley: Human Perfection at Checkers?" *Games of No Chance* 26 (1996): 115–118.

4. Shlomo Maital, "Daniel Kahneman, Nobel Laureate 2002: A Brief Comment," *SABE Newsletter* 10, no. 2 (Autumn 2002): 2.

5. Daniel Kahneman and Amos Tversky, "On the Psychology of Prediction," *Psychological Review* 80, no. 4 (July 1973): 237–251.

6. Stanley Lieberson, "Modeling Social Processes: Some Lessons from Sports," *Sociological Forum* 12, no. 1 (March 1997): 11–35.

7. Strictly speaking, sabermetrics is the study of baseball through the use of statistics, and a sabermetrician focuses only on that sport. The term comes from the acronym "SABR," which stands for the Society for American Baseball Research. I use the term more generally to reflect the study of all sports through statistics.

8. Richard A. Epstein, *The Theory of Gambling and Statistical Logic*, rev. ed. (San Diego, CA: Academic Press, 1977), xv.

Chapter 1 — Skill, Luck, and Three Easy Lessons

1. Jeffrey Young, "Gary Kildall: The DOS That Wasn't," *Forbes*, July 7, 1997.

2. Harold Evans, *They Made America: From the Steam Engine to the Search Engine: Two Centuries of Innovators* (New York: Little, Brown and Company, 2004), 402–417.

3. Peyton Whitely, "Computer Pioneer's Death Probed—Kildall Called Possible Victim of Homicide," *Seattle Times*, July 16, 1994.

4. "Bill Gates Answers Most Frequently Asked Questions," http://insidemicrosoft.blogspot.com/2004/12/bill-gates-faqd.html.

5. For example, see John Rawls's theory of distributive justice. Rawls argues that even effort—which is typically associated with skill—can be the lucky result of upbringing: "Even the willingness to make an effort, to try, and to so be

deserving in an ordinary sense is itself dependent upon happy family and social circumstances." John Rawls, *A Theory of Social Justice* (Cambridge, MA: Belknap Press, 1971). For a good summary of Rawls's argument, see Michael J. Sandel, *Justice: What's the Right Thing to Do?* (New York: Farrar, Straus and Giroux, 2009); also, "Justice and Bad Luck," Stanford Encyclopedia of Philosophy at http://plato.stanford.edu/entries/justice-bad-luck/.

6. *Webster's Ninth New Collegiate Dictionary* (Springfield, MA: Merriam-Webster, Inc., 1988).

7. Nicholas Rescher, *Luck: The Brilliant Randomness of Everyday Life* (Pittsburgh, PA: University of Pittsburgh Press, 1995).

8. Gary Smith and Joanna Smith, "Regression to the Mean in Average Test Scores," *Educational Assessment* 10, no. 4 (November 2005): 377–399.

9. Kielan Yarrow, Peter Brown, and John W. Krakauer, "Inside the Brain of an Elite Athlete: The Neural Processes that Support High Achievement in Sports," *Nature Reviews Neuroscience* 10 (August 2009): 585–596.

10. Lisa B. Kahn, "The Long-Term Labor Market Consequences of Graduating from College in a Bad Economy," *Labour Economics* 17, no. 2 (April 2010): 303–316; and Peter Coy, "The Youth Unemployment Bomb," *Bloomberg BusinessWeek*, February 2, 2011.

11. The quote, "Luck is what happens when preparation meets opportunity" is often attributed to Lucius Annaeus Seneca, the Roman Stoic philosopher, but I could find no evidence that he actually said or wrote the phrase. The quote, "I'm a great believer in luck, and I find the harder I work, the more I have of it" is attributed to Thomas Jefferson. Here, too, I found no unequivocal evidence that he said it.

12. Richard Wiseman, *The Luck Factor: Changing Your Luck, Changing Your Life: The Four Essential Principles* (New York: Miramax, 2003). Along similar lines, see Ed Smith, *Luck: What It Means and Why It Matters* (London: Bloomsbury, 2012); Steve Gillman, *Secrets of Lucky People: A Study of the Laws of Good Luck* (Denver, CO: Outskirts Press, 2008); Max Gunther, *The Luck Factor: Why Some People Are Luckier than Others and How You Can Become One of Them* (Petersfield, UK: Harriman House, 2009); Thor Muller and Lane Becker, *Get Lucky: How to Put Planned Serendipity to Work for You and Your Business* (San Francisco, CA: Jossey-Bass, 2012); and Barrie Dolnick and Anthony H. Davidson, *Luck: Understanding Luck and Improving the Odds* (New York: Harmony Books, 2007).

13. Wiseman, *The Luck Factor*, 23–27.

14. *Webster's Ninth New Collegiate Dictionary* (Springfield, MA: Merriam-Webster, Inc., 1988).

15. Testimony of Annie Duke, House Committee on the Judiciary, "Establishing Consistent Enforcement Policies in the Context of Internet Wagers," November 14, 2007; see also Steven D. Levitt and Thomas J. Miles, "The Role of Skill Versus Luck in Poker: Evidence from the World Series of Poker," NBER working paper 17023, May 2011.

16. Stan Browne, Deb Clarke, Peter Henson, Frida Hristofski, Vicki Jeffreys, Peter Kovacs, Karen Lambert, Danielle Simpson, with the assistance of the Australian Institute of Sport, *PDHPE Application & Inquiry*, 2nd ed. (Melbourne, Australia: Oxford University Press, 2009), 150–151.

17. Sian Beilock, *Choke: What the Secrets of the Brain Reveal About Getting It Right When You Have To* (New York: Free Press, 2010).

18. K. Anders Ericsson, "The Influence of Experience and Deliberate Practice on the Development of Superior Expert Performance," in *The Cambridge Handbook of Expertise and Expert Performance*, ed. K. Anders Ericsson, Neil Charness, Paul J. Feltovich, and Robert R. Hoffman (Cambridge, UK: Cambridge University Press, 2006), 683–703; and K. Anders Ericsson, Ralf Th. Krampe, and Clemens Tesch-Römer, "The Role of Deliberate Practice in Acquisition of Expert Performance," *Psychological Review* 100, no. 3 (July 1993): 363–406.

19. Ben Mezrich, *Bringing Down the House: The Inside Story of Six MIT Students Who Took Vegas for Millions* (New York: Free Press, 2003).

20. Jeffrey Ma, *The House Advantage: Playing the Odds to Win Big in Business* (New York: Palgrave McMillan, 2010), 138.

21. Philip E. Tetlock, *Expert Political Judgment: How Good Is It? How Can We Know?* (Princeton, NJ: Princeton University Press, 2005).

22. William Poundstone, *Priceless: The Myth of Fair Value (and How to Take Advantage of It)* (New York: Hill and Wang, 2010), 199.

23. National Basketball Association (2007–2011), Premier League (2007–2011), Major League Baseball (2007–2011), and National Football League (2007–2011).

24. Howard Wainer, *Picturing the Uncertain World: How to Understand, Communicate, and Control Uncertainty Through Graphical Display* (Princeton, NJ: Princeton University Press, 2009), 5–15; also Howard Wainer, "The Most Dangerous Equation," *American Scientist* (May–June 2007): 249–256.

25. Wainer, *Picturing the Uncertain World*, 8–11.

26. Ibid., 11–14.

27. Stanley Lieberson, "Small N's and Big Conclusions: An Examination of the Reasoning in Comparative Studies Based on a Small Number of Cases," *Social Forces* 70, no. 2 (December 1991): 307–320.

28. Michael E. Raynor, Mumtaz Ahmed, and Andrew D. Henderson, *A Random Search for Excellence: Why "Great Company" Research Delivers Fables and Not Facts* (Deloitte Research, December 2009); and Andrew D. Henderson, Michael E. Raynor, and Mumtaz Ahmed, "How Long Must a Firm Be Great to Rule Out Luck? Benchmarking Sustained Superior Performance Without Being Fooled By Randomness," *Strategic Management Journal* 33, no. 4 (April 2012): 387–406.

29. Stephen M. Stigler, *Statistics on the Table: The History of Statistical Concepts and Methods* (Cambridge, MA: Harvard University Press, 1999), 173–188.

30. Nassim Nicholas Taleb, *The Black Swan: The Impact of the Highly Improbable*, 2nd ed. (New York: Random House, 2010), 361–373.

Chapter 2 — Why We're So Bad at Distinguishing Skill from Luck

1. See http://www.simonsingh.net/media/online-videos/699-2/.

2. John Lewis Gaddis, *The Landscape of History: How Historians Map the Past* (Oxford: Oxford University Press, 2002), 31.

3. Jonathan Gottschall, *The Storytelling Animal: How Stories Make Us Human* (Boston, MA: Houghton Mifflin Harcourt, 2012); see also Brian Boyd, *On the Origin of Stories: Evolution, Cognition, and Fiction* (Cambridge, MA: The Belknap Press,

2009), 155–158; and Robyn M. Dawes, *Everyday Irrationality* (Boulder, CO: Westview Press, 2001).

4. Lewis Wolpert, *Six Impossible Things Before Breakfast: The Evolutionary Origins of Belief* (London: Faber and Faber, 2006); see also Wolpert's Michael Faraday lecture for the Royal Society in 2000, http://royalsociety.org/events/2001/science-belief/.

5. Michael S. Gazzaniga, *The Ethical Brain: The Science of Our Moral Dilemmas* (New York: Harper Perennial, 2006), 148.

6. Michael S. Gazzaniga, *Human: The Science Behind What Makes Us Unique* (New York: HarperCollins, 2008), 294; see also Michael S. Gazzaniga, "The Split Brain Revisited," *Scientific American*, July 1998, 50–55. For another outstanding source for this discussion, see Richard Nisbett and Lee Ross, *Human Inference: Strategies and Shortcomings of Social Judgment* (Englewood Cliffs, NJ: Prentice-Hall, 1980).

7. Steven Pinker, *The Blank Slate: The Modern Denial of Human Nature* (New York: Viking, 2002), 43.

8. Hayden White, *Metahistory: The Historical Imagination in Nineteenth-Century Europe* (Baltimore, MD: The Johns Hopkins University Press, 1973), 5–7.

9. Arthur Danto, a professor of philosophy at Columbia University who has carefully analyzed what historians do, suggests that narrative sentences are fundamental to the craft. A narrative sentence is one that contains knowledge of the outcome. For example, you might say, "Smith said his game-winning shot felt good coming out of his hands." This is a narrative sentence because describing the shot as "game-winning" makes sense only if you know that his team won the game. Smith may have felt good about the shot at the time he took it, but he could not have known with any certainty that it would win the game. Danto argues that narrative sentences are the essence of historical explanation because without them, the historian would be chronicling facts without context. As events are happening, we can't fully understand their meaning until the implications are clear. You need the story's ending to make sense of the middle.

Once we know how the story ends, we sort through the facts looking for what caused the story to end in that particular way. We can't help it. Naturally, serious historians understand that they need to be very careful when trying to find causes, but they also realize that identifying the cause of an event is essential to what they do. Common mistakes include pointing to a single cause when there are many and finding a cause where none exists. For example, if you ask the question, "What caused World War I?" you will find many different answers. The assassination of Archduke Franz Ferdinand in Sarajevo preceded the beginning of World War I, but did it cause the war? See Arthur Danto, *Analytical Philosophy of History* (Cambridge, UK: Cambridge University Press, 1965). For a terrific discussion of history and what we can learn from it, see Duncan J. Watts, *Everything Is Obvious*: *Once You Know the Answer* (New York: Crown Business, 2011), 108–134; and Edward Hallett Carr, *What Is History?* (New York: Vintage Books, 1961), 113–143. Gaddis makes three sets of distinctions when considering causality. He starts with timing: causes that preceded an outcome more immediately are generally given more weight than those that are distant from the outcome. Next he considers exceptional versus general causes. If a hiker falls off a mountain path to his death, gravity would be a general cause and the specific alignment of circumstances would be the exceptional cause. General causes are necessary but not sufficient, while exceptional causes are "missteps" that are difficult to predict. The last distinction is between factual and counterfactual, a consideration of what could have been. While events unfolded in a particular way, counterfactual thinking would ask if it is plausible that they could have unfolded in a different way. Counterfactual thinking is akin to a lab experiment and asks what outcomes we would observe if we ran this experiment repeatedly. See Gaddis, *The Landscape of History*, 91–109. For a more detailed discussion of counterfactuals, see Philip E. Tetlock, Richard Ned Lebow, and Geoffrey Parker, eds., *Unmaking the West: "What-If?" Scenarios That Rewrite World History* (Ann Arbor, MI: University of Michigan Press, 2006).

10. Nassim Nicholas Taleb, *Fooled by Randomness: The Hidden Role of Chance in Life and in the Markets*, 2nd ed. (New York: ThomsonTexere, 2004), 210.

11. Baruch Fischhoff, "Hindsight ≠ Foresight: The Effect of Outcome Knowledge on Judgment Under Uncertainty," *Journal of Experimental Psychology: Human Perception and Performance* 1, no. 3 (August 1975): 288–299.

12. John Glavin, personal correspondence with the author.

13. Jim Collins, *Good to Great: Why Some Companies Make the Leap . . . and Others Don't* (New York: Harper Business, 2001).

14. Jerker Denrell, "Vicarious Learning, Undersampling of Failure, and the Myths of Management," *Organization Science* 14, no. 3 (May–June 2003): 227–243.

15. Michael E. Raynor, *The Strategy Paradox: Why Commitment to Success Leads to Failure (and What to Do About It)* (New York: Currency Doubleday, 2007), 18–49.

16. Ibid., 37.

17. John P. A. Ioannidis, "Why Most Published Research Findings Are False," *PLoS Medicine* 2, no. 8 (August 2005): 696–701.

18. John P. A. Ioannidis, MD, "Contradicted and Initially Stronger Effects in Highly Cited Clinical Research," *Journal of the American Medical Association* 294, no. 2 (July 13, 2005): 218–228.

19. David H. Freeman, "Lies, Damned Lies, and Medical Science," *The Atlantic*, November 2010.

20. J. Bradford DeLong and Kevin Lang, "Are All Economic Hypotheses False?" *Journal of Political Economy* 100, no. 6 (December 1992): 1257–1272.

21. Don A. Moore, Philip E. Tetlock, Lloyd Tanlu, and Max H. Bazerman, "Conflicts of Interest and the Case of Auditor Independence: Moral Seduction and Strategic Issue Cycling," *Academy of Management Review* 31, no. 1 (January 2006): 10–29.

22. For a sharp rebuke of this approach, see Stephen T. Ziliak and Deidre N. McCloskey, *The Cult of Statistical Significance: How the Standard Error Costs Us Jobs, Justice, and Lives* (Ann Arbor, MI: The University of Michigan Press, 2008).

23. Fiona Mathews, Paul J. Johnson, and Andrew Neil, "You Are What Your Mother Eats: Evidence for Maternal Preconception Diet Influencing Foetal Sex in Humans," *Proceedings of the Royal Society B* 275, no. 1643 (July 22, 2008): 1661–1668.

24. S. Stanley Young, Heejung Bang, and Kutluk Oktay, "Cereal-Induced Gender Selection? Most Likely a Multiple Testing False Positive," *Proceedings of the Royal Society B* 276, no. 1660 (April 7, 2009): 1211–1212.

25. Boris Groysberg, *Chasing Stars: The Myth of Talent and the Portability of Performance* (Princeton, NJ: Princeton University Press, 2010).

26. Ibid., 63.

27. Boris Groysberg, Lex Sant, and Robin Abrahams, "When 'Stars' Migrate, Do They Still Perform Like Stars?" *MIT Sloan Management Review* 50, no. 1 (Fall 2008): 41–46.

28. Two other examples are the gambler's and hot-hand fallacies. With the *gambler's fallacy*, people expect outcomes in a random series to reverse systematically. For example, if you flip heads on a coin three times in a row, subjects assess the probability of flipping a tails next at 70 percent. The reason is that people expect a short sequence to resemble a larger population, so that heads and tails roughly balance out. The *hot-hand fallacy* is when people expect a random series to continue. For instance, a basketball player who has made her last three shots is expected to make her next shot because she has a "hot hand." Here, it appears that the streak of success prompts individuals to overestimate the degree of skill, and hence overestimate probability of ongoing success. For a theoretical discussion of these fallacies, see Matthew Rabin and Dimitri Vayanos, "The Gambler's Fallacy and Hot-Hand Fallacies: Theory and Application," *Review of Economic Studies* 77, no. 2 (April 2010): 730–778. For empirical evidence of their modest but noteworthy effects, see Rachel Croson and James Sundali, "The Gambler's Fallacy and the Hot Hand: Empirical Data from Casinos," *Journal of Risk and Uncertainty* 30, no. 3 (May 2005): 195–209.

Chapter 3—The Luck-Skill Continuum

1. See Adam Horowitz, David Jacobson, Tom McNichol, and Owen Thomas, "101 Dumbest Moments in Business," *Business 2.0*, January 2007; and John Carney, "Playboy Chicks Crush Legg Mason," *Dealbreaker*, January 4, 2007.

2. Nassim Nicholas Taleb, *The Black Swan: The Impact of the Highly Improbable*, 2nd ed. (New York: Random House, 2010), 38–50; and Michael J. Mauboussin, *Think Twice: Harnessing the Power of Counterintuition* (Boston: Harvard Business Press, 2009), 107–108.

3. Matthew Rabin and Dimitri Vayanos, "The Gambler's Fallacy and Hot-Hand Fallacies: Theory and Application," *Review of Economic Studies* 77, no. 2 (April 2010): 730–778. For a discussion of why the gambler's fallacy is not a fallacy in other areas of life, see Steven Pinker, *How the Mind Works* (New York: W.W. Norton & Company, 1997), 346–347. The classic paper on this topic is Amos Tversky and Daniel Kahneman, "Belief in the Law of Small Numbers," *Psychological Bulletin* 76, no. 2 (1971): 105–110.

4. The structure of the game is also very important. Phil Birnbaum illustrates this point by comparing professional basketball to baseball. In basketball, each team has about one hundred possessions and scores roughly half of the time; in baseball, each team has forty plate appearances and gets on base roughly 40 percent of the time. So there is more opportunity to assert superiority

in basketball than in baseball. In basketball, the team that scores the most points wins. In baseball, the team that gets more players on base may not win. Success depends on the number of players who get on base and the concentration of hitting success. In basketball, five players dictate the outcomes; in baseball the contributions are dispersed among nine players. And finally, in basketball one player can take 40 percent of his team's shots, whereas in baseball the best offense players get only a bit more than one in nine plate appearances. The last two points increase the significance of superstars. See Phil Birnbaum, "'The Wages of Wins': Right Questions, Wrong Answers," *By the Numbers* 16, no. 2 (May 2006): 3–8.

5. See William Feller, *An Introduction to Probability Theory and Its Application*, vol. 1, 2nd ed. (New York: John Wiley & Sons, 1968).

6. To be more technical, when the variance of the distribution of luck is sufficiently large relative to the variance of the distribution of skill, it is possible for skillful people to do poorly and unskillful people to do well over the short term. Variance is a measure of how far the numbers in the distribution are spread out. The higher the ratio between the two values of variance in the distributions of luck and skill, the more important luck is in shaping the outcomes. Strictly, this holds when skill and luck are distributed normally. These distributions can be expressed with only a mean (μ) and standard deviation (σ). We will also consider distributions that are not normal.

7. Batting average is the number of hits divided by the number of at-bats. *At-bat* refers to the number of times a player takes a turn at the plate, or a plate appearance, less the times he is walked to first base or hit by a pitch. See Stephen Jay Gould, *Triumph and Tragedy in Mudville: A Lifelong Passion for Baseball* (New York: W.W. Norton & Company, 2004), 151–172.

8. Evolutionary biologists describe a similar phenomenon that they call the *red queen effect*, after the Red Queen in Lewis Carroll's *Through the Looking Glass*, who says, "It takes all the running you can do, to keep in the same place." The idea is that species coevolve in a way that maintains a competitive equilibrium. For a popular treatment, see Matt Ridley, *The Red Queen: Sex and the Evolution of Human Nature* (New York: Macmillan, 1994).

9. Wilbert M. Leonard II, "The Decline of the .400 Hitter: An Explanation and a Test," *Journal of Sport Behavior* 18, no. 3 (September 1995): 226–236.

10. Phil Rosenzweig, *The Halo Effect . . . and the Eight Other Business Delusions That Deceive Managers* (New York: Free Press, 2007).

11. John Brenkus, *The Perfection Point: Sport Science Predicts the Fastest Man, The Highest Jump, and the Limits of Athletic Performance* (New York: HarperCollins, 2010), 207–222.

12. Malcolm Gladwell, *Outliers: The Story of Success* (New York: Little, Brown and Company, 2008).

13. Ibid., 37.

14. For excellent accounts of DiMaggio's streak, see Kostya Kennedy, *56: Joe DiMaggio and the Last Magic Number in Sports* (New York: Sports Illustrated Books, 2011); and Michael Seidel, *Streak: Joe DiMaggio and the Summer of '41* (New York: McGraw Hill, 1988).

15. Gould, *Triumph and Tragedy in Mudville*.

16. Ibid.

17. My example of .300 versus .200 hitters makes a lot of simplifying assumptions, including that the probability of a hit during each turn at bat is stable and independent. That is not exactly true. But the point holds: more skillful players will have more streaks of success. For the quotations, see Gould, *Triumph and Tragedy in Mudville*, 185–186.

18. The James-Stein estimator is a refinement of what is known as Stein's paradox, based on the work of Charles Stein, a statistician at Stanford University. Stein's finding was originally considered paradoxical because it provides a method for estimating true means more accurately than the arithmetic average in all cases when three or more means are being estimated. (The arithmetic average still works better when there are two or fewer means.) Stein's paradox ran counter to traditional statistical theory, which proved that no other rule for estimating is uniformly better than the observed average. For more on Stein's paradox, see Bradley Efron and Carl Morris, "Stein's Paradox in Statistics," *Scientific American*, May 1977, 119–127; Stephen M. Stigler, "The 1988 Neyman Memorial Lecture: A Galtonian Perspective on Shrinkage Estimators," *Statistical Science* 5, no. 1 (February 1990): 147–155; and Bradley Efron and Carl Morris, "Data Analysis Using Stein's Estimator and Its Generalizations," *Journal of American Statistical Association* 70, no. 350 (June 1975): 311–319.

19. Efron and Morris, "Stein's Paradox in Statistics."

Chapter 4—Placing Activities on the Luck-Skill Continuum

1. For a discussion of how to beat the house in slots, see David Sklansky, *Getting the Best of It* (Henderson, NV: Two Plus Two Publishing, 2001), 199–212.

2. See Mike J. Dixon, Kevin A. Harrigan, Rajwant Sandhu, Karen Collins, and Jonathan A. Fugelsang, "Losses Disguised as Wins in Modern Multi-line Video Slot Machines," *Addiction* 105, no. 10 (October 2010): 1819–1824.

3. David L. Donoho, Robert A. Crenian, and Matthew H. Scanlan, "Is Patience a Virtue? The Unsentimental Case for the Long View in Evaluating Returns," *Journal of Portfolio Management* (Fall 2010): 105–120.

4. This is also essential to understanding when intuition applies. See Eric Bonabeau, "Don't Trust Your Gut," *Harvard Business Review*, May 2003, 116–123; David G. Myers, *Intuition: Its Powers and Perils* (New Haven, CT: Yale University Press, 2002).

5. Walter A. Shewhart, *Statistical Method from the Viewpoint of Quality Control* (1939; rept. New York: Dover, 1985).

6. Young Hoon Kwak and Frank T. Anbari, "Benefits, Obstacles, and Future of Six Sigma Approach," *Technovation* 26, nos. 5–6 (May–June 2006): 708–715.

7. Christopher Chabris and Daniel Simons, *The Invisible Gorilla: And Other Ways Our Intuition Deceives Us* (New York: Crown, 2010), 83.

8. Philip E. Tetlock, *Expert Political Judgment: How Good Is It? How Can We Know?* (Princeton, NJ: Princeton University Press, 2005); Dan Gardner, *Future Babble: Why Expert Predictions Are Next to Worthless, and You Can Do Better* (New York: Dutton, 2011); and Dan Gardner and Philip Tetlock, "Overcoming Our Aversion to Acknowledging Our Ignorance," *Cato Unbound*, July 2011.

9. Michael J. Mauboussin, *Think Twice: Harnessing the Power of Counterintuition* (Boston: Harvard Business Press, 2009), 101–118.

10. See http://www.advancednflstats.com/2007/08/luck-and-nfl-outcomes.html.

11. William M. K. Trochim and James P. Donnelly, *The Research Methods Knowledge Base*, 3rd ed. (Mason, OH: Atomic Dog, 2008), 80–81. For a terrific discussion of the topic, see Phil Birnbaum, "On Why Teams Don't Repeat," *Baseball Analyst*, February 1989.

12. According to Wikipedia, "Tom Tango" is an alias for an unidentified expert in statistical analysis of sports. He is also coauthor of *The Book*, an excellent reference for sabermetrics. You can see the discussion of variance and skill here: http://www.insidethebook.com/ee/index.php/site/article/true_talent_levels_for_sports_leagues/. For thoughts on how to expand this beyond the binomial model, see Tom M. Tango, Mitchel G. Lichtman, and Andrew E. Dolphin, *The Book: Playing the Percentages in Baseball* (Washington, DC: Potomac Books, 2007), 365–382.

13. Ian Stewart, *Game, Set and Math: Enigmas and Conundrums* (Mineola, NY: Dover Publications, 1989), 15–30.

14. Martin B. Schmidt and David J. Berri, "On the Evolution of Competitive Balance: The Impact of an Increasing Global Search," *Economic Inquiry* 41, no. 4 (October 2003): 692–704; and David J. Berri, Stacey L. Brook, Bernd Frick, Aju J. Fenn, and Roberto Vicente-Mayoral, "The Short Supply of Tall People: Competitive Imbalance and the National Basketball Association," *Journal of Economic Issues* 39, no. 4 (December 2005): 1029–1041.

15. In reality, professional athletes are probably four or more standard deviations better than the average of the eligible population. For an excellent discussion of the distribution of talent and why results look normal even though professional athletes are drawn from the extreme right tail of the talent distribution, see Tom Tango's essay, "Talent Distributions," at http://tangotiger.net/talent.html.

16. Martin B. Schmidt and David J. Berri, "Concentration of Playing Talent: Evolution in Major League Baseball," *Journal of Sports Economics* 6, no. 4 (November 2005): 412–419.

17. The NBA height statistics come from www.basketball-reference.com.

18. Berri, Brook, Frick, Fenn, and Vicente-Mayoral, "The Short Supply of Tall People." This conclusion has been challenged. See Phil Birnbaum, "'The Wages of Wins': Right Questions, Wrong Answers," *By the Numbers* 16, no. 2 (May 2006): 3–8. Birnbaum argues that the lack of balance reflects the structure of the game versus the composition of the players.

19. Daniel H. Pink, *Drive: The Surprising Truth About What Motivates Us* (New York: Riverhead Books, 2009), 29–32.

20. Powell measured parity using a Gini coefficient. The coefficient was developed by Corrado Gini, an Italian statistician, to measure income inequality. Zero represents perfect parity and 1.00 reflects maximum disparity. Powell found that the average Gini coefficient for U.S. companies was 0.60, with a standard deviation of 0.24. He found that the nonindustrial domains had an average Gini coefficient of 0.56, with a standard deviation exactly the same as the industrial sample. See Thomas C. Powell, "Varieties of Competitive Parity," *Strategic Management Journal* 24, no. 1 (January 2003): 61–86; and Thomas C. Powell and Chris J. Lloyd, "Toward a General Theory of Competitive Dominance: Comments and Extensions on Powell (2003)," *Strategic Management Journal* 26, no. 4 (April 2005): 385–394.

21. Andrew D. Henderson, Michael E. Raynor, and Mumtaz Ahmed, "How Long Must a Firm Be Great to Rule Out Luck? Benchmarking Sustained Superior

Performance Without Being Fooled By Randomness," *Strategic Management Journal* 33, no. 4 (April 2012): 387–406.

22. Charles MacKay, *Extraordinary Delusions and the Madness of Crowds* (New York: Three Rivers Press, 1995).

23. John C. Bogle, *Common Sense on Mutual Funds: Fully Updated 10th Anniversary Issue* (Hoboken, NJ: John Wiley & Sons, 2010).

24. Werner F. M. De Bondt and Richard H. Thaler, "Anomalies: A Mean-Reverting Walk Down Wall Street," *Journal of Economic Perspectives* 3, no. 1 (Winter 1989): 189–202.

25. Mark Grinblatt and Sheridan Titman, "The Persistence of Mutual Fund Performance," *Journal of Finance* 47, no. 5 (December 1992): 1977–1984; Darryll Hendricks, Jayendu Patel, and Richard Zeckhauser, "Hot Hands in Mutual Funds: Short-Run Persistence of Relative Performance, 1974–1988," *Journal of Finance* 48, no. 1 (March 1993): 93–129; and Stephen J. Brown and William N. Goetzmann, "Performance Persistence," *Journal of Finance* 50, no. 2 (June 1995): 679–698. For a dissenting view, see Mark M. Carhart, "On the Persistence in Mutual Fund Performance," *Journal of Finance* 52, no. 1 (March 1997): 57–82. Persistence tends to fade when researchers adjust fund returns for factors in stock returns. This, of course, leaves aside the possibility that the manager sought exposure to the factor.

26. Charles D. Ellis, "The Loser's Game," *Financial Analysts Journal* 31, no. 4 (July–August 1975): 19–26.

27. Peter L. Bernstein, "Where, Oh Where Are the .400 Hitters of Yesteryear?" *Financial Analysts Journal* 54, no. 6 (November–December 1998): 6–14; and Stephen Jay Gould, *Triumph and Tragedy in Mudville: A Lifelong Passion for Baseball* (New York: W.W. Norton & Company, 2004).

28. Russ Wermers, "Mutual Fund Performance: An Empirical Decomposition into Stock-Picking Talent, Style, Transactions Costs, and Expenses," *Journal of Finance* 55, no. 4 (August 2000): 1655–1695; and Laurent Barras, Olivier Scaillet, and Russ Wermers, "False Discoveries in Mutual Fund Performance: Measuring Luck in Estimated Alphas," *Journal of Finance* 65, no. 1 (February 2010): 179–216.

Chapter 5—The Arc of Skill

1. Ronald Blum, "Werth Agrees to $126 Million, 7-yr Deal with Nats," *AP Sports*, December 5, 2010.

2. Craig Calcaterra, "Scott Boras Explains the Jayson Werth Contract," *HardballTalk*, February 3, 2011.

3. Robert K. Adair, PhD, *The Physics of Baseball: Revised, Updated, and Expanded* (New York: HarperCollins, 2002), 29–46; and Michael Sokolove, "For Derek Jeter, on His 37th Birthday," *New York Times Magazine*, June 23, 2011.

4. David Epstein, "Major League Vision," *Sports Illustrated*, August 8, 2011.

5. Irving Herman, *Physics of the Human Body* (New York: Springer, 2007), 285.

6. Compiled by author from Richard Schulz and Christine Curnow, "Peak Performance and Age Among Superathletes: Track and Field, Swimming, Baseball, Tennis, and Golf," *Journal of Gerontology* 43, no. 5 (September 1988): 113–120; Scott M. Berry, C. Shahe Reese, and Patrick Larkey, "Bridging Different Eras in Sports," in *Anthology of Statistics in Sports*, ed. Jim Albert, Jay Bennett, and James

J. Cochran (Philadelphia, and Alexandria, VA: ASA-SIAM Series on Statistics and Applied Probability, 2005), 209–224; "How Important Is Age?" www.pro-football-reference.com/articles/age.htm; Tom Tango, "Aging Patterns," www.tangotiger.net/aging.html; Brian Burke, "How Quarterbacks Age," *Advanced NFL Stats*, August 30, 2011; J. C. Bradbury, "How Do Baseball Players Age?" *Baseball Prospectus*, January 11, 2010; Alain Haché, PhD, and Pierre P. Ferguson, BSc, "Hockey Fitness with Age," www.thephysicsofhockey.com; Joe Baker, Janice Deakin, Sean Horton, and G. William Pearce, "Maintenance of Skilled Performance with Age: A Descriptive Examination of Professional Golfers," *Journal of Aging and Physical Activity* 15, no. 3 (July 2007): 299–316; and J. C. Bradbury, "When Gender Matters and When It Doesn't," www.sports-reference.com/olympics/blog/?p=115.

7. The data on peak performance yields some other interesting points. In sports that require power and speed, women reach their peak performance at an earlier age than men. The age of peak performance has been relatively stable in most sports over time. For example, hockey players have always peaked in their mid-twenties. But the absolute level of peak performance has improved over the years. This is readily apparent in sports where a clock measures performance, including running, swimming, and rowing. For example, Roger Bannister ran a mile in 3 minutes and 59.4 seconds on May 6, 1954. Today the world record for the mile is 3 minutes, 43.13 seconds, held by Hicham El Guerrouj of Morocco.

8. Melissa L. Finucane and Christina M. Gullion, "Developing a Tool for Measuring the Decision-Making Competence of Older Adults," *Psychology and Aging* 25, no. 2 (June 2010): 271–288.

9. Gary Klein, *Sources of Power: How People Make Decisions* (Cambridge, MA: MIT Press, 1998).

10. Ray C. Fair, "Estimated Age Effects in Athletic Events and Chess," *Experimental Aging Research* 33, no. 1 (January–March 2007): 37–57.

11. Daniel Kahneman and Gary Klein, "Conditions for Intuitive Expertise: A Failure to Disagree," *American Psychologist* 64, no. 6 (September 2009): 515–526.

12. Tibor Besedeš, Cary Deck, Sudipta Sarangi, and Mikhael Shor, "Age Effects and Heuristics in Decision Making," *Review of Economics and Statistics* 94, no. 2 (May 2012): 580–595; and Tibor Besedeš, Cary Deck, Sudipta Sarangi, and Mikhael Shor, "Decision-Making Strategies and Performance Among Seniors," *Journal of Economic Behavior and Organization* 81, no. 2 (February 2012): 522–533.

13. George M. Korniotis and Alok Kumar, "Do Older Investors Make Better Investment Decisions?" *Review of Economics and Statistics* 93, no. 1 (February 2011): 244–265. Researchers found similar results for mutual fund managers. See Judith Chevalier and Glenn Ellison, "Are Some Mutual Fund Investors Better Than Others? Cross-Sectional Patterns in Behavior and Performance," *Journal of Finance* 54, no. 3 (June 1999): 875–899. Chevalier and Ellison write, "Older managers seem to fare much worse than their young counterparts. A manager who is one year older than another is expected to achieve a return that is 8.6 basis points lower."

14. Raymond B. Cattell, "Theory of Fluid and Crystallized Intelligence: A Critical Experiment," *Journal of Educational Psychology* 54, no. 1 (February 1963): 1–22.

15. For the sources of decline, see Julie M. Bugg, Nancy A. Zook, Edward L. DeLosh, Deana B. Davalos, and Hasker P. Davis, "Age Differences in Fluid

Intelligence: Contributions of General Slowing and Frontal Decline," *Brain and Cognition* 62, no. 1 (October 2006): 9–16. For no decline in variability, see Timothy A. Salthouse, "What and When of Cognitive Aging," *Current Directions in Psychological Science* 13, no. 4 (August 2004): 40–144.

16. Sumit Agarwal, John C. Driscoll, Xavier Gabaix, and David I. Laibson, "The Age of Reason: Financial Decisions over the Life Cycle and Implications for Regulation," *Brookings Papers on Economic Activity* (Fall 2009): 51–117.

17. Finucane and Gullion, "Developing a Tool for Measuring the Decision-Making Competence of Older Adults."

18. Agarwal et al., "The Age of Reason."

19. David Laibson, "The Age of Reason," presentation delivered June 2011. See http://www.economics.harvard.edu/faculty/laibson/files/Age%2Bof%2BReason.pdf.

20. David W. Galenson, *Old Masters and Young Geniuses: Two Life Cycles of Artistic Creativity* (Princeton, NJ: Princeton University Press, 2006).

21. Jonah Lehrer, "Fleeting Youth, Fading Creativity," *Wall Street Journal*, February 19, 2010.

22. Keith E. Stanovich, *What Intelligence Tests Miss: The Psychology of Rational Thought* (New Haven, CT: Yale University Press, 2009), 15.

23. Ibid., 63–66.

24. Keith E. Stanovich, "The Thinking That IQ Tests Miss," *Scientific American Mind*, November/December 2009, 34–39.

25. Stanovich, *What Intelligence Tests Miss*, 145.

26. Gerd Gigerenzer, *Calculated Risks: How to Know When Numbers Deceive You* (New York: Simon & Shuster, 2002).

27. Finucane and Gullion, "Developing a Tool for Measuring the Decision-Making Competence of Older Adults."

28. Bartley J. Madden, *CFROI Valuation: A Total System Approach to Valuing the Company* (Oxford: Butterworth-Heinemann, 1999), 18–63.

29. Robert R. Wiggins and Timothy W. Ruefli, "Sustained Competitive Advantage: Temporal Dynamics and the Incidence and Persistence of Superior Economic Performance," *Organization Science* 13, no. 1 (January–February 2002): 82–105; Robert R. Wiggins and Timothy W. Ruefli, "Schumpeter's Ghost: Is Hypercompetition Making the Best of Times Shorter?" *Strategic Management Journal* 26, no. 10 (October 2005): 887–911; and L. G. Thomas and Richard D'Aveni, "The Rise of Hypercompetition from 1950–2002: Evidence of Increasing Industry Destabilization and Temporary Competitive Advantage," working paper, October 11, 2004. For the relationship between age and performance, see Claudio Loderer and Urs Waelchli, "Firm Age and Performance," working paper, January 24, 2011.

30. James G. March, "Exploration and Exploitation in Organizational Learning," *Organization Science* 2, no. 1 (February 1991): 71–87.

Chapter 6—The Many Shapes of Luck

1. Jennifer Ordonez, "Pop Singer Fails to Strike a Chord Despite Millions Spent by MCA," *Wall Street Journal*, February 26, 2002. Hennessy had a comeback as Carly Smithson (her married name), coming in sixth place in the *American Idol* competition in 2008.

2. Bill Carter, "Top Managers Dismissed at ABC Entertainment," *New York Times*, April 21, 2004; and James B. Stewart, *Disney War* (New York: Simon & Schuster, 2006), 485–487, 527.

3. Thomas Gilovich, Robert Vallone, and Amos Tversky, "The Hot Hand in Basketball: On the Misperception of Random Sequences," *Cognitive Psychology* 17, no. 3 (July 1985): 295–314.

4. Jim Albert and Jay Bennett, *Curve Ball: Baseball, Statistics, and the Role of Chance in the Game* (New York: Springer-Verlag, 2003), 111–144. I also ran the simulation using different values than 90 percent for the "switch" parameter. The parameter that best fit the empirical data was in the range of 50–60 percent, which is similar to assuming the Mr. Consistent model.

5. Jim Albert, "Streaky Hitting in Baseball," *Journal of Quantitative Analysis in Sports* 4, no. 1 (January 2008): article 3; Trent McCotter, "Hitting Streaks Don't Obey Your Rules: Evidence That Hitting Streaks Aren't Just By-Products of Random Variation," *Baseball Research Journal* 37 (2008): 62–70; http://www. hardballtimes.com/main/article/the-color-of-clutch/; and Zheng Cao, Joseph Price, and Daniel F. Stone, "Performance Under Pressure in the NBA," *Journal of Sports Economics* 12, no. 3 (June 2011): 231–252.

6. Michael Bar-Eli, Simcha Avugos, and Markus Raab, "Twenty Years of 'Hot Hand' Research: Review and Critique," *Psychology of Sport and Exercise* 7, no. 6 (November 2006): 525–553; and Alan Reifman, *Hot Hands: The Statistics Behind Sports' Greatest Streaks* (Washington, DC: Potomac Books, 2011).

7. Frank H. Knight, *Risk, Uncertainty, and Profit* (New York: Houghton and Mifflin, 1921), and http://www.econlib.org/library/Knight/knRUP.html. Benoit Mandelbrot distinguishes between "mild" and "wild" chance. These terms neatly capture the spirit of this discussion; see Benoit Mandelbrot and Richard L. Hudson, *The (Mis)Behavior of Markets* (New York: Basic Books, 2004), 32–33.

8. William Goldman, *Adventures in the Screen Trade: A Personal View of Hollywood and Screenwriting* (New York: Warner Books, 1983), 39.

9. Matthew Salganik, "Prediction and Surprise," presentation at the Thought Leader Forum, Legg Mason Capital Management, October 14, 2011.

10. More formally, a power law is expressed in the form: $p(x) = Cx^{-\alpha}$, where C and α are constants. The exponent, α, is often shown as positive, although it is negative. Since x is raised to the power of α, the distribution is called a power law. The value of the exponent is typically $2 < \alpha < 3$. See M. E. J. Newman, "Power Laws, Pareto Distributions, and Zipf's Law," *Contemporary Physics* 46, no. 5 (September–October 2005): 323–351; and Aaron Clauset, Cosma Rohilla Shalizi, and M. E. J. Newman, "Power-law Distributions in Empirical Data," *SIAM Review* 51, no. 4 (2009): 661–703.

11. Matthew 13:12 from the King James version, www.kingjamesbibleonline. org/matthew-13-12.

12. See Robert K. Merton, "The Matthew Effect in Science," *Science* 159, no. 3810 (January 5, 1968): 56–63; and Daniel Rigney, *The Matthew Effect: How Advantage Begets Further Advantage* (New York: Columbia University Press, 2010). For a more detailed and nuanced discussion of path dependence, see Scott E. Page, "Path Dependence," *Quarterly Journal of Political Science* 1, no. 1 (January 2006): 87–115.

13. Albert-László Barabási and Réka Albert, "Emergence of Scaling in Random Networks," *Science* 286, no. 5439 (October 15, 1999): 509–512; Albert-László Barabási, *Linked: The New Science of Networks* (Cambridge, MA: Perseus Publishing, 2002), 86–89; and Duncan J. Watts, *Six Degrees: The Science of a Connected Age* (New York: W.W. Norton & Company, 2003), 108–111. Preferential attachment is also related to Gibrat's Law and a Yule process, or Yule distribution; see Herbert A. Simon, "On a Class of Skew Distribution Functions," *Biometrika* 42, no. 3/4 (December 1955): 425–440.

14. In ten thousand realizations of this model, red won 54 percent of the time, black 29 percent, yellow 12 percent, green 4 percent, and blue 1 percent. Contrast that with the starting probabilities: red at 33 percent, black 27 percent, yellow 20 percent, green 13 percent, and blue 7 percent. The strong get stronger and the weak get weaker.

15. Mark Granovetter, "Threshold Models of Collective Behavior," *American Journal of Sociology* 83, no. 6 (May 1978): 1420–1443. For a more sophisticated version, see Duncan J. Watts, "A Simple Model of Global Cascades on Random Networks," *Proceedings of the National Academy of Sciences* 99, no. 9 (April 30, 2002): 5766–5771.

16. Michael A. Cusumano, Yiorgos Mylonadis, and Richard S. Rosenbloom, "Strategic Maneuvering and Mass-Market Dynamics: The Triumph of VHS over Beta," *Business History Review* 66, no. 1 (Spring 1992): 51–94; Carl Shapiro and Hal R. Varian, *Information Rules: A Strategic Guide to the Network Economy* (Boston: Harvard Business School Press, 1999); and Jeffrey H. Rohlfs, *Bandwagon Effects in High Technology Industries* (Cambridge, MA: MIT Press, 2001).

17. W. Brian Arthur, *Increasing Returns and Path Dependence in the Economy* (Ann Arbor, MI: University of Michigan Press, 1994).

18. Sherwin Rosen, "The Economics of Superstars," *American Economic Review* 71, no. 5 (December 1981): 845–858.

19. Robert H. Frank and Philip J. Cook, *The Winner-Take-All Society: How More and More Americans Compete for Ever Fewer and Bigger Prizes, Encouraging Economic Waste, Income Inequality, and an Impoverished Cultural Life* (New York: The Free Press, 1995); and Robert H. Frank, *The Darwin Economy: Liberty, Competition, and the Common Good* (Princeton, NJ: Princeton University Press, 2011).

20. Xavier Gabaix and Augustin Landier, "Why Has CEO Pay Increased So Much?" *Quarterly Journal of Economics* 123, no. 1 (February 2008): 49–100; and Carola Frydman and Dirk Jenter, "CEO Compensation," *Annual Review of Financial Economics* 2 (December 2010): 75–102.

21. For example, Sherwin Rosen wrote, "Rest assured that prospective impresarios will receive no guidance here on what makes for box office appeal, sometimes said to involve a combination of talent and charisma in uncertain proportions. The distribution of talent is assumed to be fixed in the population of potential sellers and costlessly observable to all economic agents." (Rosen, "The Economics of Superstars.")

22. Gabaix and Landier, "Why Has CEO Pay Increased So Much?"; also see Marko Terviö, "The Difference That CEOs Make: An Assignment Model Approach," *American Economic Review* 98, no. 3 (June 2008): 642–668. For a classic

paper on this topic, see James C. March and James G. March, "Almost Random Careers: The Wisconsin School Superintendency, 1940–1972," *Administrative Science Quarterly* 22, no. 3 (September 1977): 377–409.

23. Robert Morse, "Methodology: Undergraduate Ranking Criteria and Weights," *USNews.com*, September 12, 2011. See http://www.usnews.com/education/best-colleges/articles/2011/09/12/methodology-undergraduate-ranking-criteria-and-weights-2012.

24. Donald G. Saari, *Chaotic Elections! A Mathematician Looks at Voting* (Providence, RI: American Mathematical Society, 2001).

25. For a popular article on this topic, see Malcolm Gladwell, "The Order of Things," *The New Yorker*, February 14, 2011, 68–75. Also see Michael N. Bastedo and Nicholas A. Bowman, "U.S. News & World Report College Rankings: Modeling Institutional Effects on Organizational Reputation," *American Journal of Education* 116, no. 2 (February 2010): 163–183; and Ashwini R. Sehgal, MD, "The Role of Reputation in U.S. News & World Report Rankings of the Top 50 American Hospitals," *Annals of Internal Medicine* 152, no. 8 (April 20, 2010): 521–525.

26. Matthew J. Salganik, Peter Sheridan Dodds, and Duncan J. Watts, "Experimental Study of Inequality and Unpredictability in an Artificial Cultural Market," *Science* 311, no. 5762 (February 10, 2006): 854–856.

27. Donald Sassoon, *Becoming Mona Lisa: The Making of a Global Icon* (New York: Harcourt, Inc., 2001).

28. Philip E. Tetlock, *Expert Political Judgment: How Good Is It? How Can We Know?* (Princeton, NJ; Princeton University Press, 2005), 128. For an in-depth discussion of this bias, see Daniel T. Gilbert and Patrick S. Malone, "The Correspondence Bias," *Psychological Bulletin* 117, no. 1 (January 1995): 21–38.

29. Ellen J. Langer and Jane Roth, "Heads I Win, Tails It's Chance: The Illusion of Control as a Function of the Sequence of Outcomes in a Purely Chance Task," *Journal of Personality and Social Psychology* 32, no. 6 (December 1975): 951–955.

30. Rakesh Khurana, *Searching for a Corporate Savior: The Irrational Quest for Charismatic CEOs* (Princeton, NJ: Princeton University Press, 2002), 23.

Chapter 7 — What Makes for a Useful Statistic?

1. Robert C. Hill, "When the Going Gets Rough: A Baldrige Award Winner on the Line," *Academy of Management Executive* 7, no. 3 (August 1993): 75–79.

2. More technically, you can say that reliability measures: variance (skill)/[variance (skill) + variance (luck)]. If the variance of luck is zero then you are left with variance (skill)/variance (skill), or a perfect correlation. If there is no skill you are left with zero/variance(luck) and zero reliability. See William M. K. Trochim and James P. Donnelly, *The Research Methods Knowledge Base*, 3rd. ed. (Mason, OH: Atomic Dog, 2008), 80–95.

3. Chris Spatz, *Basic Statistics: Tales of Distributions*, 10th ed. (Belmont, CA: Wadsworth, 2011), 87–119.

4. Standard deviation is a measure of variation from the average. A low standard deviation signifies that the values in the distribution are close to the average, and a high standard deviation signifies that they are far from average. In a

normal, bell-shaped distribution, 68 percent of the results are within one standard deviation of the average. See Phil Birnbaum, "On Correlation, r, and r-squared," *Sabermetric Research*, August 22, 2006, and http://sabermetricresearch.blogspot. com/2006/08/on-correlation-r-and-r-squared.html.

5. Trochim and Donnelly, *The Research Methods Knowledge Base*, 20–23.

6. Jim Albert, "A Batting Average: Does It Represent Ability or Luck?" working paper, April 17, 2004. See: http://bayes.bgsu.edu/papers/paper_bavg.pdf.

7. See "When Is the Observed Data Half Real and Half Noise?" www. insidethebook.com/ee, July 13, 2011.

8. David J. Berri and Martin B. Schmidt, *Stumbling on Wins: Two Economists Expose the Pitfalls on the Road to Victory in Professional Sports* (Upper Saddle River, NJ: FT Press, 2010), 33–39.

9. Michael Lewis, *Moneyball: The Art of Winning an Unfair Game* (New York: W.W. Norton & Company, 2003), 57 and 128. For a more detailed analysis, see Ben S. Baumer, "Why On-Base Percentage Is a Better Indicator of Future Performance than Batting Average: An Algebraic Proof," *Journal of Quantitative Sports* 4, no. 2 (April 2008): article 3.

10. Branch Rickey, "Goodby to Some Old Baseball Ideas," *Life*, August 2, 1954, 79–89.

11. Michael Lewis, "The King of Human Error," *Vanity Fair*, December 2011.

12. Alfred Rappaport, *Creating Shareholder Value: A Guide for Managers and Investors, Revised and Updated* (New York: Free Press, 1998); and Anant K. Sundaram and Andrew C. Inkpen, "The Corporate Objective Revisited," *Organization Science* 15, no. 3 (May–June 2004): 350–363. William Starbuck argues that performance measures are important not because they correlate with desired factors but rather because they can alter performance; see William H. Starbuck, "Performance Measures: Prevalent and Important but Methodologically Challenging," *Journal of Management Inquiry* 14, no. 3, September 2005, 280–286.

13. Frederic W. Cook & Co., "The 2010 Top 250: Long-Term Incentive Grant Practices for Executives," October 2010, www.fwcook.com/alert_letters/The_2010_Top_250_Report.pdf.

14. "Seven Myths of Executive Compensation," Stanford Business School, Closer Look Series, June 6, 2011, www.gsb.stanford.edu/cgrp/research/.../CGRP17-MythsComp.pdf.

15. John R. Graham, Campbell R. Harvey, and Shiva Rajgopal, "Value Destruction and Financial Reporting Decisions," *Financial Analysts Journal* 62, no. 6 (November/December 2006): 27–39.

16. Alfred Rappaport and Michael J. Mauboussin, *Expectations Investing: Reading Stock Prices for Better Returns* (Boston: Harvard Business School Press, 2001), 15–16.

17. Graham, Harvey, and Rajgopal, "Value Destruction and Financial Reporting Decisions."

18. Eugene F. Fama and Kenneth R. French, "Forecasting Profitability and Earnings," *Journal of Business* 73, no. 2 (April 2000): 161–175; and Louis K. C. Chan, Jason Karceski, and Josef Lakonishok, "The Level and Persistence of Growth Rates," *Journal of Finance* 58, no. 2 (April 2003): 643–684.

19. This point is also shown in Robert L. Hagin, *Investment Management: Portfolio Diversification, Risk, and Timing—Fact and Fiction* (Hoboken, NJ: John Wiley & Sons, 2004), 75–80.

20. Christopher D. Ittner and David F. Larcker, "Coming Up Short on Nonfinancial Performance Measurement," *Harvard Business Review*, November 2003, 88–95.

21. Sanford J. Grossman and Joseph E. Stiglitz, "On the Impossibility of Informationally Efficient Markets," *American Economic Review* 70, no. 3 (June 1980): 393–408.

22. Scott D. Stewart, CFA, John J. Neumann, Christopher R. Knittel, and Jeffrey Heisler, CFA, "Absence of Value: An Analysis of Investment Allocation Decisions by Institutional Plan Sponsors," *Financial Analysts Journal* 65, no. 6 (November/December 2009): 34–51; Amit Goyal and Sunil Wahal, "The Selection and Termination of Investment Management Firms by Plan Sponsors," *Journal of Finance* 63, no. 4 (August 2008): 1805–1847; Jeffrey Heisler, Christopher R. Kittel, John J. Neuman, and Scott D. Stewart, "Why Do Plan Sponsors Hire and Fire Their Investment Managers?" *Journal of Business and Economic Studies* 13, no. 1 (Spring 2007): 88–118; Diane Del Guercio and Paula A. Tkac, "The Determinants of the Flow of Funds of Managed Portfolios: Mutual Funds Versus Pension Funds," *Journal of Financial and Quantitative Analysis* 37, no. 4 (December 2002): 523–555; and Andrea Frazzini and Owen A. Lamont, "Dumb Money: Mutual Fund Flows and the Cross-Section of Stock Returns," *Journal of Financial Economics* 88, no. 2 (May 2008): 299–322.

23. Diane Del Guercio and Paula A. Tkac, "Star Power: The Effect of Morningstar Ratings on Mutual Fund Flow," *Journal of Financial and Quantitative Analysis* 43, no. 4 (December 2008): 907–936.

24. From the Morningstar, Inc., website: "Funds are ranked within their categories according to their risk-adjusted return (after accounting for all sales charges and expenses), and stars are assigned such that the distribution reflects a classic bell-shaped curve with the largest section in the center." http://www.morningstar.com/Help/Data.html#RatingCalc.

25. Christopher B. Philips and Francis M. Kinniry Jr., "Mutual Fund Ratings and Future Performance," Vanguard Research, June 2010.

26. K. J. Martijn Cremers and Antti Petajisto, "How Active Is Your Fund Manager? A New Measure That Predicts Performance," *Review of Financial Studies* 22, no. 9, September 2009, 3329–3365; and Antti Petajisto, "Active Share and Mutual Fund Performance," working paper, December 15, 2010.

The technical definition of active share:

$$\text{Active Share} = \frac{1}{2} \sum_{i=1}^{N} \left| \omega_{fund,i} - \omega_{index,i} \right|$$

where:

$\omega fund,i$ = portfolio weight of asset i in the fund
$\omega index,i$ = portfolio weight of asset i in the index
The sum is taken over the universe of all assets.

27. Jerker Denrell, "Random Walks and Sustained Competitive Advantage," *Management Science* 50, no. 7 (July 2004): 922–934.

Chapter 8—Building Skill

1. Daniel Kahneman and Gary Klein, "Conditions for Intuitive Expertise: A Failure to Disagree," *American Psychologist* 64, no. 6 (September 2009): 515–526.

2. Daniel Kahneman, *Thinking, Fast and Slow* (New York: Farrar, Straus and Giroux, 2011).

3. Gary Klein, *Sources of Power: How People Make Decisions* (Cambridge, MA: MIT Press, 1998).

4. Kahneman and Klein, "Conditions for Intuitive Expertise."

5. Robert A. Olsen, "Professional Investors as Naturalistic Decision Makers: Evidence and Market Implications," *Journal of Psychology and Financial Markets* 3, no. 3 (2002): 161–167.

6. Kahneman, *Thinking, Fast and Slow*, 97.

7. Ibid., 24.

8. Michelene T. H. Chi, Robert Glaser, and Marshall Farr, eds., *The Nature of Expertise* (Hillsdale, NJ: Lawrence Erlbaum Associates, 1988), xvii–xx.

9. David M. Cutler, James M. Poterba, and Lawrence H. Summers, "What Moves Stock Prices?" *Journal of Portfolio Management* 15, no. 3 (Spring 1989): 4–12.

10. These books include Geoffrey Colvin, *Talent Is Overrated: What Really Separates World-Class Performers from Everybody Else* (New York: Portfolio, 2008); Daniel Coyle, *The Talent Code: Greatness Isn't Born. It's Grown. Here's How* (New York: Bantam Books, 2009); Malcolm Gladwell, *Outliers: The Story of Success* (New York: Little, Brown and Company, 2008); David Schenk, *The Genius in All of Us: New Insights into Genetics, Talent, and IQ* (New York: Doubleday, 2010); and Matthew Syed, *Bounce: Mozart, Federer, Picasso, Beckham, and the Science of Success* (New York: Harper, 2010). For a more academic treatment of the topic, see Chi, Glaser, and Farr, eds., *The Nature of Expertise*; K. Anders Ericsson, ed., *The Road to Excellence: The Acquisition of Expert Performance in the Arts and Sciences, Sports and Games* (Mahwah, NJ: Lawrence Erlbaum Associates, 1996); K. Anders Ericsson, ed., *Development of Professional Expertise: Toward Measurement of Expert Performance and Design of Optimal Learning Environments* (Cambridge, UK: Cambridge University Press, 2009); K. Anders Ericsson and Jacqui Smith, eds., *Toward a General Theory of Expertise: Prospects and Limits* (Cambridge, UK: Cambridge University Press, 1991); K. Anders Ericsson, Neil Charness, Paul J. Feltovich, and Robert R. Hoffman, eds., *The Cambridge Handbook of Expertise and Expert Performance* (Cambridge, UK: Cambridge University Press, 2006); and Paul J. Feltovich, Kenneth M. Ford, and Robert Hoffman, eds., *Expertise in Context: Human and Machine* (Menlo Park, CA, and Cambridge, MA: AAAI Press and The MIT Press, 1997).

11. This discussion relies on Colvin, *Talent Is Overrated*, 65–72.

12. K. Anders Ericsson, Ralf Th. Krampe, and Clemens Tesch-Römer, "The Role of Deliberate Practice in Acquisition of Expert Performance," *Psychological Review* 100, no. 3 (July 1993): 363–406.

13. Atul Gawande, "Personal Best: Top Athletes and Singers Have Coaches. Should You?" *The New Yorker*, October 3, 2011.

14. Guillermo Campitelli and Fernand Gobet, "Deliberate Practice: Necessary But Not Sufficient," *Current Directions in Psychological Science* 20, no. 5 (October 2011): 280–285.

15. David Z. Hambrick and Elizabeth J. Meinz, "Limits on the Predictive Power of Domain-Specific Experience and Knowledge in Skilled Performance," *Current Directions in Psychological Science* 20, no. 5 (October 2011): 275–279; and David Z. Hambrick and Randall W. Engle, "Effects of Domain Knowledge, Working Memory Capacity, and Age on Cognitive Performance: An Investigation of the Knowledge-Is-Power Hypothesis," *Cognitive Psychology* 44, no. 4 (June 2002): 339–387.

16. See David Brooks, *The Social Animal: The Hidden Sources of Love, Character, and Achievement* (New York: Random House, 2011), 165; and Gladwell, *Outliers*, 78–79.

17. Kimberly Ferriman Robertson, Stijn Smeets, David Lubinski, and Camillia P. Benbow, "Beyond the Threshold Hypothesis: Even Among the Gifted and Top Math/Science Graduate Students, Cognitive Abilities, Vocational Interests, and Lifestyle Preferences Matter for Career Choice, Performance, and Persistence," *Current Directions in Psychological Science* 19, no. 6 (December 2010): 346–351.

18. Carol S. Dweck, *Mindset: The New Psychology of Success* (New York: Random House, 2006).

19. Daniel H. Pink, *Drive: The Surprising Truth About What Motivates Us* (New York: Riverhead Books, 2009).

20. Atul Gawande, "The Checklist: If Something So Simple Can Transform Intensive Care, What Else Can It Do?" *The New Yorker*, December 10, 2007.

21. Peter Pronovost, MD PhD, and Eric Vohr, *Safe Patients, Smart Hospitals: How One Doctor's Checklist Can Help Us Change Health Care from the Inside Out* (New York: Hudson Street Books, 2010).

22. Atul Gawande, *The Checklist Manifesto: How to Get Things Right* (New York: Metropolitan Books, 2009), 114–135.

23. Daniel Boorman, "Safety Benefits of Electronic Checklists: An Analysis of Commercial Transport Accidents," *Proceedings of the 11th International Symposium on Aviation Psychology*, 2001, 5–8.

24. For additional reading on how to create a checklist, see Brigette Hales, Marius Terblanche, Robert Fowler, and William Sibbald, "Development of Medical Checklists for Improved Quality of Patient Care," *International Journal for Quality in Health Care* 20, no. 1 (February 2008): 22–30; and Michael Shearn, *The Investment Checklist: The Art of In-Depth Research* (Hoboken, NJ: John Wiley & Sons, 2012).

25. Gawande, *The Checklist Manifesto*, 114–135.

26. Pronovost and Vohr, *Safe Patients, Smart Hospitals*, 175.

27. Steven Crist, "Crist on Value," in Beyer et al., *Bet with the Best* (New York: Daily Racing Form Press, 2001), 64.

28. Benjamin Graham, *The Intelligent Investor: A Book of Practical Counsel*, 4th rev. ed. (New York: Harper & Row, 1973), 281.

29. Michael J. Mauboussin, "Size Matters: The Kelly Criterion and the Importance of Money Management," *Mauboussin on Strategy*, February 1, 2006.

30. Scott Patterson, "Old Pros Size Up the Game," *Wall Street Journal*, March 22, 2008.

31. For a good summary of the heuristics and biases research, see Max H. Bazerman and Don Moore, *Judgment in Managerial Decision Making*, 7th ed. (Hoboken, NJ: John Wiley & Sons, 2009), 13–41.

32. Kahneman, *Thinking, Fast and Slow*, 278–288; and Daniel Kahneman and Amos Tversky, eds., *Choices, Values, and Frames* (Cambridge, UK: Cambridge University Press, 2000).

33. Eldar Shafir, Peter Diamond, and Amos Tversky, "Money Illusion," *Quarterly Journal of Economics* 112, no. 2 (May 1997): 341–374.

34. Hersh Shefrin and Meir Statman, "The Disposition to Sell Winners Too Early and Ride Losers Too Long: Theory and Evidence," *Journal of Finance* 40, no. 3 (July 1985): 777–790; and Terrance Odean, "Are Investors Reluctant to Realize Their Losses?" *Journal of Finance* 53, no. 5 (October 1998): 1775–1798.

35. From Seth Klarman's speech at Columbia Business School on October 2, 2008. Reproduced in *Outstanding Investor Digest* 22, nos. 1–2 (March 17, 2009): 3.

36. Graham, *The Intelligent Investor*, 287.

37. David F. Swensen, *Unconventional Success: A Fundamental Approach to Personal Investment* (New York: Free Press, 2005), 220–222.

38. Charles D. Ellis, "Will Business Success Spoil the Investment Management Profession?" *Journal of Portfolio Management* 27, no. 3 (Spring 2001): 11–15.

39. John Maynard Keynes, *The General Theory of Employment, Interest, and Money* (New York: Harcourt, Brace and Company, 1936), 157–158.

40. David Romer, "Do Firms Maximize? Evidence from Professional Football," *Journal of Political Economy* 114, no. 2 (April 2006): 340–365.

Chapter 9—Dealing with Luck

1. Stanley Meisler, "First in 1763: Spain Lottery—Not Even a War Stops It," *Los Angeles Times*, December 30, 1977, A5.

2. The story is in 1 Samuel, chapter 17. For an excellent translation, see Robert Alter, *The David Story* (New York: W.W. Norton & Company, 1999).

3. Unlike the prisoner's dilemma, a well-known model in game theory, Colonel Blotto has had little impact on real-world decisions. Because cooperation is the preferred outcome from the prisoner's dilemma and there is a good understanding of how repeated interactions lead to cooperation, decision makers have been able to use the model in practical settings. For example, the prisoner's dilemma nicely describes the emergence of the "live-and-let-live" system in trench warfare during World War I. In numerous instances, both sides learned that there would be retaliation for any aggression. So when one side showed restraint, the other side learned to reciprocate by also showing restraint. This cooperation spared many lives. The model has also been useful in international relations and business, among other areas.

4. For a formal treatment of the Colonel Blotto game, see Brian Roberson, "The Colonel Blotto Game," *Economic Theory* 29, no. 1 (September 2006): 1–24; and Russell Golman and Scott E. Page, "General Blotto: Games of Allocative Strategic Mismatch," *Public Choice* 138, nos. 3–4 (March 2009): 279–299. For a more informal discussion, see Scott E. Page, *The Difference: How the Power of Diversity Creates*

Better Groups, Firms, Schools, and Societies (Princeton, NJ: Princeton University Press, 2007), 112–114; Jeffrey Kluger, *Simplexity: Why Simple Things Become Complex (and How Complex Things Can Be Made Simple)* (New York: Hyperion, 2008), 183–185; and John McDonald and John W. Tukey, "Colonel Blotto: A Problem of Military Strategy," *Fortune*, June 1949, 102.

5. For this example of asymmetric conflict, I selected an Xa/Xb ratio of 0.13. Using Theorem 3 from Roberson, "The Colonel Blotto Game," the expected payoff is 2.5 percent with nine battlefields. Using Theorem 2, the expected payoff is 6.7 percent with fifteen battlefields. Related to this point, see Dan Kovenock, Michael J. Mauboussin, and Brian Roberson, "Asymmetric Conflicts with Endogenous Dimensionality," *Korean Economic Review* 26, no. 2 (Winter 2010): 287–305.

6. KC Joyner, *Blindsided: Why the Left Tackle Is Overrated and Other Contrarian Football Thoughts* (Hoboken, NJ: John Wiley & Sons, 2008), 76–77; and Brian Skinner, "Scoring Strategies for the Underdog: A General, Quantitative Method for Determining Optimal Sports Strategies," *Journal of Quantitative Analysis in Sports* 7, no. 4 (October 2011): article 11.

7. Michael Lewis, "Coach Leach Goes Deep, Very Deep," *New York Times Magazine*, December 4, 2005.

8. Clayton M. Christensen, *The Innovator's Dilemma: When New Technologies Cause Great Companies to Fail* (Boston: MA: Harvard Business School Press, 1997).

9. Clayton M. Christensen and Michael E. Raynor, *The Innovator's Solution: Creating and Sustaining Successful Growth* (Boston, MA: Harvard Business School Press, 2003).

10. Clayton M. Christensen, Scott D. Anthony, and Erik A. Roth, *Seeing What's Next: Using the Theories of Innovation to Predict Industry Change* (Boston: Harvard Business School Press, 2004).

11. Michael E. Raynor, *The Innovator's Manifesto: Deliberate Disruption for Transformational Growth* (New York: Crown Business, 2011).

12. Gautam Mukunda, "We Cannot Go On: Disruptive Innovation and the First World War Royal Navy," *Security Studies* 19, no. 1 (January 2010): 124–159.

13. Ivan Arreguín-Toft, *How the Weak Win Wars* (Cambridge, UK: Cambridge University Press, 2005). Another account of how underdogs win is in Jeffrey Record, *Beating Goliath: Why Insurgencies Win* (Washington, DC: Potomac Books, 2009). Arreguín-Toft is mentioned in a popular article: Malcolm Gladwell, "How David Beats Goliath: When Underdogs Break the Rules," *New Yorker*, May 11, 2009, 40–49.

14. Kenneth Waltz, *Theory of International Politics* (New York: McGraw Hill, 1979).

15. A pair of books published in 2011 develop this theme. See Tim Harford, *Why Success Always Starts with Failure* (New York: Farrar, Straus and Giroux, 2011); and Peter Sims, *Little Bets: How Breakthrough Ideas Emerge from Small Discoveries* (New York: Free Press, 2011).

16. Even if a sales increase is correlated with the advertising, there's no way to know for sure that the advertising caused the sales increase. But a controlled experiment is a good step in the right direction.

17. Randall A. Lewis and David H. Reiley, "Does Retail Advertising Work? Measuring the Effects of Advertising on Sales via a Controlled Experiment on Yahoo!" working paper, September 29, 2010.

18. Duncan J. Watts, *Everything Is Obvious*: *Once You Know the Answer* (New York: Crown Business, 2011), 187–213.

19. Sasha Issenberg, *The Victory Lab: The Secret Science of Winning Campaigns* (New York: Crown, 2012).

20. Alan S. Gerber, James G. Gimpel, Donald P. Green, and Daron R. Shaw, "How Large and Long-lasting Are the Persuasive Effects of Televised Campaign Ads? Results from a Randomized Field Experiment," *American Political Science Review* 105, no. 1 (February 2011): 135–150.

21. Nassim Nicholas Taleb, *The Bed of Procrustes: Philosophical and Practical Aphorisms* (New York: Random House, 2010).

22. Nassim Nicholas Taleb, "Antifragility, Robustness, and Fragility Inside the 'Black Swan' Domain," SSRN working paper, February 2011.

23. Nassim Nicholas Taleb and Mark Blyth, "The Black Swan of Cairo: How Suppressing Volatility Makes the World Less Predictable and More Dangerous," *Foreign Affairs* 90, no. 3 (May/June 2011): 33–39; Emanuel Derman distinguishes between models and theories, "Models are analogies; they always describe one thing relative to something else. Models need a defense or explanation. Theories, in contrast, are the real thing. They need confirmation rather than explanation. A theory describes an essence. A successful theory can become a fact." From Emanuel Derman, *Models. Behaving. Badly: Why Confusing Illusion with Reality Can Lead to Disaster, on Wall Street and in Life* (New York: Free Press, 2011), 59.

24. Aaron Lucchetti and Julie Steinberg, "Corzine Rebuffed Internal Warnings on Risk," *Wall Street Journal*, December 6, 2011; and Bryan Burrough, William D. Cohan, and Bethany McLean, "Jon Corzine's Riskiest Business," *Vanity Fair*, February 2012.

25. More formally, Taleb calls the first type of payoff *concave* and the second type *convex*. Convexity over an interval Δx satisfies the inequality:

$$\frac{1}{2}[f(x + \Delta x) + f(x - \Delta x)] > f(x)$$

Convexity can be local (present for a Δx of a certain size) and may become concave for a different Δx. See Taleb, "Antifragility, Robustness, and Fragility Inside the 'Black Swan' Domain."

Chapter 10—Reversion to the Mean

1. Francis Galton, "Regression Towards Mediocrity in Hereditary Stature," *Journal of the Anthropological Institute* 15 (1886): 246–263.

2. Stephen M. Stigler, *Statistics on the Table: The History of Statistical Concepts and Methods* (Cambridge, MA: Harvard University Press, 1999), 174.

3. Karl Pearson and Alice Lee, "On the Laws of Inheritance in Man: I. Inheritance of Physical Characters," *Biometrika* 2, no. 4 (November 1903): 357–462.

4. Daniel Kahneman, *Thinking, Fast and Slow* (New York: Farrar, Straus and Giroux, 2011), 181–182.

5. J. Martin Bland and Douglas G. Altman, "Some Examples of Regression Towards the Mean," *British Medical Journal* 309, no. 6957 (September 24, 1994): 780.

6. Stephen M. Stigler, "Milton Friedman and Statistics," in *The Collected Writings of Milton Friedman*, ed. Robert Leeson (New York: Palgrave Macmillan, 2012 [forthcoming]).

7. Horace Secrist, *The Triumph of Mediocrity in Business* (Evanston, IL: Bureau of Business Research, Northwestern University, 1933).

8. Milton Friedman, "Do Old Fallacies Ever Die?" *Journal of Economic Literature* 30 (December 1992): 2129–2132. For another account of mistakes surrounding reversion to the mean, see Marcus Lee and Gary Smith, "Regression to the Mean and Football Wagers," *Journal of Behavioral Decision Making* 15, no. 4 (October 2002): 329–342.

9. Daniel Kahneman and Amos Tversky, "On the Psychology of Prediction," *Psychological Review* 80, no. 4 (July 1973): 237–251.

10. Andrea Frazzini and Owen A. Lamont, "Dumb Money: Mutual Fund Flows and the Cross-Section of Stock Returns," *Journal of Financial Economics* 88, no. 2, (May 2008): 299–322.

11. Scott D. Stewart, CFA, John J. Neumann, Christopher R. Knittel, and Jeffrey Heisler, CFA, "Absence of Value: An Analysis of Investment Allocation Decisions by Institutional Plan Sponsors," *Financial Analysts Journal* 65, no. 6 (November/December 2009): 34–51.

12. Bradley Efron and Carl Morris, "Stein's Paradox in Statistics," *Scientific American*, May 1977, 119–127.

13. William M. K. Trochim and James P. Donnelly, *The Research Methods Knowledge Base*, 3rd ed. (Mason, OH: Atomic Dog, 2008), 166. More accurately, since r can take a value from 1.0 to −1.0, so too can c. A negative correlation suggests that above-average results are likely to be followed by below-average results, and vice versa. I have focused on positive correlations, but negative correlations can be very useful as well.

14. For a good summary of the Tom Tango method, see http://sabermetricresearch. blogspot.com/2011/08/tango-method-of-regression-to-mean-kind.html.

15. Efron and Morris, "Stein's Paradox in Statistics," 119–127.

16. As you can see in the appendix, my estimate came out to 73 games. Rounding it to an even number makes the calculation a little simpler, so I used 74 instead of 73.

17. For the story behind Bayes's theorem, see Sharon Bertsch McGrayne, *The Theory That Would Not Die: How Bayes' Rule Cracked the Enigma Code, Hunted Down Russian Submarines & Emerged Triumphant From Two Centuries of Controversy* (New Haven, CT: Yale University Press, 2011).

Chapter 11 — The Art of Good Guesswork

1. Horace B. Barlow, "Intelligence: the Art of Good Guesswork," in *The Oxford Companion to the Mind*, ed. Richard L. Gregory (Oxford: Oxford University Press, 1987), 381–383.

2. Ibid.

3. Amos Tversky and Daniel Kahneman, "Belief in the Law of Small Numbers," *Psychological Bulletin* 76, no. 2 (August 1971): 105–110.

4. Tom M. Tango, Mitchel G. Lichtman, and Andrew E. Dolphin, *The Book: Playing the Percentages in Baseball* (Washington, DC: Potomac Books, 2007).

5. Ibid.

6. Derek Carty, "When Hitters' Stats Stabilize," *Baseball Prospectus*, June 13, 2011, http://www.baseballprospectus.com/article.php?articleid=14215.

7. Deirdre N. McCloskey and Stephen T. Ziliak, "The Standard Error of Regressions," *Journal of Economic Literature* 34 (March 1996): 97–114.

8. Stephen T. Ziliak and Deirdre N. McCloskey, "Size Matters: The Standard Error of Regressions in the American Economic Review," *Journal of Socio-Economics* 33, no. 5 (November 2004): 527–546.

9. Andrew Mauboussin and Samuel Arbesman, "Differentiating Skill and Luck in Financial Markets With Streaks," SSRN working paper, February 3, 2011.

10. Gary Loveman, Interview on NPR's *Planet Money*, November 16, 2011. See http://www.npr.org/blogs/money/2011/11/15/142366953/the-tuesday-podcast-from-harvard-economist-to-casino-ceo.

11. Brian J. Hall and Jeffrey B. Liebman, "Are CEOs Really Paid Like Bureaucrats?" *Quarterly Journal of Economics* 113, no. 3 (August 1998): 653–691; and "2004 CEO Compensation Survey and Trends," *Wall Street Journal/Mercer Human Resource Consulting*, May 2005.

12. Alfred Rappaport, "New Thinking on How to Link Executive Pay with Performance," *Harvard Business Review*, March–April 1999, 91–101.

13. Philip E. Tetlock, Richard Ned Lebow, and Geoffrey Parker, eds., *Unmaking the West: "What-If?" Scenarios That Rewrite World History* (Ann Arbor, MI: University of Michigan Press, 2006).

14. Brigette Hales, Marius Terblanche, Robert Fowler, and William Sibbald, "Development of Medical Checklists for Improved Quality of Patient Care," *International Journal for Quality in Health Care* 20, no. 1 (December 11): 2007, 22–30.

15. Atul Gawande, MD, MPH, et al., "A Surgical Safety Checklist to Reduce Morbidity and Mortality in a Global Population," *New England Journal of Medicine* 360, no. 5 (January 29, 2009).

16. Peter Pronovost, MD, PhD, and Eric Vohr, *Safe Patients, Smart Hospitals: How One Doctor's Checklist Can Help Us Change Health Care from the Inside Out* (New York: Hudson Street Books, 2010).

17. Philip E. Tetlock, *Expert Political Judgment: How Good Is It? How Can We Know?* (Princeton, NJ: Princeton University Press, 2005), 129–143.

18. Clayton M. Christensen, *The Innovator's Dilemma: When New Technologies Cause Great Companies to Fail* (Boston: MA: Harvard Business School Press, 1997).

19. Daniel Kahneman, presentation at the Thought Leader Forum, October 7, 2011, http://thoughtleaderforum.com/957443.pdf.

BIBLIOGRAPHY

Adair, Robert K., PhD. *The Physics of Baseball: Revised, Updated, and Expanded*. New York: HarperCollins, 2002.

Agarwal, Sumit, John C. Driscoll, Xavier Gabaix, and David I. Laibson. "The Age of Reason: Financial Decisions over the Life Cycle and Implications for Regulation." *Brookings Papers on Economic Activity* (Fall 2009): 51–117.

Albert, Jim. "A Batting Average: Does It Represent Ability or Luck?" Working paper, April 17, 2004, http://bayes.bgsu.edu/papers/paper_bavg.pdf.

———. "Streaky Hitting in Baseball." *Journal of Quantitative Analysis in Sports* 4, no. 1 (January 2008): Article 3.

Albert, Jim, and Jay Bennett. *Curve Ball: Baseball, Statistics, and the Role of Chance in the Game*. New York: Springer-Verlag, 2003.

Alter, Robert. *The David Story*. New York: W.W. Norton & Company, 1999.

Arreguín-Toft, Ivan. *How the Weak Win Wars*. Cambridge, UK: Cambridge University Press, 2005.

Arthur, W. Brian. *Increasing Returns and Path Dependence in the Economy*. Ann Arbor, MI: University of Michigan Press, 1994.

Baker, Joe, Janice Deakin, Sean Horton, and G. William Pearce. "Maintenance of Skilled Performance with Age: A Descriptive Examination of Professional Golfers." *Journal of Aging and Physical Activity* 15, no. 3 (July 2007): 299–316.

Barabási, Albert-László. *Linked: The New Science of Networks*. Cambridge, MA: Perseus Publishing, 2002.

Barabási, Albert-László, and Réka Albert. "Emergence of Scaling in Random Networks." *Science* 286, no. 5439 (October 15, 1999): 509–512.

Bar-Eli, Michael, Simcha Avugos, and Markus Raab. "Twenty Years of 'Hot Hand' Research: Review and Critique." *Psychology of Sport and Exercise* 7, no. 6 (November 2006): 525–553.

Barlow, Horace B. "Intelligence: The Art of Good Guesswork." In *The Oxford Companion to the Mind*, ed. Richard L. Gregory. Oxford, UK: Oxford University Press, 1987, 381–383.

Barras, Laurent, Olivier Scaillet, and Russ Wermers. "False Discoveries in Mutual Fund Performance: Measuring Luck in Estimated Alphas." *Journal of Finance* 65, no. 1 (February 2010): 179–216.

Bastedo, Michael N., and Nicholas A. Bowman. "*U.S. News & World Report* College Rankings: Modeling Institutional Effects on Organizational Reputation." *American Journal of Education* 116, no. 2 (February 2010): 163–183.

Baumer, Ben S. "Why On-Base Percentage Is a Better Indicator of Future Performance than Batting Average: An Algebraic Proof." *Journal of Quantitative Sports* 4, no. 2 (April 2008): Article 3.

Bazerman, Max H., and Don Moore. *Judgment in Managerial Decision Making.* 7th ed. Hoboken, NJ: John Wiley & Sons, 2009.

Beilock, Sian. *Choke: What the Secrets of the Brain Reveal About Getting It Right When You Have To.* New York: Free Press, 2010.

Belsky, Gary. "A Checkered Career: Marion Tinsley Hasn't Met a Man or Machine That Can Beat Him at His Game." *Sports Illustrated*, December 28, 1992.

Bernstein, Peter L. "Where, Oh Where Are the .400 Hitters of Yesteryear?" *Financial Analysts Journal* 54, no. 6 (November–December 1998): 6–14.

Berri, David J., and Martin B. Schmidt. *Stumbling on Wins: Two Economists Expose the Pitfalls on the Road to Victory in Professional Sports.* Upper Saddle River, NJ: FT Press, 2010.

Berri, David J., Stacey L. Brook, Bernd Frick, Aju J. Fenn, and Roberto Vicente-Mayoral. "The Short Supply of Tall People: Competitive Imbalance and the National Basketball Association." *Journal of Economic Issues* 39, no. 4 (December 2005): 1029–1041.

Berry, Scott M., C. Shahe Reese, and Patrick Larkey. "Bridging Different Eras in Sports." In *Anthology of Statistics in Sports*, ed. Jim Albert, Jay Bennett, and James J. Cochran. Philadelphia, PA, and Alexandria, VA: ASA-SIAM Series on Statistics and Applied Probability, 2005, 209–224.

Bertsch McGrayne, Sharon. *The Theory That Would Not Die: How Bayes' Rule Cracked the Enigma Code, Hunted Down Russian Submarines & Emerged Triumphant From Two Centuries of Controversy.* New Haven, CT: Yale University Press, 2011.

Besedeš, Tibor, Cary Deck, Sudipta Sarangi, and Mikhael Shor. "Age Effects and Heuristics in Decision Making." *Review of Economics and Statistics* 94, no. 2 (May 2012): 580–595.

———. "Decision-Making Strategies and Performance Among Seniors." *Journal of Economic Behavior and Organization* 81, no. 2 (February 2012): 522–533.

Birnbaum, Phil. "On Why Teams Don't Repeat." *Baseball Analyst*, February 1989.

———. "'The Wages of Wins': Right Questions, Wrong Answers." *By the Numbers* 16, no. 2 (May 2006): 3–8.

———. "On Correlation, r, and r-squared." *Sabermetric Research* (August 22, 2006).

Blum, Ronald. "Werth Agrees to $126 Million, 7-yr Deal with Nats." *AP Sports*, December 5, 2010.

Bogle, John C. *Common Sense on Mutual Funds: Fully Updated 10th Anniversary Issue.* Hoboken, NJ: John Wiley & Sons, 2010.

Bonabeau, Eric. "Don't Trust Your Gut." *Harvard Business Review*, May 2003, 116–123.

Boorman, Daniel. "Safety Benefits of Electronic Checklists: An Analysis of Commercial Transport Accidents." *Proceedings of the 11th International Symposium on Aviation Psychology* (2001): 5–8.

Boyd, Brian. *On the Origin of Stories: Evolution, Cognition, and Fiction.* Cambridge, MA: The Belknap Press, 2009.

Bradbury, J. C. "How Do Baseball Players Age?" *Baseball Prospectus*, January 11, 2010.

Bland, J. Martin, and Douglas G. Altman. "Some Examples of Regression Towards the Mean." *British Medical Journal* 309, no. 6957 (September 24, 1994): 780.

Brenkus, John. *The Perfection Point: Sport Science Predicts the Fastest Man, The Highest Jump, and the Limits of Athletic Performance.* New York: HarperCollins, 2010.

Brooks, David. *The Social Animal: The Hidden Sources of Love, Character, and Achievement.* New York: Random House, 2011.

Brown, Stephen J., and William N. Goetzmann. "Performance Persistence." *Journal of Finance* 50, no. 2 (June 1995): 679–698.

Browne, Stan, Deb Clarke, Peter Henson, Frida Hristofski, Vicki Jeffreys, Peter Kovacs, Karen Lambert, Danielle Simpson, with the assistance of the Australian Institute of Sport. *PDHPE Application & Inquiry.* 2nd ed. Melbourne, Australia: Oxford University Press, 2009.

Bugg, Julie M., Nancy A. Zook, Edward L. DeLosh, Deana B. Davalos, and Hasker P. Davis. "Age Differences in Fluid Intelligence: Contributions of General Slowing and Frontal Decline." *Brain and Cognition* 62, no. 1 (October 2006): 9–16.

Burke, Brian. "How Quarterbacks Age." *Advanced NFL Stats*, August 30, 2011.

Burrough, Bryan, William D. Cohan, and Bethany McLean. "Jon Corzine's Riskiest Business." *Vanity Fair*, February 2012.

Calcaterra, Craig. "Scott Boras Explains the Jayson Werth Contract." *HardballTalk*, February 3, 2011.

Campitelli, Guillermo, and Fernand Gobet. "Deliberate Practice: Necessary But Not Sufficient." *Current Directions in Psychological Science* 20, no. 5 (October 2011): 280–285.

Cao, Zheng, Joseph Price, and Daniel F. Stone. "Performance Under Pressure in the NBA." *Journal of Sports Economics* 12, no. 3 (June 2011): 231–252.

Carhart, Mark M. "On the Persistence in Mutual Fund Performance." *Journal of Finance* 52, no. 1 (March 1997): 57–82.

Carney, John. "Playboy Chicks Crush Legg Mason." *Dealbreaker*, January 4, 2007.

Carr, Edward Hallett. *What Is History?* New York: Vintage Books, 1961.

Carter, Bill. "Top Managers Dismissed at ABC Entertainment." *New York Times*, April 21, 2004.

Carty, Derek. "When Hitters' Stats Stabilize." *Baseball Prospectus*, June 13, 2011.

Cattell, Raymond B. "Theory of Fluid and Crystallized Intelligence: A Critical Experiment." *Journal of Educational Psychology* 54, no. 1 (February 1963): 1–22.

Chabris, Christopher, and Daniel Simons. *The Invisible Gorilla: And Other Ways Our Intuition Deceives Us.* New York: Crown, 2010.

Chan, Louis K. C., Jason Karceski, and Josef Lakonishok. "The Level and Persistence of Growth Rates." *Journal of Finance* 58, no. 2 (April 2003): 643–684.

Chevalier, Judith, and Glenn Ellison. "Are Some Mutual Fund Investors Better Than Others? Cross-Sectional Patterns in Behavior and Performance." *Journal of Finance* 54, no. 3 (June 1999): 875–899.

Chi, Michelene T. H., Robert Glaser, and Marshall Farr, eds. *The Nature of Expertise.* Hillsdale, NJ: Lawrence Erlbaum Associates, 1988.

Christensen, Clayton M. *The Innovator's Dilemma: When New Technologies Cause Great Companies to Fail.* Boston: MA: Harvard Business School Press, 1997.

Christensen, Clayton M., and Michael E. Raynor. *The Innovator's Solution: Creating and Sustaining Successful Growth.* Boston, MA: Harvard Business School Press, 2003.

Christensen, Clayton M., Scott D. Anthony, and Erik A. Roth. *Seeing What's Next: Using the Theories of Innovation to Predict Industry Change.* Boston, MA: Harvard Business School Press, 2004.

Clauset, Aaron, Cosma Rohilla Shalizi, and M. E. J. Newman. "Power-Law Distributions in Empirical Data." *SIAM Review* 51, no. 4 (2009): 661–703.

Collins, Jim. *Good to Great: Why Some Companies Make the Leap . . . and Others Don't.* New York: Harper Business, 2001.

Colvin, Geoffrey. *Talent Is Overrated: What* Really *Separates World-Class Performers from Everybody Else.* New York: Portfolio, 2008.

Coy, Peter. "The Youth Unemployment Bomb." *Bloomberg Business Week,* February 2, 2011.

Coyle, Daniel. *The Talent Code: Greatness Isn't Born. It's Grown. Here's How.* New York: Bantam Books, 2009.

Cremers, K. J. Martijn, and Antti Petajisto. "How Active Is Your Fund Manager? A New Measure That Predicts Performance." *Review of Financial Studies* 22, no. 9 (September 2009): 3329–3365.

Crist, Steven. "Crist on Value." In Beyer et al., *Bet with the Best.* New York: Daily Racing Form Press, 2001.

Croson, Rachel, and James Sundali. "The Gambler's Fallacy and the Hot Hand: Empirical Data from Casinos." *Journal of Risk and Uncertainty* 30, no. 3 (May 2005): 195–209.

Cusumano, Michael A., Yiorgos Mylonadis, and Richard S. Rosenbloom. "Strategic Maneuvering and Mass-Market Dynamics: The Triumph of VHS over Beta." *Business History Review* 66, no. 1 (Spring 1992): 51–94.

Cutler, David M., James M. Poterba, and Lawrence H. Summers. "What Moves Stock Prices?" *Journal of Portfolio Management* 15, no. 3 (Spring 1989): 4–12.

Danto, Arthur. *Analytical Philosophy of History.* Cambridge: Cambridge University Press, 1965.

Dawes, Robyn M. *Everyday Irrationality.* Boulder, CO: Westview Press, 2001.

De Bondt, Werner F. M., and Richard H. Thaler. "Anomalies: A Mean-Reverting Walk Down Wall Street." *Journal of Economic Perspectives* 3, no. 1 (Winter 1989): 189–202.

Del Guercio, Diane, and Paula A. Tkac. "The Determinants of the Flow of Funds of Managed Portfolios: Mutual Funds Versus Pension Funds." *Journal of Financial and Quantitative Analysis* 37, no. 4 (December 2002): 523–555.

———. "Star Power: The Effect of Morningstar Ratings on Mutual Fund Flow." *Journal of Financial and Quantitative Analysis* 43, no. 4 (December 2008): 907–936.

DeLong, J. Bradford, and Kevin Lang. "Are All Economic Hypotheses False?" *Journal of Political Economy* 100, no. 6 (December 1992): 1257–1272.

Denrell, Jerker. "Vicarious Learning, Undersampling of Failure, and the Myths of Management." *Organization Science* 14, no. 3 (May–June 2003): 227–243.

———. "Random Walks and Sustained Competitive Advantage." *Management Science* 50, no. 7 (July 2004): 922–934.

Derman, Emanuel. *Models. Behaving. Badly: Why Confusing Illusion with Reality Can Lead to Disaster, on Wall Street and in Life.* New York: Free Press, 2011.

Dixon, Mike J., Kevin A. Harrigan, Rajwant Sandhu, Karen Collins, and Jonathan A. Fugelsang. "Losses Disguised as Wins in Modern Multi-line Video Slot Machines." *Addiction* 105, no. 10 (October 2010): 1819–1824.

Dolnick, Barrie, and Anthony H. Davidson. *Luck: Understanding Luck and Improving the Odds.* New York: Harmony Books, 2007.

Donoho, David L., Robert A. Crenian, and Matthew H. Scanlan. "Is Patience a Virtue? The Unsentimental Case for the Long View in Evaluating Returns." *Journal of Portfolio Management* (Fall 2010): 105–120.

Duke, Annie. "Establishing Consistent Enforcement Policies in the Context of Internet Wagers." Testimony Before the House Committee on the Judiciary November 14, 2007.

Dweck, Carol S. *Mindset: The New Psychology of Success.* New York: Random House, 2006.

Efron, Bradley, and Carl Morris. "Data Analysis Using Stein's Estimator and Its Generalizations." *Journal of American Statistical Association* 70, no. 350 (June 1975): 311–319.

———. "Stein's Paradox in Statistics." *Scientific American*, May 1977, 119–127.

Ellis, Charles D. "The Loser's Game." *Financial Analysts Journal* 31, no. 4 (July–August 1975): 19–26.

———. "Will Business Success Spoil the Investment Management Profession?" *Journal of Portfolio Management* 27, no. 3 (Spring 2001): 11–15.

Epstein, David. "Major League Vision." *Sports Illustrated*, August 8, 2011.

Epstein, Richard A. *The Theory of Gambling and Statistical Logic.* Rev. ed. San Diego, CA: Academic Press, 1977.

Ericsson, K. Anders, ed. *The Road to Excellence: The Acquisition of Expert Performance in the Arts and Sciences, Sports and Games.* Mahwah, NJ: Lawrence Erlbaum Associates, 1996.

———. "The Influence of Experience and Deliberate Practice on the Development of Superior Expert Performance." In *The Cambridge Handbook of Expertise and Expert Performance*, K. Anders Ericsson, Neil Charness, Paul J. Feltovich, and Robert R. Hoffman, eds. Cambridge: Cambridge University Press, 2006, 683–703.

———. ed. *Development of Professional Expertise: Toward Measurement of Expert Performance and Design of Optimal Learning Environments.* Cambridge, UK: Cambridge University Press, 2009.

Ericsson, K. Anders, and Jacqui Smith, eds. *Toward a General Theory of Expertise: Prospects and Limits.* Cambridge, UK: Cambridge University Press, 1991.

Ericsson, K. Anders, Ralf Th. Krampe, and Clemens Tesch-Römer. "The Role of Deliberate Practice in Acquisition of Expert Performance." *Psychological Review* 100, no. 3 (July 1993): 363–406.

Ericsson, K. Anders, Neil Charness, Paul J. Feltovich, and Robert R. Hoffman, eds. *The Cambridge Handbook of Expertise and Expert Performance.* Cambridge, UK: Cambridge University Press, 2006.

Evans, Harold. *They Made America: From the Steam Engine to the Search Engine: Two Centuries of Innovators.* New York: Little, Brown and Company, 2004.

Fair, Ray C. "Estimated Age Effects in Athletic Events and Chess." *Experimental Aging Research* 33, no. 1 (January–March 2007): 37–57.

Fama, Eugene F., and Kenneth R. French. "Forecasting Profitability and Earnings." *Journal of Business* 73, no. 2 (April 2000): 161–175.

Feller, William. *An Introduction to Probability Theory and Its Application.* Vol. 1. 2nd ed. New York: John Wiley & Sons, 1968.

Feltovich, Paul J., Kenneth M. Ford, and Robert Hoffman, eds. *Expertise in Context: Human and Machine.* Menlo Park, CA, and Cambridge, MA: AAAI Press and The MIT Press, 1997.

Finucane, Melissa L., and Christina M. Gullion. "Developing a Tool for Measuring the Decision-Making Competence of Older Adults." *Psychology and Aging* 25, no. 2 (June 2010): 271–288.

Fischhoff, Baruch. "Hindsight ≠ Foresight: The Effect of Outcome Knowledge on Judgment Under Uncertainty." *Journal of Experimental Psychology: Human Perception and Performance* 1, no. 3 (August 1975): 288–299.

Frank, Robert H. *The Darwin Economy: Liberty, Competition, and the Common Good.* Princeton, NJ: Princeton University Press, 2011.

Frank, Robert H., and Philip J. Cook. *The Winner-Take-All Society: How More and More Americans Compete for Ever Fewer and Bigger Prizes, Encouraging Economic Waste, Income Inequality, and an Impoverished Cultural Life.* New York: The Free Press, 1995.

Frazzini, Andrea, and Owen A. Lamont. "Dumb Money: Mutual Fund Flows and the Cross-Section of Stock Returns." *Journal of Financial Economics* 88, no. 2 (May 2008): 299–322.

Freeman, David H. "Lies, Damned Lies, and Medical Science." *The Atlantic*, November 2010.

Friedman, Milton. "Do Old Fallacies Ever Die?" *Journal of Economic Literature* 30 (December 1992): 2129–2132.

Frydman, Carola, and Dirk Jenter. "CEO Compensation." *Annual Review of Financial Economics* 2 (December 2010): 75–102.

Gabaix, Xavier, and Augustin Landier. "Why Has CEO Pay Increased So Much?" *The Quarterly Journal of Economics* 123, no. 1 (February 2008): 49–100.

Galenson, David W. *Old Masters and Young Geniuses: Two Life Cycles of Artistic Creativity.* Princeton, NJ: Princeton University Press, 2006.

Galton, Francis. "Regression Towards Mediocrity in Hereditary Stature." *Journal of the Anthropological Institute* 15 (1886): 246–263.

Garcia, Michelle. "Fortune Cookie Has Got Their Numbers." *Washington Post*, May 12, 2005.

Gardner, Dan. *Future Babble: Why Expert Predictions Are Next to Worthless, and You Can Do Better.* New York: Dutton, 2011.

Gardner, Dan, and Philip Tetlock. "Overcoming Our Aversion to Acknowledging Our Ignorance." *Cato Unbound*, July 2011.

Gawande, Atul. "The Checklist: If Something So Simple Can Transform Intensive Care, What Else Can It Do?" *The New Yorker*, December 10, 2007.

———. *The Checklist Manifesto: How to Get Things Right.* New York: Metropolitan Books, 2009.

———. "Personal Best: Top Athletes and Singers Have Coaches. Should You?" *The New Yorker*, October 3, 2011.

Gawande, Atul, MD, MPH, et al. "A Surgical Safety Checklist to Reduce Morbidity and Mortality in a Global Population." *New England Journal of Medicine* 360, no. 5 (January 29): 2009.

Gazzaniga, Michael S. "The Split Brain Revisited." *Scientific American*, July 1998, 50–55.

———. *The Ethical Brain: The Science of Our Moral Dilemmas.* New York: Harper Perennial, 2006.

———. *Human: The Science Behind What Makes Us Unique.* New York: HarperCollins, 2008.

Gerber, Alan S., James G. Gimpel, Donald P. Green, and Daron R. Shaw. "How Large and Long-lasting Are the Persuasive Effects of Televised Campaign Ads? Results from a Randomized Field Experiment." *American Political Science Review* 105, no. 1 (February 2011): 135–150.

Gigerenzer, Gerd. *Calculated Risks: How to Know When Numbers Deceive You.* New York: Simon & Shuster, 2002.

Gilbert, Daniel T., and Patrick S. Malone. "The Correspondence Bias." *Psychological Bulletin* 117, no. 1 (January 1995): 21–38.

Gillman, Steve. *Secrets of Lucky People: A Study of the Laws of Good Luck.* Denver, CO: Outskirts Press, 2008.

Gilovich, Thomas, Robert Vallone, and Amos Tversky. "The Hot Hand in Basketball: On the Misperception of Random Sequences." *Cognitive Psychology* 17, no. 3 (July 1985): 295–314.

Gladwell, Malcolm. *Outliers: The Story of Success.* New York: Little, Brown and Company, 2008.

———. "How David Beats Goliath: When Underdogs Break the Rules." *The New Yorker*, May 11, 2009, 40–49.

———. "The Order of Things." *The New Yorker*, February 14, 2011, 68–75.

Goldman, William. *Adventures in the Screen Trade: A Personal View of Hollywood and Screenwriting.* New York: Warner Books, 1983.

Golman, Russell, and Scott E. Page. "General Blotto: Games of Allocative Strategic Mismatch." *Public Choice* 138, nos. 3–4 (March 2009): 279–299.

Gottschall, Jonathan. *The Storytelling Animal: How Stories Make Us Human.* Boston, MA: Houghton Mifflin Harcourt, 2012.

Gould, Stephen Jay. *Triumph and Tragedy in Mudville: A Lifelong Passion for Baseball.* New York: W.W. Norton & Company, 2004.

Goyal, Amit, and Sunil Wahal. "The Selection and Termination of Investment Management Firms by Plan Sponsors." *Journal of Finance* 63, no. 4 (August 2008): 1805–1847.

Graham, Benjamin. *The Intelligent Investor: A Book of Practical Counsel, Fourth Revised Edition.* New York: Harper & Row, 1973.

Graham, John R., Campbell R. Harvey, and Shiva Rajgopal. "Value Destruction and Financial Reporting Decisions." *Financial Analysts Journal* 62, no. 6 (November/December 2006): 27–39.

Granovetter, Mark. "Threshold Models of Collective Behavior." *American Journal of Sociology* 83, no. 6 (May 1978): 1420–1443.

Grinblatt, Mark, and Sheridan Titman. "The Persistence of Mutual Fund Performance." *Journal of Finance* 47, no. 5 (December 1992): 1977–1984.

Grossman, Sanford J., and Joseph E. Stiglitz. "On the Impossibility of Informationally Efficient Markets." *American Economic Review* 70, no. 3 (June 1980): 393–408.

Groysberg, Boris. *Chasing Stars: The Myth of Talent and the Portability of Performance.* Princeton, NJ: Princeton University Press, 2010.

Groysberg, Boris, Lex Sant, and Robin Abrahams. "When 'Stars' Migrate, Do They Still Perform Like Stars?" *MIT Sloan Management Review* 50, no. 1 (Fall 2008): 41–46.

Gunther, Max. *The Luck Factor: Why Some People Are Luckier than Others and How You Can Become One of Them.* Petersfield, UK: Harriman House, 2009.

Hagin, Robert L. *Investment Management: Portfolio Diversification, Risk, and Timing—Fact and Fiction.* Hoboken, NJ: John Wiley & Sons, 2004.

Hales, Brigette, Marius Terblanche, Robert Fowler, and William Sibbald. "Development of Medical Checklists for Improved Quality of Patient Care." *International Journal for Quality in Health Care* 20, no. 1 (February 2008): 22–30.

Hall, Brian J., and Jeffrey B. Liebman. "Are CEOs Really Paid Like Bureaucrats?" *Quarterly Journal of Economics* 113, no. 3 (August 1998): 653–691.

Hambrick, David Z., and Randall W. Engle. "Effects of Domain Knowledge, Working Memory Capacity, and Age on Cognitive Performance: An Investigation of the Knowledge-Is-Power Hypothesis." *Cognitive Psychology* 44, no. 4 (June 2002): 339–387.

Hambrick, David Z., and Elizabeth J. Meinz. "Limits on the Predictive Power of Domain-Specific Experience and Knowledge in Skilled Performance." *Current Directions in Psychological Science* 20, no. 5 (October 2011): 275–279.

Harford, Tim. *Why Success Always Starts with Failure.* New York: Farrar, Straus and Giroux, 2011.

Heisler, Jeffrey, Christopher R. Kittel, John J. Neuman, and Scott D. Stewart. "Why Do Plan Sponsors Hire and Fire Their Investment Managers?" *Journal of Business and Economic Studies* 13, no. 1 (Spring 2007): 88–118.

Henderson, Andrew D., Michael E. Raynor, and Mumtaz Ahmed. "How Long Must a Firm Be Great to Rule Out Luck? Benchmarking Sustained Superior Performance Without Being Fooled By Randomness." *Strategic Management Journal* 33, no. 4 (April 2012): 387–406.

Hendricks, Darryll, Jayendu Patel, and Richard Zeckhauser. "Hot Hands in Mutual Funds: Short-Run Persistence of Relative Performance, 1974–1988." *Journal of Finance* 48, no. 1 (March 1993): 93–129.

Herman, Irving. *Physics of the Human Body.* New York: Springer, 2007.

Hill, Robert C. "When the Going Gets Rough: A Baldrige Award Winner on the Line." *Academy of Management Executive* 7, no. 3 (August 1993): 75–79.

Horowitz, Adam, David Jacobson, Tom McNichol, and Owen Thomas. "101 Dumbest Moments in Business." *Business 2.0,* January 2007.

Ioannidis, John P. A., MD. "Contradicted and Initially Stronger Effects in Highly Cited Clinical Research." *Journal of the American Medical Association* 294, no. 2 (July 13, 2005): 218–228.

———. "Why Most Published Research Findings Are False." *PLoS Medicine* 2, no. 8 (August 2005): 696–701.

Issenberg, Sasha. *The Victory Lab: The Secret Science of Winning Campaigns.* New York: Crown, 2012.

Ittner, Christopher D., and David F. Larcker. "Coming Up Short on Nonfinancial Performance Measurement." *Harvard Business Review*, November 2003, 88–95.

Joyner, KC. *Blindsided: Why the Left Tackle Is Overrated and Other Contrarian Football Thoughts.* Hoboken, NJ: John Wiley & Sons, 2008.

Kahn, Lisa B.. "The Long-Term Labor Market Consequences of Graduating from College in a Bad Economy." *Labour Economics* 17, no. 2 (April 2010): 303–316.

Kahneman, Daniel, *Thinking, Fast and Slow.* New York: Farrar, Straus and Giroux, 2011.

Kahneman, Daniel, and Gary Klein. "Conditions for Intuitive Expertise: A Failure to Disagree." *American Psychologist* 64, no. 6 (September 2009): 515–526.

Kahneman, Daniel, and Amos Tversky. "On the Psychology of Prediction." *Psychological Review* 80, no. 4 (July 1973): 237–251.

———. eds. *Choices, Values, and Frames.* Cambridge, UK: Cambridge University Press, 2000.

Kennedy, Kostya. *56: Joe DiMaggio and the Last Magic Number in Sports.* New York: Sports Illustrated Books, 2011.

Keynes, John Maynard. *The General Theory of Employment, Interest, and Money.* New York: Harcourt, Brace and Company, 1936.

Khurana, Rakesh. *Searching for a Corporate Savior: The Irrational Quest for Charismatic CEOs.* Princeton, NJ: Princeton University Press, 2002.

Klarman, Seth. Speech at Columbia Business School on October 2, 2008. Reproduced in *Outstanding Investor Digest* 22, nos. 1–2 (March 17, 2009): 3.

Klein, Gary. *Sources of Power: How People Make Decisions.* Cambridge, MA: MIT Press, 1998.

Kluger, Jeffrey. *Simplexity: Why Simple Things Become Complex* (and *How Complex Things Can Be Made Simple*). New York: Hyperion, 2008.

Knight, Frank H. *Risk, Uncertainty, and Profit.* New York: Houghton and Mifflin, 1921.

Korniotis, George M., and Alok Kumar. "Do Older Investors Make Better Investment Decisions?" *Review of Economics and Statistics* 93, no. 1 (February 2011): 244–265.

Kovenock, Dan, Michael J. Mauboussin, and Brian Roberson. "Asymmetric Conflicts with Endogenous Dimensionality." *Korean Economic Review* 26, no. 2 (Winter 2010): 287–305.

Kwak, Young Hoon, and Frank T. Anbari. "Benefits, Obstacles, and Future of Six Sigma Approach." *Technovation* 26, nos. 5–6 (May–June 2006): 708–715.

Langer, Ellen J., and Jane Roth. "Heads I Win, Tails It's Chance: The Illusion of Control as a Function of the Sequence of Outcomes in a Purely Chance Task." *Journal of Personality and Social Psychology* 32, no. 6 (December 1975): 951–955.

Lee, Jennifer 8. "Who Needs Giacomo? Bet on a Fortune Cookie." *New York Times*, May 11, 2005.

———. *The Fortune Cookie Chronicles: Adventures in the World of Chinese Food.* New York: Twelve, 2008.

Lee, Marcus, and Gary Smith. "Regression to the Mean and Football Wagers." *Journal of Behavioral Decision Making* 15, no. 4 (October 2002): 329–342.

Lehrer, Jonah. "Fleeting Youth, Fading Creativity." *Wall Street Journal*, February 19, 2010.

Leonard, Wilbert M. II. "The Decline of the .400 Hitter: An Explanation and a Test." *Journal of Sport Behavior* 18, no. 3 (September 1995): 226–236.

Levitt, Steven D., and Thomas J. Miles. "The Role of Skill Versus Luck in Poker: Evidence from the World Series of Poker." NBER Working Paper 17023, May 2011.

Lewis, Michael. *Moneyball: The Art of Winning an Unfair Game*. New York: W.W. Norton & Company, 2003.

———. "Coach Leach Goes Deep, Very Deep." *New York Times Magazine*, December 4, 2005.

———. "The King of Human Error." *Vanity Fair*, December 2011.

Lewis, Randall A., and David H. Reiley. "Does Retail Advertising Work? Measuring the Effects of Advertising on Sales via a Controlled Experiment on Yahoo!" Working paper, September 29, 2010.

Lieberson, Stanley. "Small N's and Big Conclusions: An Examination of the Reasoning in Comparative Studies Based on a Small Number of Cases." *Social Forces* 70, no. 2 (December 1991): 307–320.

———. "Modeling Social Processes: Some Lessons from Sports." *Sociological Forum* 12, no. 1 (March 1997): 11–35.

Loderer, Claudio, and Urs Waelchli. "Firm Age and Performance." Working paper, January 24, 2011.

Lucchetti, Aaron, and Julie Steinberg. "Corzine Rebuffed Internal Warnings on Risk." *Wall Street Journal*, December 6, 2011.

Ma, Jeffrey. *The House Advantage: Playing the Odds to Win Big in Business*. New York: Palgrave McMillan, 2010.

MacKay, Charles. *Extraordinary Delusions and the Madness of Crowds*. New York: Three Rivers Press, 1995.

Madden, Bartley J. *CFROI Valuation: A Total System Approach to Valuing the Company*. Oxford, UK: Butterworth-Heinemann, 1999.

Maital, Shlomo. "Daniel Kahneman, Nobel Laureate 2002: A Brief Comment." *SABE Newsletter* 10, no. 2 (Autumn 2002).

Mandelbrot, Benoit, and Richard L. Hudson. *The (Mis)Behavior of Markets*. New York: Basic Books, 2004.

March, James C., and James G. March. "Almost Random Careers: The Wisconsin School Superintendency, 1940–1972." *Administrative Science Quarterly* 22, no. 3 (September 1977): 377–409.

March, James G. "Exploration and Exploitation in Organizational Learning." *Organization Science* 2, no. 1 (February 1991): 71–87.

Mathews, Fiona, Paul J. Johnson, and Andrew Neil. "You Are What Your Mother Eats: Evidence for Maternal Preconception Diet Influencing Foetal Sex in Humans." *Proceedings of the Royal Society B* 275, no. 1643 (July 22, 2008): 1661–1668.

Mauboussin, Andrew, and Samuel Arbesman. "Differentiating Skill and Luck in Financial Markets With Streaks." SSRN working paper, February 3, 2011.

Mauboussin, Michael J. "Size Matters: The Kelly Criterion and the Importance of Money Management." *Mauboussin on Strategy*, February 1, 2006.

————. *Think Twice: Harnessing the Power of Counterintuition.* Boston, MA: Harvard Business Press, 2009.

McCloskey, Deirdre N., and Stephen T. Ziliak. "The Standard Error of Regressions." *Journal of Economic Literature* 34 (March 1996): 97–114.

McCotter, Trent. "Hitting Streaks Don't Obey Your Rules: Evidence That Hitting Streaks Aren't Just By-Products of Random Variation." *Baseball Research Journal* 37 (2008): 62–70.

McDonald, John, and John W. Tukey. "Colonel Blotto: A Problem of Military Strategy." *Fortune*, June 1949, 102.

Meisler, Stanley. "First in 1763: Spain Lottery—Not Even a War Stops It." *Los Angeles Times*, December 30, 1977.

Merton, Robert K. "The Matthew Effect in Science." *Science* 159, no. 3810 (January 5, 1968): 56–63.

Mezrich, Ben. *Bringing Down the House: The Inside Story of Six MIT Students Who Took Vegas for Millions.* New York: Free Press, 2003.

Mlodinow, Leonard. *The Drunkard's Walk: How Randomness Rules Our Lives.* New York: Pantheon Books, 2008.

Moore, Don A., Philip E. Tetlock, Lloyd Tanlu, and Max H. Bazerman. "Conflicts of Interest and the Case of Auditor Independence: Moral Seduction and Strategic Issue Cycling." *Academy of Management Review* 31, no. 1 (January 2006): 10–29.

Mukunda, Gautam. "We Cannot Go On: Disruptive Innovation and the First World War Royal Navy." *Security Studies* 19, no. 1 (January 2010): 124–159.

Muller, Thor, and Lane Becker. *Get Lucky: How to Put Planned Serendipity to Work for You and Your Business.* San Francisco, CA: Jossey-Bass, 2012.

Myers, David G. *Intuition: Its Powers and Perils.* New Haven, CT: Yale University Press, 2002.

Newman, M. E. J. "Power Laws, Pareto Distributions, and Zipf's Law." *Contemporary Physics* 46, no. 5 (September–October 2005): 323–351.

Nisbett, Richard, and Lee Ross. *Human Inference: Strategies and Shortcomings of Social Judgment.* Englewood Cliffs, NJ: Prentice-Hall, 1980.

Odean, Terrance. "Are Investors Reluctant to Realize Their Losses?" *Journal of Finance* 53, no. 5 (October 1998): 1775–1798.

Olsen, Robert A. "Professional Investors as Naturalistic Decision Makers: Evidence and Market Implications." *Journal of Psychology and Financial Markets* 3, no. 3 (2002): 161–167.

Ordonez, Jennifer. "Pop Singer Fails to Strike a Chord Despite Millions Spent by MCA." *Wall Street Journal*, February 26, 2002.

Page, Scott E. "Path Dependence." *Quarterly Journal of Political Science* 1, no. 1 (January 2006): 87–115.

————. *The Difference: How the Power of Diversity Creates Better Groups, Firms, Schools, and Societies.* Princeton, NJ: Princeton University Press, 2007.

Patterson, Scott. "Old Pros Size Up the Game." *Wall Street Journal*, March 22, 2008.

Pearson, Karl, and Alice Lee. "On the Laws of Inheritance in Man: I. Inheritance of Physical Characters." *Biometrika* 2, no. 4 (November 1903): 357–462.

Petajisto, Antti. "Active Share and Mutual Fund Performance." Working paper, December 15, 2010.

Philips, Christopher B., and Francis M. Kinniry Jr. "Mutual Fund Ratings and Future Performance." Vanguard Research, June 2010.

Pink, Daniel H. *Drive: The Surprising Truth About What Motivates Us*. New York: Riverhead Books, 2009.

Pinker, Steven. *How the Mind Works*. New York: W.W. Norton & Company, 1997.

———. *The Blank Slate: The Modern Denial of Human Nature*. New York: Viking, 2002.

Poundstone, William. *Priceless: The Myth of Fair Value (and How to Take Advantage of It)*. New York: Hill and Wang, 2010.

Powell, Thomas C. "Varieties of Competitive Parity." *Strategic Management Journal* 24, no. 1 (January 2003): 61–86.

Powell, Thomas C., and Chris J. Lloyd. "Toward a General Theory of Competitive Dominance: Comments and Extensions on Powell (2003)." *Strategic Management Journal* 26, no. 4 (April 2005): 385–394.

Pronovost, Peter, MD, PhD, and Eric Vohr. *Safe Patients, Smart Hospitals: How One Doctor's Checklist Can Help Us Change Health Care from the Inside Out*. New York: Hudson Street Books, 2010.

Rabin, Matthew, and Dimitri Vayanos. "The Gambler's Fallacy and Hot-Hand Fallacies: Theory and Application." *Review of Economic Studies* 77, no. 2 (April 2010): 730–778.

Rappaport, Alfred. *Creating Shareholder Value: A Guide for Managers and Investors, Revised and Updated*. New York: Free Press, 1998.

———. "New Thinking on How to Link Executive Pay with Performance." *Harvard Business Review*, March–April 1999, 91–101.

Rappaport, Alfred, and Michael J. Mauboussin. *Expectations Investing: Reading Stock Prices for Better Returns*. Boston, MA: Harvard Business School Press, 2001.

Rawls, John. *A Theory of Social Justice*. Cambridge, MA: Belknap Press, 1971.

Raynor, Michael E. *The Strategy Paradox: Why Commitment to Success Leads to Failure (and What to Do About It)*. New York: Currency Doubleday, 2007.

———. *The Innovator's Manifesto: Deliberate Disruption for Transformational Growth*. New York: Crown Business, 2011.

Raynor, Michael E., Mumtaz Ahmed, and Andrew D. Henderson. *A Random Search for Excellence: Why "Great Company" Research Delivers Fables and Not Facts*. Deloitte Research, December 2009.

Record, Jeffrey. *Beating Goliath: Why Insurgencies Win*. Washington, DC: Potomac Books, 2009.

Reifman, Alan. *Hot Hands: The Statistics Behind Sports' Greatest Streaks*. Washington, DC: Potomac Books, 2011.

Rescher, Nicholas. *Luck: The Brilliant Randomness of Everyday Life*. Pittsburgh, PA: University of Pittsburgh Press, 1995.

Rickey, Branch. "Goodby to Some Old Baseball Ideas." *Life*, August 2, 1954, 79–89.

Ridley, Matt. *The Red Queen: Sex and the Evolution of Human Nature*. New York: Macmillan, 1994.

Rigney, Daniel. *The Matthew Effect: How Advantage Begets Further Advantage*. New York: Columbia University Press, 2010.

Roberson, Brian. "The Colonel Blotto Game." *Economic Theory* 29, no. 1 (September 2006): 1–24.

Robertson, Kimberly Ferriman, Stijn Smeets, David Lubinski, and Camillia P. Benbow. "Beyond the Threshold Hypothesis: Even Among the Gifted and Top Math/Science Graduate Students, Cognitive Abilities, Vocational Interests, and Lifestyle Preferences Matter for Career Choice, Performance, and Persistence." *Current Directions in Psychological Science* 19, no. 6 (December 2010): 346–351.

Rohlfs, Jeffrey H. *Bandwagon Effects in High Technology Industries*. Cambridge, MA: MIT Press, 2001.

Romer, David. "Do Firms Maximize? Evidence from Professional Football." *Journal of Political Economy* 114, no. 2 (April 2006): 340–365.

Rosen, Sherwin. "The Economics of Superstars." *American Economic Review* 71, no. 5 (December 1981): 845–858.

Rosenzweig, Phil. *The Halo Effect . . . and the Eight Other Business Delusions That Deceive Managers*. New York: Free Press, 2007.

Saari, Donald G. *Chaotic Elections! A Mathematician Looks at Voting*. Providence, RI: American Mathematical Society, 2001.

Salganik, Matthew J. "Prediction and Surprise." Presentation at the Thought Leader Forum, Legg Mason Capital Management, October 14, 2011.

Salganik, Matthew J., Peter Sheridan Dodds, and Duncan J. Watts. "Experimental Study of Inequality and Unpredictability in an Artificial Cultural Market." *Science* 311, no. 5762 (February 10, 2006): 854–856.

Salthouse, Timothy A. "What and When of Cognitive Aging." *Current Directions in Psychological Science* 13, no. 4 (August 2004): 40–144.

Sandel, Michael J. *Justice: What's the Right Thing to Do?* New York: Farrar, Straus and Giroux, 2009.

Sassoon, Donald. *Becoming Mona Lisa: The Making of a Global Icon*. New York: Harcourt, Inc., 2001.

Schaeffer, Jonathan. "Marion Tinsley: Human Perfection at Checkers?" *Games of No Chance* 26 (1996): 115–118.

Schenk, David. *The Genius in All of Us: New Insights into Genetics, Talent, and IQ*. New York: Doubleday, 2010.

Schmidt, Martin B., and David J. Berri. "On the Evolution of Competitive Balance: The Impact of an Increasing Global Search." *Economic Inquiry* 41, no. 4 (October 2003): 692–704.

———. "Concentration of Playing Talent: Evolution in Major League Baseball." *Journal of Sports Economics* 6, no. 4 (November 2005): 412–419.

Schulz, Richard, and Christine Curnow. "Peak Performance and Age Among Superathletes: Track and Field, Swimming, Baseball, Tennis, and Golf." *Journal of Gerontology* 43, no. 5 (September 1988): 113–120.

Secrist, Horace. *The Triumph of Mediocrity in Business*. Evanston, IL: Bureau of Business Research, Northwestern University, 1933.

Sehgal, Ashwini R., MD. "The Role of Reputation in *U.S. News & World Report* Rankings of the Top 50 American Hospitals." *Annals of Internal Medicine* 152, no. 8 (April 20, 2010): 521–525.

Seidel, Michael. *Streak: Joe DiMaggio and the Summer of '41*. New York: McGraw Hill, 1988.

Shafir, Eldar, Peter Diamond, and Amos Tversky. "Money Illusion." *Quarterly Journal of Economics* 112, no. 2 (May 1997): 341–374.

Shapiro, Carl, and Hal R. Varian. *Information Rules: A Strategic Guide to the Network Economy*. Boston, MA: Harvard Business School Press, 1999.

Shearn, Michael. *The Investment Checklist: The Art of In-Depth Research*. Hoboken, NJ: John Wiley & Sons, 2012.

Shefrin, Hersh, and Meir Statman. "The Disposition to Sell Winners Too Early and Ride Losers Too Long: Theory and Evidence." *Journal of Finance* 40, no. 3 (July 1985): 777–790.

Shewhart, Walter A. *Statistical Method from the Viewpoint of Quality Control*. New York: Dover, 1985.

Simon, Herbert A. "On a Class of Skew Distribution Functions." *Biometrika* 42, no. 3/4 (December 1955): 425–440.

Sims, Peter. *Little Bets: How Breakthrough Ideas Emerge from Small Discoveries*. New York: Free Press, 2011.

Skinner, Brian. "Scoring Strategies for the Underdog: A General, Quantitative Method for Determining Optimal Sports Strategies." *Journal of Quantitative Analysis in Sports* 7, no. 4 (October 2011): article 11.

Sklansky, David. *Getting the Best of It*. Henderson, NV: Two Plus Two Publishing, 2001.

Smith, Ed. *Luck: What It Means and Why It Matters*. London: Bloomsbury, 2012.

Smith, Gary, and Joanna Smith. "Regression to the Mean in Average Test Scores." *Educational Assessment* 10, no. 4 (November 2005): 377–399.

Sokolove, Michael. "For Derek Jeter, on His 37th Birthday." *New York Times Magazine*, June 23, 2011.

Spanier, David. *Easy Money: Inside the Gambler's Mind*. New York: Penguin Books, 1987.

Spatz, Chris. *Basic Statistics: Tales of Distributions, Tenth Edition*. Belmont, CA: Wadsworth, 2011.

Stanovich, Keith E. *What Intelligence Tests Miss: The Psychology of Rational Thought*. New Haven, CT: Yale University Press, 2009.

———. "The Thinking That IQ Tests Miss." *Scientific American Mind*, November/December 2009, 34–39.

Starbuck, William H. "Performance Measures: Prevalent and Important but Methodologically Challenging." *Journal of Management Inquiry* 14, no. 3 (September 2005): 280–286.

Stewart, Ian. *Game, Set & Math: Enigmas and Conundrums*. Mineola, New York: Dover Publications, 1989.

Stewart, James B. *Disney War*. New York: Simon & Schuster, 2006.

Stewart, Scott D., CFA, John J. Neumann, Christopher R. Knittel, and Jeffrey Heisler, CFA. "Absence of Value: An Analysis of Investment Allocation Decisions by Institutional Plan Sponsors." *Financial Analysts Journal* 65, no. 6 (November/December 2009): 34–51.

Stigler, Stephen M. "The 1988 Neyman Memorial Lecture: A Galtonian Perspective on Shrinkage Estimators." *Statistical Science* 5, no. 1 (February 1990): 147–155.

————. *Statistics on the Table: The History of Statistical Concepts and Methods.* Cambridge, MA: Harvard University Press, 1999.

————. "Milton Friedman and Statistics." In *The Collected Writings of Milton Friedman*, ed. Robert Leeson. New York: Palgrave Macmillan, 2012, forthcoming.

Sundaram, Anant K., and Andrew C. Inkpen. "The Corporate Objective Revisited." *Organization Science* 15, no. 3 (May–June 2004): 350–363.

Swensen, David F. *Unconventional Success: A Fundamental Approach to Personal Investment.* New York: Free Press, 2005.

Syed, Matthew. *Bounce: Mozart, Federer, Picasso, Beckham, and the Science of Success.* New York: Harper, 2010.

Taleb, Nassim Nicholas. *Fooled by Randomness: The Hidden Role of Chance in Life and in the Markets.* 2nd ed. New York: ThomsonTexere, 2004.

————. *The Black Swan: The Impact of the Highly Improbable, Second Edition.* New York: Random House, 2010.

————. *The Bed of Procrustes: Philosophical and Practical Aphorisms.* New York: Random House, 2010.

————. "Antifragility, Robustness, and Fragility Inside the 'Black Swan' Domain." SSRN working paper, February 2011.

Taleb, Nassim Nicholas, and Mark Blyth. "The Black Swan of Cairo: How Suppressing Volatility Makes the World Less Predictable and More Dangerous." *Foreign Affairs* 90, no. 3 (May/June 2011): 33–39.

Tango, Tom M., Mitchel G. Lichtman, and Andrew E. Dolphin. *The Book: Playing the Percentages in Baseball.* Washington, DC: Potomac Books, 2007.

Terviö, Marko. "The Difference That CEOs Make: An Assignment Model Approach." *American Economic Review* 98, no. 3 (June 2008): 642–668.

Tetlock, Philip E. *Expert Political Judgment: How Good Is It? How Can We Know?* Princeton, NJ: Princeton University Press, 2005.

Tetlock, Philip E., Richard Ned Lebow, and Geoffrey Parker, eds. *Unmaking the West: "What-If?" Scenarios That Rewrite World History.* Ann Arbor, MI: The University of Michigan Press, 2006.

Thomas, L. G., and Richard D'Aveni. "The Rise of Hypercompetition from 1950–2002: Evidence of Increasing Industry Destabilization and Temporary Competitive Advantage." Working paper, October 11, 2004.

Trochim, William M. K., and James P. Donnelly. *The Research Methods Knowledge Base.* 3rd ed. Mason, OH: Atomic Dog, 2008.

Tversky, Amos, and Daniel Kahneman. "Belief in the Law of Small Numbers." *Psychological Bulletin* 76, no. 2 (1971): 105–110.

Wainer, Howard. "The Most Dangerous Equation." *American Scientist* (May–June 2007): 249–256.

————. *Picturing the Uncertain World: How to Understand, Communicate, and Control Uncertainty Through Graphical Display.* Princeton, NJ: Princeton University Press, 2009.

Waltz, Kenneth. *Theory of International Politics.* New York: McGraw Hill, 1979.

Watts, Duncan J. "A Simple Model of Global Cascades on Random Networks." *Proceedings of the National Academy of Sciences* 99, no. 9 (April 30, 2002): 5766–5771.

————. *Six Degrees: The Science of a Connected Age*. New York: W.W. Norton & Company, 2003.

————. *Everything Is Obvious*: *Once You Know the Answer*. New York: Crown Business, 2011.

Wermers, Russ. "Mutual Fund Performance: An Empirical Decomposition into Stock-Picking Talent, Style, Transactions Costs, and Expenses." *Journal of Finance* 55, no. 4 (August 2000): 1655–1695.

White, Hayden. *Metahistory: The Historical Imagination in Nineteenth-Century Europe*. Baltimore, MD: The Johns Hopkins University Press, 1973.

Whitely, Peyton. "Computer Pioneer's Death Probed—Kildall Called Possible Victim of Homicide." *Seattle Times*, July 16, 1994.

Wiggins, Robert R., and Timothy W. Ruefli. "Sustained Competitive Advantage: Temporal Dynamics and the Incidence and Persistence of Superior Economic Performance." *Organization Science* 13, no. 1 (January–February 2002): 82–105.

————. "Schumpeter's Ghost: Is Hypercompetition Making the Best of Times Shorter?" *Strategic Management Journal* 26, no. 10 (October 2005): 887–911.

Wiseman, Richard. *The Luck Factor: Changing Your Luck, Changing Your Life: The Four Essential Principles*. New York: Miramax, 2003.

Wolpert, Lewis. *Six Impossible Things Before Breakfast: The Evolutionary Origins of Belief*. London: Faber and Faber, 2006.

Yarrow, Kielan, Peter Brown, and John W. Krakauer. "Inside the Brain of an Elite Athlete: The Neural Processes that Support High Achievement in Sports." *Nature Reviews Neuroscience* 10 (August 2009): 585–596.

Young, Jeffrey, "Gary Kildall: The DOS That Wasn't." *Forbes*, July 7, 1997.

Young, S. Stanley, Heejung Bang, and Kutluk Oktay. "Cereal-Induced Gender Selection? Most Likely Multiple Testing False Positive." *Proceedings of the Royal Society B* 276, no. 1660 (April 7, 2009): 1211–1212.

Ziliak, Stephen T., and Deirdre N. McCloskey. "Size Matters: The Standard Error of Regressions in the American Economic Review." *Journal of Socio-Economics* 33, no. 5 (November 2004): 527–546.

————. *The Cult of Statistical Significance: How the Standard Error Costs Us Jobs, Justice, and Lives*. Ann Arbor, MI: The University of Michigan Press, 2008.

INDEX

Note: *f* refers to figures and *t* refers to tables

ABOUT THE AUTHOR

Michael J. Mauboussin is an investment strategist who has been in the financial services industry for more than twenty-five years. He has also taught at the Columbia Graduate School of Business since 1993, and is on the board of trustees at the Santa Fe Institute.

He is the author of two previous books, *Think Twice: Harnessing the Power of Counterintuition* and *More Than You Know: Finding Financial Wisdom in Unconventional Places* and is coauthor, with Alfred Rappaport, of *Expectations Investing: Reading Stock Prices for Better Returns.*

He lives in Darien, CT, with his family.

For more, see www.michaelmauboussin.com and www.success-equation.com.